Swaledale

Valley of the Wild River

by

Andrew Fleming

WINDgather
PRESS

Windgather Press
is an imprint of
Oxbow Books, Oxford

ISBN 978-1-84217-372-5

A CIP record for this book is available from the British Library

This book is available direct from

Oxbow Books, Oxford, UK
(Phone: 01865-241249; Fax: 01865-794449)

and

The David Brown Book Company
PO Box 511, Oakville, CT 06779, USA
(Phone: 860-945-9329; Fax: 860-945-9468)

or from our website

www.oxbowbooks.com

Printed in China by
Kwong Fat Offset Printing Co Ltd

In memory of John and Barbara, my parents, who introduced me to landscape

The name is related to swallow *(the bird) and belongs to the root* svel – *'to move, plash' … the meaning of the name seems to be 'whirling, rushing river'.*

Eilert Ekwall

Contents

Preface to the first edition (1998)

'The archaeology of the Yorkshire dales is one of Britain's best-kept secrets'. These are the words of Bob Bewley, an archaeologist who flew over the Pennines many times in the course of his work at the York office of the Royal Commission on Ancient and Historic Monuments. Bob was talking about the breathtaking diversity of what is prosaically known as 'the archaeological record' – everything from old field-banks to charming seventeenth-century farmhouses, from deserted medieval villages to abandoned smelt-mills. He was talking also about the often excellent state of preservation of archaeological sites in the dales, and their ability to surprise even the seasoned archaeologist. And he was also talking about the potential of these sites to provide evidence for the history of the lovely landscapes in which they are located.

Certainly the landscape history of Swaledale, the northernmost of the Yorkshire Pennine dales, has been a well-kept secret. I have been trying to unravel it for ten years or so – intermittently and on a low budget, as a university teacher usually must. I have been fortunate to work with Tim Laurie, who lives not far from Swaledale, and has made many archaeological discoveries there, and in the support I have received from Robert White, the Park's archaeological conservation officer. Tim and I have worked on the 'ancient landscape' of the area around Reeth – the old walls and earthworks of later prehistoric and Roman times.

Landscape archaeology is an approach which cannot be contained within narrow boundaries. While working on the ancient landscape, the humps and bumps of the late prehistoric and Roman periods, I began to realise that there was a story of woodland management to be teased out, a story which might prove to be more interesting than that of the famous walls and haybarns. I started to have problems with Arthur Raistrick's idea that the Grinton-Fremington dykes, two large banks and ditches crossing the dale near Reeth, were constructed as part of a rebellion against the Romans. Instead of thinking about Swaledale's footpaths as amenities for ramblers, I started to think about their historical origins. And I began to wonder about another of Swaledale's well-loved images – the sturdy self-reliance symbolised by the family farm, isolated on the daleside; how did that square with the evidence for large areas of common land in the past, not to mention the exercise of common rights in the present?

I began to move into a different area of enquiry, getting involved with documents, and with maps old and new, as well as with bumps in the ground. I started to understand the importance of *place-names* to the landscape history of the last 1,500 years or so. It is interesting to find out the early forms of the names and *translate* them, from their Old Norse or Old English roots. But the names of places and of parcels of land also say a great deal about past attitudes to the land. Different kinds of names make coherent patterns in relation to the terrain, patterns which can only have historical roots. Historical questions are raised by places which have more than one name, and places whose names as currently interpreted do not make sense in terms of the local landscape. In other words, there is an archaeology of names.

These were the thoughtpaths which led me to write this book. I wanted to move away from the long silences of prehistory towards the more richly textured stores which may be told when there are written documents as well as archaeology – 'text-aided' periods, as archaeologists call them. In the research which fires the telling of the tale, there is no greater satisfaction than the discovery that different, independent categories of evidence are all pointing in the same direction. Landscape archaeologists will always be dissatisfied with accounts of local and regional history which simply use the archaeology of the landscape to illustrate what they already know from written sources. The landscape is full of archaeological evidence, which is worth deploying in its own right; but in any case, the places and landscapes where people have lived and worked can never be viewed simply as scenery or treated as stage-sets.

I could have written the book in chronological sequence, as a narrative account of the history of the Swaledale landscape, from handaxes to heritage management – a neat package in a familiar framework. But this would be a trickster's approach, blurring the diversity of a wide range of sources, which are rich and reliable in different degrees; I need space to explain about that. Research has been like the zoom lens which I have often used in Swaledale, to photograph one side of the dale from the other. It has brought some areas of enquiry into sharp focus. But there are other topics about which I cannot claim to know a great deal – mining, for example, or building history. So the book is about some aspects of the Swaledale landscape, at the expense of others. I wanted to take the reader 'into my workshop', to share some of the arguments and approaches of landscape historians and archaeologists. That is why I have sometimes digressed from the detail of Swaledale itself, to set an argument into its general context, or to try to convey a sense of Swaledale as part of a wider world, historically and geographically.

I have not tried to 'cover' all aspects of Swaledale's landscape history. Those who are interested in the history of lead-mining, or in the development of the town of Richmond, will be deeply disappointed in this book. In largely ignoring lead-mining, I do not wish to belittle its importance; it is simply that I have not pursued the topic very much, and consequently have nothing fresh to say about it. There is certainly plenty of scope for an archaeology of mining and quarrying; I hope someone will attempt it. I should also say that this book cannot in any sense 'cover' the history of every township, hamlet or farm; readers who know Swaledale well may look in vain for historical news about their pet locality. Obviously, it would be possible to write at least a dozen 'local histories' at least as long as this book. But sometimes one can become a little too obsessed by a particular area; this book has tried to stand back a bit, to address some general themes as well as to try and explain how to go about writing landscape history in detail.

I am indebted to many people and institutions – among others most notably Tim and Eileen Laurie, Robert White, Bill Godfrey, Tom Gledhill, Ros Nichol, Catharina Mascher, Pår Connelid, Elizabeth Livett, Colin Merrony, Pat Foster, Kate Edwards, Sarah Whiteley, Anna Badcock, Mark Simmons, the late Don Spratt, Oliver Rackham, Richard Tipping, Graeme Guilbert, Robin Minnitt, Richard Smith, Roy Switsur, Lawrence Barker, Dave and Val Lowson, several Swaledale farmers and landowners, numerous volunteers who helped with excavation and survey work, the staff of North Yorkshire County Record Office and North Yorkshire Sites and Monuments Record (both at Northallerton), Yorkshire Dales National Park Committee, the Universities of Sheffield and Wales, the Prehistoric Society, Richard Purslow, and Nicola Carr and the staff at Edinburgh University Press. I hope they will forgive me for not having found the time yet to publish the more detailed results of fieldwork, and that they will enjoy this book, for whose inadequacies they are in no way responsible.

Talsarn, Ceredigion

Preface to the 2010 edition

This book was the first to be written about the landscape history of one of the best-loved and most beautiful Yorkshire Pennine dales. Iconic images of Swaledale feature intricate patterns of drystone walls and stonebuilt field-barns, and the mute, evocative remains of the lead-mining industry. *Swaledale: Valley of the Wild River* takes the reader beneath this recent historical surface, further back in history, to times when the management of common land and woodland, for instance, played much more important roles in Swaledale. Taking advantage of clues provided by a rich store of local place-names, documentary references, and archaeological features visible on the ground, I have picked up traces of settlements long-abandoned, much-diminished, or re-located; some have even changed their names. I have explored the network of roads and paths which connected these places. Still further back in time I have argued that there was a well-defined Dark Age 'kingdom' in Upper Swaledale; before that, in the Romano-British period, the dalesides were covered in farms and field-walls forming patterns not unlike those of more recent centuries. I found the process of getting to grips with this landscape absolutely fascinating, an absorbing exercise in detective work. So it's a pleasure to introduce the new, colour edition of this book. The original monochrome version was out of print for several years, and second-hand copies were becoming increasingly expensive. I have made only small amendments to the text of the first edition, mostly for the sake of increased clarity.

Before this book appeared, anyone curious about the landscape history of Swaledale had to mine the copious writings of the late Arthur Raistrick. Swaledale was not the dale Raistrick knew best (he lived in Wharfedale), and he tended to treat it mostly as a contributor to a more general narrative about the Yorkshire Dales. Arguably, the landscape history of Swaledale looks north-west or north as much as south – if not more so – and has a good deal in common with that of the old county of Westmorland, or even parts of southern Scotland. This emerges clearly, I think, from the writings of Angus Winchester (e.g. *The Harvest of the Hills* (Edinburgh University Press 2000)) which are well worth reading both for their own sake and to set this book in a wider context. Although he knows his landscapes well, Winchester tends to place more emphasis on the documentary record than an archaeologist would. Where my treatment of fiscal and legal relationships is relatively vague, his is more clearly defined, providing a sharp-edged portrayal of the nexus of power, and complementing, I believe, my own sense of the workings of the face-to-face local community.

When I started writing, then, there was little conventional wisdom about the history of the Swaledale landscape, beyond the general narratives which Raistrick had provided for the Yorkshire dales. The field was open, and I was able to introduce and develop plenty of new ideas. Some of these – like my suggestion that Upper Swaledale was a Dark Age 'kingdom', or my belief that wood-pasture and its decline form a significant part of the story – are supported by a good deal of evidence and argument. At the other end of the scale, some – such as particular interpretations of place-names – are single speculations, offered on a 'take it or leave it' basis. I am not going to apologise for these, even the ones which turn out to be misguided. In refuting them, or bringing forward evidence in their support, we will learn more than would have been the case had they never appeared in print.

When I wrote this book, I was explicitly aware that landscape historians' narratives – and also, I fear, their potential – are often deeply influenced by the nature of the sources available; the reader will certainly notice the difference between my treatments of the Roman, Dark Age and late medieval periods. On re-reading my text after ten years or so, I am more struck, however, by the different *scales* at which the landscape historian has to work. Sometimes the mode is observational, responsive, and deeply empirical, as when one is brought up short by encountering an ancient pollard, an odd kink in a line on a map, a previously unfamiliar place-name in a document. At the other extreme, what is observed in the landscape may be discussed and interpreted in terms of more abstract theory. In this book, the most conspicuous case is that of commons management, where I have had to think about the 'Tragedy of the Commons' theory; I also put forward my own three-stage theory of commons evolution, from the co-operative phase to the competitive via the regulated. I'm also interested in the distinction between how people should behave in theory (in legal terms, or in relation to anthropologists' generalisations) and what actually happens; at one point I turn to anthropological studies of farmers in the Tirol in order to get to grips with the impact of partible and impartible inheritance on farm size and the continuing livelihood of families.

However, much of the argument of this book takes place in the broad space *between* the abstract and the empirical, as I utilise diverse materials and arguments to construct interwoven narratives which deal with territory, land use, commons management, farming practice, communications, and the decline of wood pasture, among other things. This book, I believe, says as much about *method* in the investigation of landscape history as it says about Swaledale's history. Some commentators – who have become more insistent during the course of the past decade – complain variously that landscape history is too empirical, and not adequately 'theorised'; that we use maps and air photos too much, at the expense of sensuous engagement with the landscape; and that we should concern ourselves less with reconstructing the material conditions of past existence, and more with imagining past perceptions of landscape and the cosmos. These ideals are attractive, though their advocates do not help their case by so frequently setting up false polar oppositions and demanding that we make unrealistic choices between them. Such commentators might characterise this book as mostly an exercise in what they would call 'mere reconstruction'. In response, I would simply point out that if they are to realise their ideals in relation to any particular area, they will have to go through some sort of exercise in 'reconstruction' of the type attempted here. Only then will they have any hope of knowing roughly what they are talking about; they may then go on, perhaps, to reap the harvest of their own rhetoric.

There is still plenty to do in Swaledale. For instance, since this book was written, the keen eyes of Tim Laurie have spotted many more burnt mounds in and around the dale. These discoveries will have a major impact on our view of the nature of prehistoric settlement in the area, especially during the Bronze Age, and I hope Tim will at some stage publish his own ideas on this topic. Looking back over my text, I realise that I should probably have made more effort to penetrate and elucidate the meaning (in terms of landscape) of the place-names hagg, park, and *gehaeg* (the word which has generated most of the names ending in 'ay' or 'ey'). Thanks to the recent writings of Della Hooke, I now understand that the English place-name element *leāh* should not necessarily be read as 'clearing'; it is just as likely to refer to a zone of woodland, or wood pasture. This mostly affects – and tends to support – what I have written about Healaugh. And as far as wood pasture is concerned, it is possible that some readers of this book may feel that I have made too much of the Swaledale elm pollards; should they not be seen simply as the product of casual, relatively recent tree-lopping practices, rather than as representing the tail end of a venerable tradition of wood pasture? I must confess to having entertained occasional doubts myself – not about the Swaledale wood pasture hypothesis in general, but rather about my characterisation of the role of the elm pollards within that story. However, my current work in Powys (in eastern Wales) is revealing a range of stages and episodes in the decline of wood pasture which supply good insights into the survival of elm pollards in Swaledale. In fact comparison between the two areas persuades me that when I was working in northern England I was actually quite perceptive to be thinking about the 'survivorship' of very old trees and of ways of treating them, and about the fragmentary nature of evidence for wood pasture in its final manifestations. Alas, some of the dead elm pollards which I visited and photographed in the 1980s have fallen victim to the chain-saw, and most if not all of those still alive then have since died.

If we are to cherish and conserve our most beautiful and interesting landscapes, it is vital that we understand their history. If this book helps, in the case of Swaledale, I will be more than satisfied.

Andrew Fleming
Talsarn,
Ceredigion
April 2009

List of Illustrations

CHAPTER ONE

All Features Great and Small: Landscape Archaeology in Herriot Country

Most people take two days to walk through Swaledale. It is a little less than 30 miles (48km) from the bustle of the market-place in Richmond to the end of the dale, the desolate spot near Hollow Mill Cross from which you may look across the upper valleys of the Eden and the Lyvennet to the mountains of the Lake District. Most of the walk can be done on public footpaths; and you should be on foot, and probably by yourself, to see the fox leap out of the heather a few feet in front of you, the flurry of young wrens in the lane, the brown hare leaving quietly through the gate at the top of the field. You may come here on a chill, still February afternoon, and see a deer standing still as a statue in a meadow beside the Swale; or on a warm and hazy July evening, with shadows lengthening across the shorn, flaxen hayfields. Out on the moors, the landscape is often bleak and forbidding. But in the dale, it is the familiar detail, crafted by people, that Swaledale's visitors have come to love: the clustering of stone-built, slate-roofed houses beside the roaring beck, the neatly constructed stone stiles along the path through the fields, the smell of new-mown hay. This landscape has been created by past generations of Swaledale people, and in appreciating the dale's beauty, we are celebrating its history.

Swaledale is marketed as 'Herriot country' (though the original Herriot country is forty miles to the east); it is a landscape which has come to symbolise the enduring virtues of Yorkshire folk – their tenacity, self-reliance and capacity for hard work, as well as the warmth of their hospitality. It is all very heart-warming. But as we purchase yet another pot of 'Mrs Applethwaite's Traditional Dales Marmalade', we might just pause to question our fondness for this word 'traditional', and ask whether it is destroying our historical understanding. We may be thinking of the people of the Dales rather as we used to think of the Australian aborigines before archaeologists got on the case – as 'timeless' people who have practised a simple, unchanging way of life since time out of mind, people essentially without history.

It isn't true. In fact, Swaledale's 'traditional' landscape of walls and field-barns (Fig. 1.1) is no more than three or four hundred years old. Most of the field-barns, like many of the houses, were built or, more likely, rebuilt in the nineteenth century, and we don't know very much about what their predecessors looked like. Also, we have to remember that not very long ago this idyllic valley was beset by an industry notorious for noise, dirt and suffering. Whitaker, writing in the early nineteenth century, did not mince words:[1]

In Swaledale and the adjoining districts, where mining prevails, habits of subterraneous toil and danger, together with seclusion from light and society, while they harden the constitution in general, steel the nerves, and necessarily produce a degree of ferocity very formidable when highly excited. In the mining villages only of Richmondshire are to be found those appearances of squalid neglect about the persons of the inhabitants, and those external accumulations of domestic filth about their dwellings, which sicken every stranger in the worst parts of Lancashire and the West Riding of Yorkshire.

It is not unlikely that the hardships of mining were affecting the social attitudes of the miners and smelters; they were certainly affecting their health and life expectancy. And lead-mining did a great deal of environmental damage. Whitaker reported that 'hushing' (releasing water downhill to remove overburden from the ore) was:

> detrimental to the spawn by impregnating the water with filth, poisonous minerals, and particles of lead. This for many miles in its descent so pollutes and discolours the river with its thick dirty mud; that it gives it very much the appearance of the washings of the turnpike road after a heavy shower of rain.[2]

Floods in Swaledale still have a tendency to poison the pastures.

When Whitaker was writing, there were over 1,500 people living in Arkengarthdale alone. And when they took the census in 1851, the little

FIGURE 1.1. The classic Swaledale landscape: walls and haybarns.

hamlet of Healaugh (pronounced 'Hee-law') was occupied by no less than 51 lead-miners, plus a further 11 men occupied in lead-smelting, ore-carrying or as mining agents. And these figures take no account of the women and girls working on the dressing-floors.[3] It is all rather a far cry from winning the best-kept village competition! The demise of the lead industry, not much more than a century ago, with the inevitable emigration which followed, created social traumas as harsh as those resulting from the decline of coal-mining in other parts of Yorkshire today.

So this is a landscape which is only 'traditional' up to a point. Traces of very different pasts are there to be observed, discovered and celebrated; even the number of holes in an old stone gate-stoop may have a story to tell (Fig. 10.3). Swaledale's landscape is intricately bound up with Swaledale's history, so that without some knowledge of landscape history, the visitor is half-blind – or perhaps we should say semi-literate, in the face of a landscape which is there to be read and understood. This book is about the landscape history of Swaledale. But I want to make it clear that the emphasis is on *history* rather than landscape, because I do not want to write simply about changing scenery. History is about humans. And landscape history may be rather a special area for writing about human history – especially long-term history – because it is a good meeting-ground for ideas and concrete data, for writing about fantasy as well as hard work; landscape is where, sooner or later, most historical changes and processes make their mark.

So how should we approach the task of reading and writing landscape? An archaeologist may use my own discipline, landscape archaeology, which deals with immensely variable kinds of evidence, from a collection of prehistoric flint implements recovered from a peat-covered moorland to the layout of an eighteenth-century garden. And Swaledale is full of opportunities for the landscape archaeologist. This is mostly because of the nature of the archaeological record here, and the way it has survived. The frequent use and reuse of stone makes archaeological features such as buildings and boundary-walls more durable and visible. On the steep daleside, it is often necessary to cut a platform before erecting a building or an enclosure; many such platforms can still be seen. In the early sixteenth century, John Leland wrote that 'little corne growith in Swaledale'[4] and although medieval ploughing has clearly been very destructive, particularly in Lower Swaledale, the regime of cattle and sheep-farming in recent centuries has allowed archaeological sites to survive as 'humps and bumps'; their counterparts in lowland England have mostly been flattened by centuries of ploughing. For various reasons, Swaledale farming has tended to be fairly conservative, and landowners, who have usually lived elsewhere, have been more concerned to collect the rents than to promote advanced farming systems. The mining and smelting of lead have been destructive, but the impact of these activities has been mostly on the moorlands. In any case, the mines and associated structures are themselves a valuable and interesting part of the archaeological record.

Landscape archaeologists identify sites and study their relationships, building up historical sequences from humps and hollows. A set of old field boundaries maybe shown to pre-date an earthwork, which itself must be earlier than the roadway which cuts through it. More information can be obtained from these methods than most people imagine. We are still refining our powers of observation and deduction, enjoying the sense of fulfilment which comes from 'decoding' new landscapes. But these methods simply provide us with a framework, a stage set without people. Our challenge is to find ways of encountering the people of the past, of making them perform upon our stage. How can we meet this challenge?

For times for which written documents are available – text-aided periods, as archaeologists call them – we can turn to the archives in an attempt to make contact with the people of the past. For Swaledale, the contents of nine hundred years of documents have been summarised in *A History of Richmond and Swaledale,* published by Roger Fieldhouse and Bernard Jennings in 1978.[5] This is a very useful book, the result of a great deal of hard work, much of it by evening class students – five hundred pages packed with information. But it is like quite a lot of document-based local histories. We encounter people as landowners and tenants, heirs and testators, litigants, recusants, traders and wage-earners. This is Swaledale of the scribes; there is not too much action, except in the court cases. We know enough past people's names to keep the most assiduous Mormon happy, and there are numerous references to sums of money, which seem rather meaningless even after one has worked out what they mean at today's prices. And how do these people relate to their landscape? It turns out that places are simply where named people happen to have lived or owned property; Swaledale itself is represented mainly by fourteen photographs, and the closest encounter with the material world is that fascinating bit where the authors work out the contents of seventeenth-century houses, room by room, using the wills made by their occupants.

And this, it seems to me, is how local history should be. Humans organise and manipulate their world. There is a great deal of meaning in the way a room is furnished and decorated, the layout of rooms within a house, buildings in a farmyard, houses on a street, settlements and parcels of land within a township. Places have many meanings, involving myth and history, work and recreation, hopes, fears and fantasies. Change in the layout of houses, fields and farms often reflects profound change in other spheres. Documents rarely convey the sense of a Swaledale township as a theatre for action, as a land for work and dreams, reaching from the meadows by the Swale to the cluster of houses around the green and out to the 'stone men' on the moorland horizon.

In this book, then, I will try to work with those bits of the documentary record which reflect the actions and thoughts of people in their landscape. But I have also been working with another source of evidence, one which has proved surprisingly interesting and informative – toponyms (the names of places), fields and natural features. Names have their own archaeology. The experts often remind us that names change drastically, so we must seek the early forms. The way Yorkshire surnames have changed over the centuries is a vivid illustration of this point, reminding us that common speech has no respect for history! Thus Baxenden can become Baxendale and then Bassinder, Catlowe becomes Tatlow, Stancliffe becomes Stankley and then Stankler, and so on.[6] Swaledale place-names are much the same. One cannot guess that Barney Beck was once Bernopbeck (or Bernolfbeck), or that Straw Beck was once Trow Beck. A 1718 list of boundaries shows Little Pinsett Standard not far from Little Punshot Standard.[7] It is disconcerting to realise that modern 'Pinseat' and 'Punchard' are probably versions of the same name, their bogus difference fixed a long time ago by lawyers' clerks and mapmakers, who are liable in any case to mishear or misunderstand the names which they are given. There are pitfalls for the unwary here.

But we have to try to get to grips with place-names. As our leading expert, Margaret Gelling, has shown, they are not simply puzzles for linguists; knowledge of the local landscape can be crucial in deciding between different interpretations, or understanding the particular meanings of certain names. Individual place-names are like historical snap-shots, but they can also be grouped into patterns, forming a rich historical source. Unfortunately, the standard work on North Yorkshire place-names was published nearly seventy years ago.[8] But the place-name study for Westmorland, a county with much the same history as Swaledale, was published in 1967; I have found that volume, and the one for Cumberland, much more useful.[9]

Toponyms are a fascinating, under-explored field of study. Finding out the meaning of individual names is rewarding in itself, especially when one is trying to think about the relationship between people and landscape in an area like northern England, where Britons, Angles, Scandinavians and Normans all made their linguistic contributions. There are several different words for woods, clearings and outlying pasture stations, for instance. What was important about a place, when it was named? Its physical character – the shape of a hill, for instance? Its vegetation – characteristic or unusual? Something distinctive about the wildlife of the locality? The names of its owners or occupiers? The use to which it was put? Or was it best defined by its man-made structures?

In Swaledale, names set puzzles. Why are there certain patterns in the way places have been given their names – and why the exceptions? Why do some places have more than one name? Why do some names not fit the places which they are supposed to describe, or seem to have got displaced? Why do old names hang around for hundreds of years after they have apparently been superseded – and, if they can do this, why are they supplanted at all? Some historians say that names stabilise when title to land starts to become document-based ('book-

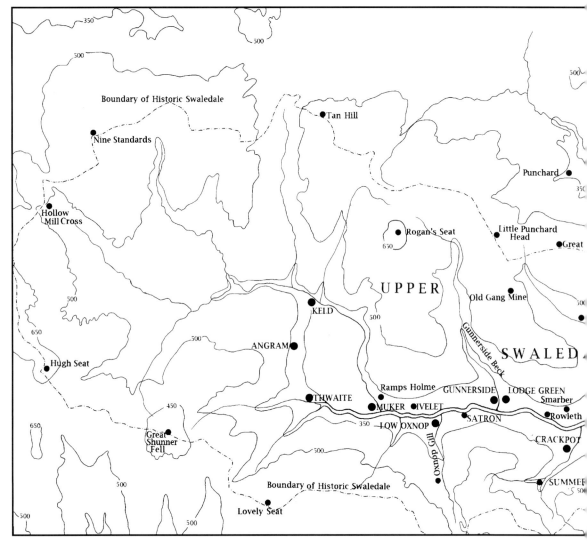

FIGURE I.2. General map of Swaledale, indicating places mentioned in Chapter I.

land'); but this is an oversimplification. (In west Wales, in the late twentieth century, the names of farms are still being changed.) Clearly, toponyms are not static things, to be pigeon-holed with the words 'oh, so that's what it means, then'. They are picked up in documents, but they reflect historical relationships between human beings, land and landscape which are very far from the concerns of clerks and mapmakers. These early recorded toponyms give documents their own form of prehistory. Landscape too has its prehistory, of course, and when we get back to the period which even place-names cannot reach, we have only archaeological evidence to work with – the results of archaeological excavations as well as the findings of the landscape archaeologist. In prehistory, we have no hope of discovering the past meaning of landscape in any direct sense; but prehistorians have quite a number of ideas about it, which they have borrowed from anthropologists.

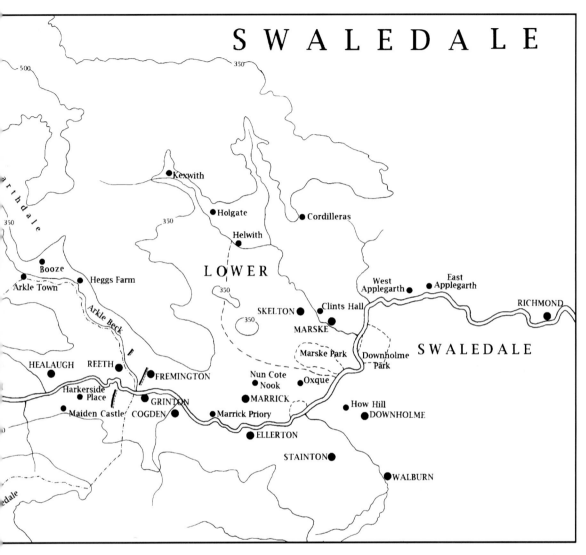

So what is the landscape of Swaledale like? Most Pennine rivers have British names, but the Swale's name is Old English, translating roughly as the tumultuous river,[10] 'the wild one'. The Swale got its name not from its sluggish lower passage through the Vales of York and Mowbray, but from its upper section, in Swaledale, where the river is said to have the steepest gradient of any major English river – about 1 in 160. The rapid rise of its waters is notorious, and has sometimes caused destructive and dramatic floods; a game worth playing in Swaledale is to stand on a bridge and see if you can spot the remains of its predecessor. Christopher Clarkson, Swaledale's other early nineteenth-century historian, recorded three major floods in a period of about seventy years.[11] After prolonged rainfall, the destructive rise of the Swale and its tributaries is awesome. Not long after the rains of January 1995, I saw how the banks of Gunnerside Beck had been sharply scoured and cut back, causing several land-slips. The Swale's tributary, the Arkle Beck, has washed away the church at Arkle Town, leaving behind a desolate kirk-garth, with its scattering of eighteenth-century tombstones.

The Swale has cut its course through sedimentary rocks, the sandstones and limestones of the Yoredale series. But Swaledale is not really limestone country like Upper Wharfedale, or the area around Malham. There *are* small areas of limestone scenery, for instance around the head of Oxnop Gill or on narrow shelves above Smarber and Ivelet, but generally the limestone is most prominent in the form of high crags towering above the daleside, as on Fremington Edge or between Richmond and Marske. In places, the dark shapes of yews may be seen on these cliffs, and on the screes below. This ecological preference may have given Ivelet its name, from Norse words meaning 'yew-stream slope'.[12] (I'm sure that the interpretation of the name offered by A. H. Smith in 1928 – 'Ifo's slope' – must be wrong; once you know the character of a place, you can sometimes take issue with the place-name experts!)

Swaledale lies among dark, heather-clad moorlands grazed by sheep and grouse. The moors carry a peat cover, shallow on shelves and shoulders above the daleside, but three or four feet deep on the watershed, where networks of rivulets have cut down to the base of the peat, and the going is hard. It is a tough walk north to the valley of the Greta, or south to Wensleydale, trudging over sodden, peat-clad moors or picking a way through a lunar landscape of miners' spoil-heaps, over ground still bare, poisoned by lead-smelting. But the wildest, most desolate stretch of moorland lies north of the head of Arkengarthdale, Swaledale's main tributary valley. From Tan Hill a great dark heather plain stretches north; in the distance, a stream of tiny white container lorries glints in the sun as they cross Stainmoor. Somewhere out there is the place where Erik Bloodaxe met his death in 954. These moors are desolate today; they are dedicated to the rearing of grouse, and their subsequent slaughter by the rich and famous, who have been hunting here since the Middle Ages.

Swaledale's isolation has always been relative. People who needed to cross the moor have always been able to do so, using established routes. They also had business on the moors. There was lead and coal to be won, peat to be cut, stone to be quarried, sheep and cattle to be tended; in the eighteenth century Scottish drovers took their cattle through. Swaledale people went to market at Hawes; young men went south to raid Wensleydale rabbit warrens or to court Wensleydale girls. In bad weather, even people who knew the moor like the back of their hand could lose their way, and who knew what tricks the *barghaists* or *boggles* might get up to in the mists? It was for travellers lost on the moors that a 'curfew bell' was once rung at Grinton church, every minute between eight and a quarter past eight, every night except Sundays from 25 October until 25 March.[13] Fifteen minutes was presumably enough time, in most cases, to walk or ride out of trouble, and woe betide anyone lost on the moors on the Sabbath.

The present main road from Richmond into Swaledale was constructed as a turnpike road in the 1830s. The older route from Richmond to Reeth followed the northern side of the dale, and went through Marske. In 1304 Thomas Robertson of Applegarth and Isabella his wife were accused of obstructing a certain road in West Applegarth 'leading from the town of Richmond to the pasture in Mersk and beyond into Swaledale'.[14] (I will explain later why the road was not yet in Swaledale when it was passing through Marske). This is likely to be a record of the medieval road, which went through East and West Applegarth. Later, and before the construction of the turnpike road on the other side of the Swale, the line of this road was rerouted to roughly its present course over the hills, across what would then have been moorland.

There was an easier way into Swaledale from the south-east, a route which ran through an opening in the hills, between Stainton and Downholme (the name Downholme means 'in the hills').[15] This route was Swaledale's most direct link with the outside world, or at least with Lower Wensleydale. Swaledale and Wensleydale are very different. Swaledale is narrow; it is easy to photograph archaeological sites on the opposite daleside. Wensleydale is much broader, and contains several large villages, including places like East Witton which were carefully planned in the Middle Ages, with its tofts and crofts at right angles to a long and broad village green. Most of Swaledale's settlements are best described as hamlets. Wensleydale is much more 'seigneurial' than Swaledale, in landscape terms; it had resident landlords who built great houses and laid out large landscape parks, such as those at Bolton Hall, Danby Hall and Jervaulx. Swaledale's landlords, by contrast, tended to live elsewhere. Middleham Castle has no counterpart in Swaledale, and Swaledale's two medieval nunneries, at Marrick and Ellerton, were much poorer than the Wensleydale monasteries of Jervaulx and Coverham.

It is the area around Downholme and Marske which is most like Wensleydale. There are no castles here, but there was a large planned medieval village at Walburn, deserted and now beautifully preserved as a complex pattern of grassy banks; the remains of the houses, tofts and crofts are all clearly visible (Fig. 7.4). There are three deer parks in close proximity to one another, at Downholme, Marske and Marrick; they are all probably medieval. The little village of Marske is now dominated by Marske Hall, effectively the only standing eighteenth-century building in Swaledale which can be described as 'polite' architecture. The hall's owners, the Hutton family, aspired to a set of cultural values shared by many of the landed gentry in other parts of England, although their love of architecture did not stop them demolishing Clints Hall, not far away, shortly after they had purchased it in 1843. It was a lovely house – a tall, sturdy seventeenth-century building of three storeys, with large mullioned windows, battlements and a three-decker porch in the centre of the facade.[16]

When the shadows lengthen on a summer evening, or when the snow takes a long time to melt, one can see that Marske lies in an area which was heavily cultivated in the Middle Ages – a zone which stretches across the river to

Downholme, and further south. On sloping land, almost everywhere there are strip lynchets – long, terraced fields. Hungry for cultivable land, the men of medieval Downholme drove their ploughs up the slopes of How Hill, destroying most of the rampart of a prehistoric hill-fort. The ploughmen even took land on the steep upper slopes of Downholme Park; when the leaves are off the trees it is possible to look across from Marske and see strip lynchets running along the contour, among the trees. Downholme Park was established as a deer park by Richard le Scrope under a licence granted in 1377, after the recession of the early fourteenth century, when this kind of land was no longer required for cultivation.[17]

North of Marske, Swaledale is separated from the valley of the Greta by a broad, high plateau, much of which was 'improved' and enclosed in the early nineteenth century; it is now range land, used by the army. The map confronts us with an exotic name – Cordilleras – a reminder that Swaledale's remoteness is strictly relative. The rich and powerful were always involved in the wider world. The chieftains of the Iron Age were caught up in tribal politics. The fate of some of Swaledale's lead-miners depended on the corporate strategy of the London Lead Company. In the middle of the seventeenth century a chunk of Arkengarthdale was bought by the City of London, which held on to it for twenty-eight years before selling it to Dr Charles Bathurst, Oliver Cromwell's physician, who donated the mystic initials 'C. B.' to Swaledale's mining (and beer-drinking) history.[18] Cordilleras, too, once offered a vision of distant horizons. A map of 1824, produced for the Hutton family of Marske, who owned the property, shows that all the recently enclosed fields had been given Latin-American names – nineteen of them, including Chimboracca, Sierra Pedrogosa, Maria Galante, Cotopaxi and Venezuela.[19] How the locals coped with these names is not recorded! This is a desolate, rather wild area; out here lie some of the most isolated farms in Swaledale, in the deep, narrow valleys of the streams which flow into Marske Beck – places like Kexwith, Holgate and Hellwith. Going west, up the main valley of the Swale, the most striking features are the two church towers of the medieval nunneries, both built on natural terraces just above the river – the tall, slender tower of ruined Ellerton, where the nuns' graves are now covered in cow-muck, and Marrick, rising above a cluster of farm buildings. Then the valley becomes broader. Around here it is possible to make out where the river has cut through great banks of gravel and stones, moraines left by the Swaledale glacier in the last Ice Age, as it paused in its retreat, melting every spring and summer into lakes which formed behind the moraines.

Here, on a shelf above the confluence of the Swale and the Arkle Beck, is Reeth, the 'capital' of Swaledale. With its large square green, Reeth now looks like a vast market-place. But the market is dead, and there are scarcely any shops. In the later Middle Ages this must have been a populous place, surrounded by extensive zones of arable land and subdivided meadow. Just west of Reeth, below the school, can be seen impressive flights of strip lynchets, the terraces

FIGURE 1.3. Medieval
strip lynchets at Reeth.

on which cereals were grown at that time (Fig. 1.3) An obvious challenge for
the landscape archaeologist is to work out what Reeth was like before the green
was laid out. We might also ask why there is no church here – and why was
the medieval parish church on the other side of the dale, at Grinton, associated
with a settlement on a north-facing slope and without much good land? General
books about Swaledale all mention the Corpse Way, along which the dead were
carried in wicker coffins from further up the dale, for burial at Grinton.[20] Before
the chapel of ease at Muker was granted a licence for burial (in 1580[21]) many
people's final journey was a long one, grim in bad weather; they were forced
to make it because Grinton was the only parish in Upper Swaledale. Grinton's
eastern boundary was less than twenty minutes' walk from the parish church,
but its western boundary was 16 miles (25km) away! Surely there must be a
good historical reason for this inconvenient state of affairs?

Running right across the dale here are two great earthworks, the Grinton-
Fremington dykes (Fig. 2.1). They are about 500 yards (c.500m) apart, each
with a massive bank and ditch. They are best seen to the west of Grinton,
though they crop up again on the north side of the dale, one running up
through Fremington and the other on the north side of the Arkle Beck,
further west. These earthworks might have had a defensive purpose, or they
might have marked a frontier. Either way, there are questions to be asked.
How can the zone which contains the largest settlement and the medieval

parish church, two obvious 'central places' for Upper Swaledale, also be a boundary zone? Not far away to the west is the big earthwork enclosure or 'hill-fort' known as Maiden Castle. Its dark rampart is often almost invisible from a distance; it is set in a sea of heather, on a narrow bench on the hillside just above and to the west of Harkerside Place. There were no medieval fortifications in Swaledale, apparently, but there were prehistoric defended enclosures, such as Maiden Castle, and the one on How Hill, Downholme, which I have already mentioned.

It is worth pausing on the road below Maiden Castle, or just beside Reeth School, and looking across the river. The weather has to be grim indeed to hide all traces of the old field-banks and platforms, large and small, which are mostly all that remains of the Iron Age and Roman landscape. They may not look spectacular – unless you catch them in just the right light (Fig. 1.4) – but it is a different story when they are all brought together and assembled on a map (Fig. 1.5). Further west, we move into Upper Swaledale. Between Reeth and Muker are the classic landscapes of walls and stone field-barns (Fig. 1.1). Easily seen from the road, the pattern of walls and barns in Gunnerside Bottoms, just south of Lodge Green, is so well known that it is almost embarrassing to be seen photographing it. If you want to experience this landscape, it is best to take one of the numerous footpaths through the fields. Every one of these rights of way challenges the landscape archaeologist to make sense of its origins; for these paths, with their beautifully constructed stiles, were established long before the Ramblers' Association got going. Historical explanations are also required for the patterns of the walls on the dalesides. These are striking in the landscape and even more obvious on the map – the ruler-straight walls on the daleside south of Muker (Fig. 4.1); the irregular jigsaw above Lodge Green, high on the eastern slopes of the valley of Gunnerside Beck; and the islands of enclosed land a little further east, each separated from its neighbours by a tortuous passage to the open pasture above (Fig. 4.3). One or two daleside pastures still display large zones of undivided grazing land below the top walls which separate them from the moors above. The best example is Ivelet Pasture, on the eastern side of that beautiful stretch of the dale between Keld and Muker, where road and river part company. There are many Norse place-names in the western part of Upper Swaledale – Thwaite, Angram, Satron, and Gunnerside, which was originally Gunnersett, the *saetr* or pasture of Gunnar.[22] Sometimes, on a warm summer evening when they are cutting the hay, with members of the family helping out by working the steep meadow-edges which machines cannot reach, one might almost be in Norway, or perhaps in the Alps. Swaledale looks in more than one direction; if Lower Swaledale has affinities with Wensleydale and the lands further east, Upper Swaledale is like a version of Westmorland.

One has to go out on to the moors and up the side-valleys to see Swaledale's industrial landscapes – the spoil-heaps, the smelt-mills, the long flue tunnels leading up the hillsides to carry away noxious fumes. Upstream from Surrender Bridge is the Old Gang smelt-mill complex, and on the shoulder above, the two long rows of stone pillars which supported the roof of the peat store – in its prime perhaps the biggest thatched building in Europe? Further upstream were the Old Gang Mines. Then there are the evocative ruins and spoil-heaps in the valley of Gunnerside Beck, to all appearance not long abandoned (Fig. 10.1). And if lead-mining has declined here, so has the small family farm. High on the dalesides, many farms and cottages have been deserted, and fine nineteenth-century building traditions lie in ruins; wrecked field-walls, buildings half open to the sky, distorted beams about to avalanche packs of stone slates on to the nettle-covered manure-heaps below.

West of Angram and Keld, the landscape is much wilder. There is no more daleside; the route to the pass which leads into Westmorland runs mostly across open moorland. The streams which make up the headwaters of the Swale trickle and ooze from deep peat into a network of becks which flow into a basin like the palm of an outstretched hand. Tracks gashed out by bulldozers lead to distant black shooting-huts made of corrugated iron. There are a few islands of enclosed pasture and meadow land, some attached to now derelict smallholdings. Here one can look around and see the higher hills which enclose the upper Swale watershed. Shunner Fell means 'Lookout Hill',[23] and there are names like Rogan's Seat, Hugh Seat, Lovely Seat – the *saetr* names given to upland pastures by speakers of Old Norse. Out here is the high-altitude pub at Tan Hill, once a refuge for drovers and coal-miners, and that lonely line of strange and sturdy drystone pillars known as the Nine Standards, Swaledale's remotest boundary marks (Fig. 1.6). And there are reminders of national history even in these remote hills. Some maps mark Hugh Morville Seat, recalling the name of one of the knights who murdered Thomas à Becket, and there is a boundstone inscribed 'AP 1664'. This was the boundary of land belonging to the redoubtable Lady Anne Clifford, Countess of Pembroke, who in her youth, before her epic fight to recover her estates, was well known in fashionable London circles.

At the far western end of the dale, one misses the woodlands. Many of Swaledale's deeper gills and side-valleys are wooded, and so are the steepest parts of the dalesides, where trees are the natural crop. The woods may be dominated by oak (in Lower Swaledale), wych elm, ash, sycamore, birch, hazel or alder; there is a good deal of holly, and rowan and bird-cherry are also found. The woodlands are at their best in May – the time of the bluebells, and the flowering of the bird-cherry, when the wild garlic really shows, first as a dark green carpet beneath trees still barely coming into leaf, then as a sheet of dazzling white. Some places derive their names from woodland detail; there is Heggs Farm, on the route from Fremington into Arkengarthdale, which is named after the bird-cherry (Old Norse, *heggr)*, and Ramps Holme, just across the Swale from Muker, which takes its name from Old English *hramsa,* the wild garlic.[24]

In Lower Swaledale, the woods tend to be managed, with clearly defined boundaries. Further west, patches of woodland are often unfenced; it is

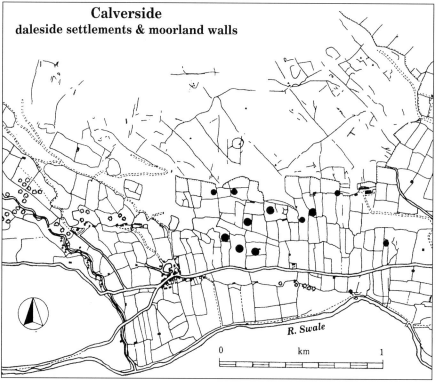

Calverside
daleside settlements & moorland walls

R. Swale

0   km   1

FIGURE 1.4 *(above)*.
Ancient and modern:
recent barns in an
ancient settlement
enclosure, with traces
of old field-banks
underlying the modern
walls – near Ivelet Bridge.

FIGURE 1.5 *(left)*.
Moorland walls (above
the modern field-
walls) and daleside
settlement-platforms
(black spots) between
Reeth and Healaugh
(the village marked on
the map). Individual
house-platforms are
not shown. The area of
best preservation on the
daleside lies between the
medieval arable lands of
Reeth and Healaugh.

FIGURE 1.6. The Nine Standards ('standers') at the far north-west corner of Swaledale.

not unusual to come across sheep among the trees, or to see cattle happily devouring leaves, as their wild ancestors must have done, several thousand years ago in the deciduous forests of Europe. Nowadays much of the woodland, in Upper Swaledale at least, appears to be rather casually managed, not greatly valued. Yet there are signs that trees were once more carefully looked after. In the central part of the dale, one can pick out the distinctive profiles of certain elms, *aums* as they were called locally, which were once pollards (Figs 6.1, 6.2). Until about 150 years ago, when pollarding mostly went out of fashion, their branches were regularly lopped a little above head height, to produce thick, knobbly crowns from which the main stems now spring. They occur on boundary-walls or sometimes in woods such as those beside the main road near Downholme Bridge. On steep slopes they are cut lower down on the trunk, forming 'stubs'; there are good examples in Rowleth Wood. Recently, elm pollards have suffered terribly from the ravages of Dutch elm disease and then from chain-saw massacres. And despite the dominance of walls, there are signs of a tradition of hedges in the dale. In some places, for example between Ivelet and Calvert Houses, one may suddenly come across ash trees whose branches have been trained to grow along the boundaries on which they stand. So, in a landscape famous for walls and haybarns, where do pollards and hedgerows come in?

Most of the woods lie apart from the places where people live. Swaledale's hamlets, and the two or three settlements which might be called villages, are an essential part of the Yorkshire Dales scenery package. The heart has gone out of some of these places, with their holiday cottages and second homes, and it is hard to imagine how full of life they once were. They challenge the landscape archaeologist to work out their origins. Why are settlements where they are? Were they once somewhere else? How did they work, as communities of farmers and lead-miners? There are few maps early enough to show what these places were like three hundred years ago, let alone in the Middle Ages; if we are to work out their earlier layout, we have to use more recent maps, and look for clues on the ground.

Swaledale's settlements vary a great deal. What historical factors lie behind the basic layout of places as different as Reeth, with its great square green; or Downholme and Grinton, with their houses mostly set along a single street; or places like Lodge Green or Low Row, straggling along a rather irregular green? Fortunately, because settlements contain so many continuously inhabited properties, often side by side, the basic layout of a place – particularly its property boundaries, its building lines and its network of lanes and paths – is more likely to be added to, with 'infilling' and 'ribbon development', rather than drastically changed. This allows us to work out a sequence of growth – or sometimes of decline. Swaledale's main settlements are important; they should tell us a good deal about social and economic change, about family structures and population, and about changing styles and fashions.

A book about the history of places runs the risk of losing sight of people. In these circumstances, I feel that I must let the past people of Swaledale speak their own language, if only briefly. Much of their distinctive identity was defined by the way they pronounced the English language, and the words they used. Fortunately, the language of Swaledale is not entirely lost to us. In 1870 Captain John Harland, of Reeth, compiled a Swaledale-English dictionary.[25] Another Reeth man, Newton Whitehead, who died in 1988, left a manuscript for a Swaledale dialect dictionary; quite by chance, I happened to come across it in a secondhand bookshop in Ilkley.[26] The language of Swaledale drew on a colourful vocabulary. How can we do without words like *pazzocking* (prowling about), *rummleduster* (an unruly or troublesome person) or *moame* (quiet, as in 'moame as a mouse', or 'keep mum')?

Just as the Eskimos have numerous words for different kinds of snow, Swaledale people had words for different kinds of weather. They could talk about a *glishy* morning (a bright sunlit morning – 'often followed by a wet day', notes Whitehead gloomily), and then there was a *girsy* day, a mild moist day which helped the grass to grow. Naturally there are plenty of words for precipitation, such as *mizzle* (light rain), *maiging* (drizzling), *daggy* (drizzly), a *clashy* (wet) day; *pash* was the heavy rain in a thunderstorm; *fremd* was a stormy day, perhaps ushered in by a *rack* ('clouds driven rapidly by wind'). An extremely wet day was described as *evendoon*. After this sort of weather, things were liable to become *dozzened* or *droked* (sodden). It might be worse: a *hap-up* was heavy snow *(hap* meaning to cover), and one might well have to *teeave* (wade) through *drife* (drifting snow). And there were plenty of words for other sorts of weather; for instance, a day could be *rooky* (misty) or *growy* (warm, moist and dull); *lound* or *lown* meant a calm, quiet day, after the wind had died down. The weather affected work on the farm: haytime could be *fortherly* (early) or *backerly* (late).

Then there are words which seem to go back to the very roots of the language – words like *gotherly* (sociable), *fore-elders* (ancestors) or *onbethink* (to recollect). There were words for the less fortunate members of a community – a *pockard* who had survived an attack of smallpox, or a *lovebegot* (an illegitimate child); a simpleton was a *mazelin*, a *donnat*, or a *gawvison*. There are words for animals, plants and insects which must make us regret the rise of standard English – words like *attercop* (spider), *daker hen* (corncrake), *crake* (crow), *foulmart* (polecat), *grey hen* (female black grouse), *hewlet* (owl)*, moudiwarp* (mole), *piat* or *piannet* (magpie), *ask* (lizard), *bummlekite* (a blackberry), *fellfaw* (fieldfare), *frosk* (frog), *pate* (badger), *glead* (kite), *simmeren* (primrose) and *kelk-keksy* (a large meadow-plant).

In this book, I want to describe the process of landscape reconstruction – which starts by recognising landscape patterns which are well known, and using them as a basic framework. Then it is a question of trying to find traces of fainter, underlying patterns, and of observing what has barely been noticed before. The appearance of a particular piece of landscape reflects its history. For instance, on the footpath from Oxque to Nun Cote Nook, just north of Marrick, one cannot help noticing the differences between the landscapes on either side of Ellers (otherwise Dales) Beck. To the north lies the early nineteenth-century landscape of 'improvement' – large rectangular fields with ruler-straight boundaries, laid out by a surveyor. The look of the walls and buildings and the character and spacing of the trees result from an estate management policy, implemented by landowners and managers who could afford to care about the appearance of the landscape, and were expected to invest in it. On the south side of the beck, the landscape looks a good deal rougher, more 'organic'; there are stretches of half tumbledown walling, ash trees of various different ages and conditions, and lines of tall straggly thorn trees which look as if they have never made up their mind whether they are proper hedges. This is the penny-pinched, none too secure landscape of tenant farming.

Appearance is one thing; the framework of analysis is something else. Usually, in England, we can start by reconstructing the landscape of the later Middle Ages, from about 1100 to 1400. When William the Conqueror seized and redistributed England among a hierarchy of subordinate feudal lords, later producing the giant land register of vills or manors which we call Domesday Book (1086), he bequeathed a framework for the holding of land, and later its 'ownership', which was to have an enduring influence on the scale and character of the English landscape. Increasingly, land-holding became a matter of legal entitlement, and written documents became more important than the testimony of old men; there was therefore quite a strong presumption against the changing of names and boundaries. When change did occur, as the late medieval population rose, it usually involved *subdivision* of existing manors, townships or parishes, and we can pick this up quite readily from maps, documents and patterns of names. As we will see, when names do change, the older ones are often mentioned as alternatives, to make the legal situation quite clear.

In the later Middle Ages the population was expanding rapidly; the countervailing pressures of so many claims upon the land tended to stabilise boundaries. This population peak has left its mark upon the landscape, in the form of deserted and shrunken settlements, with abandoned fields and ploughlands on what we would regard as uncultivable or marginal land today. These pressures also meant that the land was comprehensively *named* – some of these names have been lost or distorted, but many have survived.

Among communities highly dependent on arable land, the archaeological evidence for clear and rather predictable patterns of intensive land-use within township boundaries is impressive (although between Domesday and the Black Death there were many changes). We can usually reconstruct the late medieval landscape in a good deal of detail, and we can then use this as a basic framework for working out the sequence of settlement, moving backwards or forwards from this chronological horizon. Usually, the boundaries of post-Conquest manors and parishes respected those of existing townships, and as we go back into the pre-Conquest period, hypotheses about the stability of boundaries and the preservation of old names are often crucial to the argument. The boundaries of townships, manors and parishes may or may not coincide; studying the relationships between them often leads to valuable historical insights. Above all, confidence depends on being able to show that particular patterns and relationships recur in different places.

We can also work *forwards* in time, noting how manors were subdivided and how new settlements became established. We can also study how the demise of the medieval community affected the landscape, with drastic social and economic changes which led to the concentration of land in fewer and fewer hands, the growth of a class of landless labourers, and the extinction of common rights and other long-standing entitlements. The appearance of the landscape has changed dramatically since the Middle Ages; most obviously, open fields divided into furlongs of ridge-and-furrow have been replaced by parcels of enclosed land. But the changes have been carried out within the basic framework of old township and parish boundaries, units of analysis which we cannot ignore.

A major theme in Swaledale's landscape history is the rise and decline of the township community. In this Pennine valley, communities were tenacious in maintaining and perpetuating their rights, and in defence of more communal lifeways than most of us know today. It is a major challenge to the landscape historian to imagine this more communal, interdependent world, which is largely lost to us now. In a historical perspective, the isolated farm on the daleside is quite a recent phenomenon; what we must try to understand is the township, and the workings of old Swaledale communities.

Notes

1. Whitaker 1823, 9.
2. Whitaker 1823, 399.
3. North Yorkshire County Record Office (NYCRO): census returns for Healaugh, 1851.
4. Toulmin Smith 1906–10, 26.
5. Fieldhouse and Jennings 1978.
6. Redmonds 1973.
7. NYCRO ZQAI7/1.
8. Smith, 1928.
9. Smith 1967; Armstrong *et al.* 1950.
10. Ekwall 1960, 455.
11. Clarkson 1821, 306.
12. Smith 1928, 272; Armstrong *et al.* 1950, 480.
13. Whitehead nd [the author died in 1988].
14. Harrison 1879, 211.
15. Smith 1928, 270.
16. Waterson and Meadows, 1990, 50.
17. NYCRO ZBO.
18. Fieldhouse and Jennings 1978, 121.
19. NYCRO ZAZ (M) 11.
20. Pontefract 1934, chapter XIV.
21. Cooper 1948, 30.
22. For the meanings of Norse place-names in Upper Swaledale, see Smith 1928, though a better and fuller understanding of Norse place-names comes from a later work by the same author (Smith 1967).
23. Ekwall 1960, 421.
24. Smith 1967, 260; Ekwall 1960, 380.
25. Harland 1873.
26. Whitehead nd.

CHAPTER TWO

In the Kingdom
of the Swale

The first clue to the origins of medieval Swaledale is provided by a couple of quite well-known earthworks, the Grinton-Fremington dykes. They are about 500 yards (c.500m) apart. From their position on the dalesides, they appear to be defending both Upper Swaledale and Arkengarthdale against intruders advancing from the east, since each dyke consists of a high, broad bank with a ditch on its eastern side. The earthworks are best seen on the southern side of the dale. The eastern dyke, which is only about 300 yards (c.500m) west of Grinton church, carries a row of dead elm pollards; walk on west, past Swale Hall and Scar House, and you will reach the western dyke, which is bare of trees at its upper end (Fig. 2.1). From here, good eyesight and a map are needed to pick out the northern ends of each of the two earthworks, on the other side of the dale. The map also marks a couple of earthworks to the south, on Grinton Moor, and a third dyke which also cuts across the valley nearly 2 miles (3km) further east, just across the river from Marrick Priory. I will call this the Rue Dyke, since this was its name in the twelfth century.[1] The earthworks have not been excavated, so we do not really know what they looked like originally, or how often they may have been repaired and refurbished. On the westernmost dyke, immediately south of the lane running west from just below Swale Hall, a modern break in the earthwork reveals that its eastern side had a carefully built stone face. When I first came to Swaledale, I had no idea that the Grinton-Fremington dykes would prove crucial to the understanding of Swaledale's past. It was the late Don Spratt, an outstanding amateur archaeologist, who introduced me both to the dale and to Tim Laurie, who also lived locally, and had begun to take a serious interest in the ruined, heather-covered walls on the moors around Reeth. Tim had some black-and-white air photographs, taken by Mike Griffiths of the North Yorkshire county archaeology section, which showed that these walls were relatively long and straight, with the main ones running parallel to one another and separated by perhaps 100 yards (c.100m) or so, apparently forming large systems of land division. On the ground, the walls proved to be broad and low, often faced with upright slabs or large stone blocks, the wall cores being made up of smaller stones-very like the prehistoric walls, known as reaves, which I was studying on Dartmoor, in Devon.[2] The Dartmoor reaves also defined and subdivided very large areas of land, using a dominant if not very rigid axis of orientation; one of the Dartmoor 'reave systems' where I worked was about 4 miles (6.5km) from end to end, and covered about 18,500 acres (7,500 hectares). I had taken to using the word 'coaxial' to describe field systems of this type, and when I came to Swaledale I was interested in finding out about other coaxial systems. How old were they, and what did they have in common?

Although a few archaeological features in Swaledale were listed in Fieldhouse and Jennings' History of Richmond and Swaledale, no-one had done any sustained archaeological work here. In Upper Wharfedale, Ribblesdale and around Malham Tarn, ancient settlement sites and field boundaries were quite well known, thanks to the work of Arthur Raistrick and Alan King;[3] they were variously thought to be Iron Age, Romano-British, perhaps even Bronze Age in places, but no-one could be very confident about their dating. For Swaledale (and Wensleydale for that matter), the literature was largely silent about the prehistoric and Roman periods; lists of sites arranged in chronological order were a poor substitute for a narrative account based on archaeology. Tim and I decided to start the Swaledale Ancient Land Boundaries Project, and to do some work on these coaxial systems. But we soon realised that the moors were not the only interesting area. When the evening sun hung low in the sky, we started to notice low banks, casting long shadows in the daleside pastures and meadows – fragments of land divisions which must pre-date the present pattern of walled fields. Tim already knew of one or two old settlement sites on the daleside. Nevertheless, it was an exciting day when we first took a walk through the fields to the east of Healaugh, and came across a zone of ancient settlement – old field-banks visible beneath the present-day walls, and sizeable platforms cut back into the hillside to accommodate settlements. There were smaller platforms for individual buildings – some round, some oval, some rectangular. Some of these 'house-platforms' were on larger settlement-platforms originally enclosed by walls; others were apparently in the open, by themselves or in small groups. We had discovered quite a well-preserved 'ancient landscape' (Fig. 2.2).

The state of preservation of these daleside features was variable. It was best in areas of old pasture, and at its worst where medieval ploughmen had been most active. Nevertheless, it was fairly clear that the daleside between Reeth and Healaugh, and across the Swale to the west of Grinton and around Harkerside Place, had been quite fully occupied at some time before the later Middle Ages. Settlements, not necessarily all inhabited at the same time, had been distributed among a pattern of fields laid out coaxially on much the same axis as the land divisions on the moors above (Fig. 1.5). However, the daleside fields were much narrower, forming a pattern altogether more complex than the one on the moors – where very few obvious house sites were visible. We took the view that, even if these settlements and land boundaries originated in the prehistoric period, the landscape which we were looking at was essentially Romano-British. This is partly because many of the settlement sites look like others in the North which have produced Roman pottery, coins and so on. Also, in the later Roman period the province of Britannia experienced a considerable growth of population, and a high density of settlements in many areas. Field systems and settlements

surviving from the Iron Age would have been substantially reorganised. That seems to be the message from Roman Britain in general.

How do the Grinton-Fremington dykes relate to this 'ancient' landscape? In the literature, these earthworks have been labelled 'Brigantian', after the Brigantes, the Latinised Celtic name used by the Romans to describe the loose tribal confederacy inhabiting much of North and West Yorkshire in the Iron Age. (The name is supposed to mean something like 'highlanders',[4] so perhaps the Pennines were their original homeland.) Arthur Raistrick[5] suggested that the dykes were constructed in the early 70s AD, during the struggle of the Brigantes against the Romans, which was led by Venutius, the estranged husband of queen Cartimandua, who had reached an accommodation with the invaders. Raistrick must have been influenced by the excavations carried out by Sir Mortimer Wheeler in 1951–2 at the enormous embanked enclosures at Stanwick, 4 miles (6.5km) north of Scotch Corner.[6] Wheeler attributed two major episodes of enlargement at Stanwick to Venutius. It was certainly a very important place in the first century AD.

FIGURE 2.1. The westernmost of the Grinton-Fremington dykes, looking south from Reeth.

However, there is a problem with dating the Swaledale earthworks to the end of the Iron Age. Immediately in front of the western earthwork, in a field which was called Dyke House Close in the early nineteenth century,[7] are some grass-covered banks which appear to represent a small Romano-British farm (Fig. 2.1). The ditch of the earthwork has cut through at least one of the banks marking out this farm complex, and has sliced through one of the boundaries of the long, narrow strip-fields running downslope from the farm. If this is a Roman settlement, the earthwork must be no earlier than late Roman in date. On the other side of the earthwork, a field-bank of the 'ancient' type converges to meet it at an acute angle. If the bank was contemporary with, or later than, the earthwork, it would have enclosed a very odd-shaped piece of land; clearly, the field-bank pre-dates the earthwork. The upper end of the earthwork lies just west of Dyke House. It stops at the point where the ground rises more steeply, just below the moor; and on this grassy slope, in the right light conditions, it can be seen that the dyke has followed the line of one of the old 'coaxial' walls on Harkerside Moor. In other words, the Harkerside coaxial system was already in being when the earthwork was constructed.

FIGURE 2.2. Old fields and settlement sites near Cogden Hall, photographed in winter. The obvious settlement-platform at the bottom left-hand corner of the field has a large rectangular settlement site above it; there are also traced of two different field systems.

So is it possible that the Grinton-Fremington dykes are post-Roman, and belong to another great time of earthwork construction in Britain, the early post-Roman period? A hundred miles (160km) to the south, near Bradwell in the Peak District of Derbyshire, there's a similar earth-work running across a valley, just like the Swaledale dykes. It is called the Grey Ditch, and is about a mile (1,600m) long, although it is not continuous. Here, during a recent archaeological excavation,[8] an old ploughsoil sealed beneath the bank of the earthwork contained sherds of Roman pottery dating from the mid-second to the fourth century. The excavator, Graeme Guilbert, has pointed out that the dyke cuts across Batham Gate, a Roman road leading to the fort of Navio not far away. Since Navio was still in use in the mid-fourth century, the dyke can

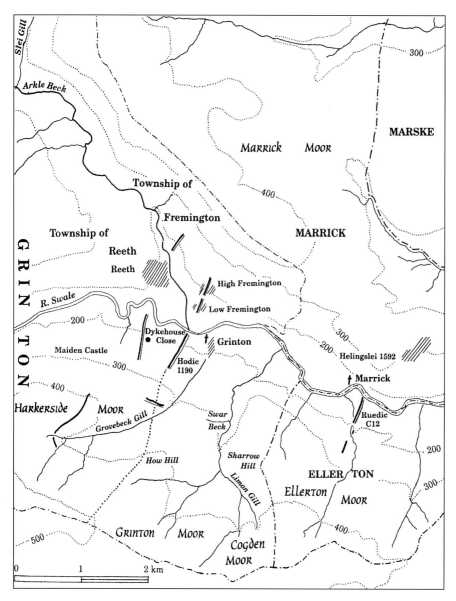

FIGURE 2.3. Map illustrating the linear earthworks at the east end of Old Swaledale, including places mentioned in the text.

hardly be earlier than the final decades of Roman occupation; Guilbert suggests that it was actually built sometime in the middle of the first millennium AD.

What other arguments might help to fix the date of the earthworks more precisely? In this area, there are three townships with names in tun – Grinton, Fremington and Ellerton (Fig. 2.3). According to our leading place-name expert Margaret Gelling, most of the tun names in England date from about 750–950.[9] Certainly these three *tūns* were in existence by 1086, as they are mentioned in Domesday Book.[10] Now the boundaries of these townships were laid out mostly without reference to the dykes, which cut through the middle of Fremington township. Both Grinton and Ellerton, too, have a dyke within their boundaries. Nor does the old Grinton-Ellerton parish boundary follow the line of a dyke; it runs in fact just where you would expect it, more or less halfway between the settlements. (In the case of Ellerton, I'm referring to the abandoned medieval hamlet, which was located to the west of the nunnery). Furthermore, the hamlet of Grinton is about 250 yards (c.250m) outside the ditch of the eastern dyke; across the valley, Fremington is even closer to the earthwork – and also situated on its eastern, undefended side. It looks as if when these *tūn* settlements were established, probably around AD 800–900, the dykes were no longer in effective use.

We have succeeded in boxing the earthworks in, chronologically, between the end of the Roman period and the period of *tūn* place-names. So what were they? Might they have been put up not long after the withdrawal of the Roman army, to defend the local people, speakers of Old Welsh, against Anglians from northern Germany, who spoke Old English and had already taken over in East Yorkshire? Or were they constructed by people already under Anglian rule, defending themselves against the incursions of other Anglians?

Taking the enquiry further involves documents and place-names. Let us start with Marrick. The name means 'boundary ridge'.[11] But there is no plausible 'boundary ridge' near Marrick village. In any case, as I shall explain later, this village formerly had a different name; the original Marrick was down by the Swale, where Marrick Priory was established. The 'boundary ridge' must have been Rue Dyke, just across the river. According to Margaret Gelling, the second element in Marrick's name is Old English *ric* or the hypothetical word *raec*. Names derived from *raecan* are to do with the idea of straightness;[12] hence Escrick, in the Vale of York (the 'ridge' being a moraine), and Reach, in Cambridgeshire, located at the north end of the Devil's Ditch, a long, straight post-Roman linear earthwork, which is cut by Newmarket racecourse. At Marrick the northern end of the Rue Dyke is certainly straight enough, although the earthwork is a little confusing, because its ditch is also a hollow way (now a bridle way) leading to a ford across the Swale. It is also on the line of a moraine, where Swaledale's glacier paused in its slow retreat.[13] South of the main road, near Hags Gill Farm, the boundary makers were content to modify the moraine, although as it climbs the slope to the south, the boundary becomes a bank and ditch again.

Not far away, just off the Grinton-Leyburn road, is a limestone bluff called Sharrow Hill. 'Sharrow' is *scearu* and *hōh* – 'the heel-shaped hill on the boundary'.[14] The old parish boundary between Grinton and Ellerton (or rather Downholme, since Ellerton is not an ancient parish) does indeed run over this hill on its way to Snowden Man, on the watershed to the south. But it is unlikely to be the parish boundary which is commemorated here. Like Marrick, Sharrow is a fairly early English name; so it is likely to refer to a boundary set up before the establishment of parishes, about a century on either side of the Norman Conquest. Is it possible, then, that the enormous medieval parish of Grinton, which extended from Sharrow Hill all the way to the head of the dale, was based on an earlier territory, whose eastern boundary ran through the zone of old, now disused linear earthworks?

This is where we come to the documents. In the later Middle Ages, Bridlington Priory, some 70 miles (110km) away on the East Yorkshire coast, had property in Upper Swaledale. The priory's records, preserved in the Bridlington Cartulary, refer to Grinton church as 'the church of Swaledale'. There are also references to 'the church of Swaldale with the vill of Grenton' and 'the vill of Grenton and Swaldal'.[15] An early eighteenth-century map describes Grinton as 'the parish Town of Swaledale'.[16] So 'Swaledale' must have been the old name for what was later known as the parish of Grinton. But that is not all; it was also the old name for the manor of Healaugh. For this part of Swaledale, Domesday Book lists the vills of Marrick, Ellerton, Grinton, Fremington and Reeth;[17] settlements further west must have been included under the entry for Reeth. But when Walter de Gaunt took control in the early twelfth century, the manor which he established was named from Healaugh, and it occupied the whole of the upper dale. And in medieval and later documents, both Reeth and Swaledale are frequently listed as alternative names for the manor; in the most complete examples, the wording is 'the manor of Healaugh alias the manor of Reeth alias the manor of Swaledale'.[18] We also find names like 'John de Rithe of Swaldale' and 'William de Ellerton in Swaldal'.[19]

So it is clear, from its persistence as an alternative name for Grinton parish and Healaugh manor, that 'Swaledale' was not just a general geographical label. It was the name of a well-defined political or administrative area, similar to others in Yorkshire, like Elmet, Morthen and Balne (as in Barwick in Elmet, Laughton en le Morthen, and Thorpe in Balne). Quite frequently in the documentary record, the suffix 'in Swaledale' is tacked on to place-names.[20] We find places as far west as Keld and West Stonesdale being identified in this way, and relatively unimportant places such as Folyng-in-Swaledale (Foal Ing, a former common meadow just below Low Row). Occasionally there are triple names, such as 'Somerlodge in Grinton in Swaledale'. To this day, the guide leaflet to Grinton church refers to the place as Grinton in Swaledale. Eventually, 'in Swaledale' did come to be understood, or rather misunderstood, as a simple geographical label, sometimes with comical results; thus there is at least one late sixteenth-century document which refers to the manors of Helagh-in-Swaledale, Grinton-in-Swaledale and also Swaledale-in-Swaledale![21] There is also a 1620 sale of 'all those manors or lordships of Helaughe and Swaldale and Swaudale in Swauldale', which seems to be trying to represent all possible pronunciations as well as all possible names![22]

In the archives at Northallerton is a map dated 1738 (Fig. 2.4).[23] It depicts the Swale valley above Reeth and Grinton, with the river and its tributaries, various settlements and an external boundary, mostly marked by points on the surrounding watersheds. There is no caption; but 'Swaldale' is written right across the area enclosed. The absorbing question arises: who, as late as the eighteenth century, would have been interested in making a map, not of Healaugh Manor or Grinton parish, but of 'Swaledale'? There's a clue on the

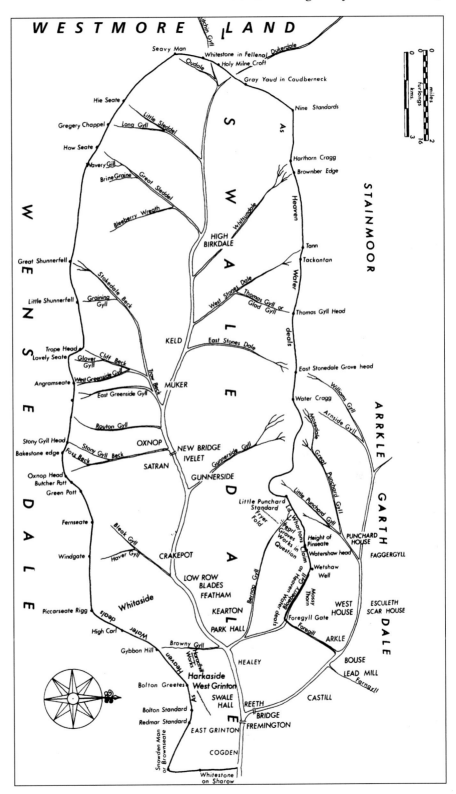

FIGURE 2.4. Map of Old Swaledale in the early eighteenth century (redrawn from the original).

map itself; a label indicates 'the works in question', which were located at or near Forefield Rake, just west of Great Pinseat, part of a long series of rakes which stretch westwards into Gunnerside Gill and beyond. So the map was made in connection with lead-mining; evidently 'Swaledale' was still the name of a recognised lead-mining district in the eighteenth century. Since 'Swaldal' existed before Grinton parish and Healaugh Manor, we may have to conclude that lead-mining was going on here before the Norman Conquest, as it was in Derbyshire. As Arthur Raistrick pointed out a long time ago, some of the technical terms used by the lead-miners of the Yorkshire Pennines are Norse words.[24] *Groove*, the north-country word for a mine, comes from an Old Norse word meaning to dig. The bale hill, where lead was smelted on a knoll deliberately exposed to the wind, gets its name from the Old Norse *bál* and fire or beacon.[25] And the boose teme, or ore hopper, was also a Norse name.

The making of this map, the insistence on using the old name in documents, and the continuing use of the place-name suffix 'in Swaledale' testify to the strength and persistence of historical memory in the dale. The tradition finds echoes even today. In 1984 a sociologist, Scott Phillips, wrote a doctoral dissertation on the parish of Muker. Discussing the 'world view' of Muker people, he wrote:[26]

> The generally-agreed axiom is that the further one goes up the dale from Richmond ... the broader and – so Muker people imply – the more authentic the dialect becomes, and vice versa. Locals especially consider that there are 'two Swaledales, each having a distinct culture history, landscape and economy'. People in and below Reeth ... are considered to speak 'in a more civilised way' than Muker people...

Far be it from me to comment on levels of civilisation in different parts of Swaledale! As we have seen, the distinctive character of the upper dale has deep roots in history. From a historical point of view, one might question whether Richmond should describe itself as 'the gateway to Swaledale'. From now on, I will use the term 'Old Swaledale' or 'historic Swaledale' to refer to the land beyond the dykes.

As the word 'dale' is English as well as Norse, I thought at first that the English name for the land behind the dykes must also have been something like 'Swaldal'. But then Margaret Gelling pointed out to me that Norse speakers tended to use the word 'dale' to describe a long valley; for the early English, a dale was usually much shorter. So perhaps the incoming English did what they did in other areas, and used the name of the river to describe themselves and the name of their territory, like the Wissa in Norfolk who lived by the river Wissey.[27] Steve Bassett has suggested that these small early English territories should be described as 'kingdoms',[28] which does at least reflect their political independence (rather short-lived in the case of the smaller ones). I propose to call this small early English realm 'the kingdom of the Swale', though if there was a local leader, he or she would have been more like a chieftain than a king. As a matter of fact, the word 'Swale' does occasionally crop up as a place-name, as in a document of about 1170, which refers to 'Reyth in le Swale'.[29]

Eventually, probably in the tenth century, the kingdom of the Swale was settled by Norse speakers from further west. For several generations, English and Norse traditions must have co-existed, sometimes separate, sometimes merging, as in other parts of northern England. Old Norse contributed to the northern version of Middle English, and to north Yorkshire dialect. Scandinavian personal names survived in northern England well into the thirteenth century. Occasionally, place-name evidence drops a hint about the situation around the time of the Norman Conquest. For instance, a document of 1254 mentions Ferrinden Beck which was evidently somewhere in lower Arkengarthdale, towards the northern end of Fremington township.[30] In the early nineteenth century, Anthony Clarkson's map of Swaledale marks 'Farndale' in the same area.[31] Now 'Ferrinden' and 'Farndale' mean 'fern valley' in English and Norse respectively. Here we get a glimpse of a Norse translation of the English name for the short, steep-sided valley now marked on the map as Slei Gill, and a sense of interplay between the two languages.

There are hints that the name of Swale had a certain mystique in Swaledale; perhaps some knowledge of the valley's early history was handed down from generation to generation. Although the surname 'Swaledale' seems to have died out (unlike Teesdale), the name Swale has survived, though I'm not sure if there are any Swales living in the dale now. One of Swaledale's most interesting historical figures was Sir Solomon Swale, who arrived here soon after the restoration of Charles II.[32] Sir Solomon was a Royalist, apparently the first person to suggest to Parliament that Charles should be proclaimed king, for which political service he obtained his baronetcy. This sounds familiar enough to modern ears! As Roebuck has written:[33]

> a generous guardian, lucrative marriage, and success at the bar increased his [Solomon Swale's] means, enabling him to purchase his ancestral home, Swale Hall. However, despite grants and interest-free loans totalling £4,000 from Charles II, his prosperity was short-lived. He became embroiled in fruitless attempts to mine lead in Swaledale and by 1700 the family was bankrupt...

The Swales sought, unsuccessfully, and with the aid of a bogus document, to establish their claim to a phoney 'manor of West Grinton'. During one of these lawsuits, in 1697, one of the witnesses said he had heard from his father that John Swale was 'the ancientest gentleman in Yorkshire'.[34] Despite the lawsuits and document-faking, the Swales were evidently thought of as an 'old' family, and before they went bankrupt they certainly seem to have conducted themselves like old-fashioned gentry.

The Swales claimed a distinguished ancestry in Swaledale, and their story got into the history books. According to the Victoria County History (1914) which based its account on the work of Christopher Clarkson in the early nineteenth century:[35]

> the tradition is that Alice sister of Walter de Gant married John de Swale and became mother of Alured de Swaledale (living 1157) ... Alured [Alfred] is an historical personage ... William Over Swale held 1 carucate of land in Reeth in 1273–4, and

was assessed for the subsidy in Grinton in 1301–2. In 1316 Robert Swakk (?Swale) was even returned as joint lord of the vill of Grinton. The Swales continued to live here for some centuries, apparently without claiming manorial rights; but in 1578 John Swale made a settlement of the 'manor of Swale'…

Clarkson also believed that the Swale arms (Swale of Swale, as the Victoria County History described them) of 'three bucks' heads caboshed, two and one, argent', were given by Walter de Gant to Alured (Alfred) de Swale.

So what is the truth? It is tempting to suggest that when the de Gaunts arrived and established the Manor of Healaugh in the early twelfth century, they found a large family of Swales, perhaps mostly in the Reeth area, some of whom claimed to be descendants of the old chiefly family. Perhaps Walter de Gaunt did find it politic to marry his sister to one of the leading male members of the older 'aristocracy' – especially if his arrival had deprived the Swales of some of their traditional rights, their title to land for example. On the other hand, the seventeenth-century Swales would have had good reason to fabricate the evidence, and it seems that somebody did fake a document; perhaps someone leaned on one or two witnesses as well. Historians such as Christopher Clarkson depended on the patronage of the rich and famous to pay for the publication of their work; there was little to be gained by questioning the historical pedigree of 'old' local families. But then again, if the seventeenth-century Swales were fabricating or embellishing some of the evidence, that does not necessarily mean that their family traditions were untrue; they were trying to establish legal title, which meant getting it all put down in writing. Would they have attempted to 'get away with it' unless their claim was plausible in terms of local tradition?

We will never know whether the Swales really were descended from the old chiefly family of the Swale. In a sense it does not matter; in questions of identity, people believe what they want to believe. The mystique which has gathered around the name is fascinating. After the demise of the family in the eighteenth century, there were other claimants to the Swale title. In recent years a memorial plaque to the family has been placed in Grinton church, inscribed 'in memory of the family of Swale of Swale Hall, Grinton AD 1138–1733. The family was founded by Alured de Swale, the nephew of Walter de Gaunt, a kinsman of William the Conqueror'. In the light of the discussion above, it may be ironic that the plaque emphasises the family's supposed kinship with William the Conqueror!

To summarise: after the departure of the Roman armies, there was a 'British' period, followed by the arrival of the Anglians, the formation of the kingdom of the Swale and then the incursions of the Norse. What else can be said about this period of over six hundred years, between the Romans and the Normans? I believe that the Grinton-Fremington dykes, and Rue Dyke further east, were probably constructed by the British, whose immediate ancestors had lived within the Roman province of Britannia; although it is conceivable that one or more of the dykes was built and/or repaired under Anglian orders. It is possible to argue that they were constructed over a period of years or decades, in sequence from west to east.[36] It may be that the earthworks on the moors, in and above the valley of the Grovebeck, on Harkerside to the south, were also part of an anti-Anglian defence system. As a result of work on names and boundaries, various other British 'kingdoms' and territorial units are being recognised in the Pennines. In West Yorkshire there was Elmet ('elmwood') and Loidis (the district which gave its name to Leeds). There was Craven (the 'scraped' land, a reference to its bare limestone pavements) which took in the upper valleys of the Ribble, the Aire and the Wharfe. There was Dentdale, which was Dunutinga in the seventh century, and may have taken its name from a ruler called Dunawt.[37] The early medieval territorial jigsaw is taking shape. One wonders how the area now known as Wensleydale, formerly Uredale, fitted into this picture; is there evidence somewhere whose significance we have yet to recognise?

It seems that the British in the Pennines made determined efforts to keep out the Anglians. In West Yorkshire, Grim's Ditch, an earthwork to the east of Leeds,[38] which was over 5 miles (8km) long, was probably one of the defences of Elmet. Some of the other West Yorkshire earthworks, around Aberford, may also reflect British/Anglian conflict. Other earthworks in North Yorkshire could be interpreted in the same terms. Perhaps the most ambitious one is Scot's Dyke, a long earthwork whose southern end reaches the Swale near Easby, just east of Richmond. From here it travels north, passing to the east of Gilling, through Melsonby and then just east of the extensive Late Iron Age earthworks at Stanwick. It seems to be heading for the Tees, but it does not seem possible to prove a course for it north of Stanwick. Has it been comprehensively destroyed, or was it unfinished? The completed section of the dyke is 'defending' the areas most likely to have been well populated, with well-motivated labour forces – the Stanwick area (an old Iron Age heartland) and the valleys of Gilling Beck and Hutton Beck. Gilling was once an important place. At the time of the Norman Conquest it was held by the powerful Edwin, Earl of Mercia; under the Normans it became the chief manor of Count Alan, lord of the newly created Richmondshire, a lordship intended to act as a bulwark against the Scots. It was the centre of one of the old 'shires', and the manor had many outlying townships attached to it – which makes it likely to have been a territorial entity rather like the one in Upper Swaledale, an early English petty kingdom perhaps with older roots.[39]

It's possible to interpret Scot's Dyke as the work of a powerful British ruler such as Urien, Lord of Rheged, who was eulogised (mythologised?) by the Welsh poet Taliesin. Rheged was a British kingdom whose heartland is supposed to have lain somewhere in south-west Scotland, or around Carlisle.[40] Urien is also described as Lord of Catraeth, which is agreed by most scholars to refer to Catterick, which derives its name from Cataractonium, the Roman town located at Catterick Bridge. Cataractonium was probably the Latin version of a British name, meaning 'place of the battle-ramparts'.[41]

Taking the literature at face value, we could interpret Scot's Dyke as the work of a powerful ruler who had extended Rheged's boundaries into the Vale of Mowbray, to include the Catraeth area. The blocking of the Tees-Swale watershed by Scot's Dyke would obstruct the Roman road over Stainmore (the modern A66) and thus prevent the Anglians from taking the fast route into the heart of Rheged. South of the southern end of the dyke, the Swale could have continued as a natural frontier, flowing from Easby to its junction with the Ure near Boroughbridge. From here, it is tempting to take Rheged's southern boundary up the Ure as far as the West Tanfield area – which would correspond to the later boundary of the North Riding – and then west across the Ure-Wharfe watershed. It's also tempting to bring in Tor Dyke, the substantial earthwork which obstructs the pass into Coverdale from Upper Wharfedale. Because the area behind the Tor Dyke is bleak moorland, a long way from the fertile part of Coverdale, one could imagine this earthwork being commissioned by someone whose strategic outlook was regional, rather than strictly local.

A passage from Taliesin, the Welsh poet, suggests that the defence of linear earthworks was part and parcel of British warfare in the region:

> If there's an enemy on the mountain
> Urien will bruise him.
> If there's an enemy on the dyke
> Urien will strike him down.

The works of the Welsh poets Taliesin and Aneirin (who wrote the *Gododdin*) have persuaded some scholars that it was the disastrous loss of the battle of Catraeth (Catterick), fought around 600, which finally ended British resistance. As Aneirin put it:

> After the wine, after the mead, they left us, wearing mail:
> I have never known a death that was so grey, as theirs was,
> for that open-handed multitude, that went to Catraeth,
> from Mynddog's bodyguard, there to meet with great sadness,
> was three hundred strong: but only one returned.

The English were in Westmorland by the early seventh century, probably travelling through Swaledale to get there. The Kingdom of the Swale had been born.

That is one scenario. But these poems were written by entertainers, not historians; how much of their account of Rheged approximates to historical truth? And there is some argument about where Catraeth really was. The name may not have applied to the former Roman town at Catterick Bridge, but rather to its hinterland (regio), which might have formed a post-Roman kingdom rather like the one in Upper Swaledale. In fact Sir Ifor Williams once suggested that Catraeth was Swaledale, although on very dubious grounds. And the idea that the Catterick area was 'British' until the time of the battle of Catraeth has been disputed by Leslie Alcock, who argued that the unsuccessful British expeditionary force described in the Gododdin seems to have been trying to get Catraeth back, and that the archaeological record at Catterick itself suggests that 'Anglians' may have arrived there in the mid-fifth century and maintained a continuous presence thereafter.[46] Perhaps we should treat the Old Welsh poetry as literature rather than history. On the other hand, we have to take the Yorkshire earthworks seriously; no doubt the Grinton-Fremington dykes are quite an important part of the story. But which story? This period isn't called the Dark Ages for nothing!

In Swaledale, only a handful of names survive to attest the British presence. There is Walburn ('the stream of the Welsh').[47] There is Marske Beck, which was called the Esk in the Middle Ages;[48] and there is Lemon Gill, which flows into Cogden Beck; evidently the beck was named after the elm, like other rivers such as the Lymn, the Leam and the Scottish Leven.[49] (If Cogden Moor today seems an unlikely place for elm trees, it is worth noting that on the other side of the watershed, in the army range beside the Leyburn-Grinton road, an elm and three oaks grow today at much the same altitude (1,100 feet; c.330m); and the elms in the crags above the Swale, to the east of Kisdon Hill, must be about 1300 feet (400m) above sea level).

According to Margaret Gelling, the earliest English names tend to refer to natural features of the landscape.[50] The name of the river – *swalwe*, meaning tumultuous or torrential – is English.[51] In about 730 it was mentioned by the Venerable Bede as the river in which St Paulinus baptised some early Christian converts, probably in the Catterick area. There are other rivers Swale in Berkshire and Kent, as well as in Angeln, the north German district from which the Anglians came. Other early names may include names in *hop*, which normally means a secluded valley. In Upper Swaledale there is Oxnop, and also Ewelop Hill (between Fremington and Marrick), which was called Yaudhope ('horse clearing') a couple of centuries ago. There was also Bernopbeck (the medieval name for Barney Beck), but it was also called Bernolfsbeck.[52] Was Beornwulf the name of the leader of a group of early English colonists? And was 'Haverdale' another example, involving the personal name Haefer or Heahfrid? *Hōh*, denoting a 'heel-shaped' hill with a profile steep on one side and gentler on the other, has given its name to several places (as in How Hill). But there is also the word for a more dome-like hill – *dūn* – which fits Kisdon very well. The word *denu*, for a fairly long and sinuous valley, is a good description for Cogden. Much further west, we find 'Sleddale' – a valley with numerous short side-valleys of the kind called by the Early English name *slaed*. Somewhat later, apparently, are names in *tūn* (Kearton, Grinton, Fremington and so on) and in *leāh* (a clearing, probably associated with wood pasture) such as Healaugh. As a late sixteenth-century map shows, the hamlet now known as Marrick was once called Hellingsley or perhaps Hellensley; as I mentioned earlier, the name Marrick originally referred to the place by the riverside, where the priory was located. Place-names might be replaced, of course, especially in times when they did not have to stay the same because title to property depended on its mention in documents. In the western part of Upper Swaledale most of the English names must have been replaced by Norse ones, but a few survive.

Thinking generally about the Anglo-Saxon 'invasion', some archaeologists and historians have suggested that relatively small numbers of 'Anglians' could have taken control, imposing their language quickly on the local population. They may also have taken over existing earthwork defences; ironically, the original inspiration for Offa's Dyke may have derived from frontier earthworks erected by speakers of Old Welsh!

In northern England, nineteenth-century barrow-digging and twentieth-century archaeological excavation have picked up a considerable number of 'Anglian' burials, inserted into earlier burial mounds. In Swaledale there are one or two interesting scraps of information which might fit into this picture. Bogg, writing in 1908,[53] mentioned a mound just west of Melbecks Vicarage, near the mouth of Haverdale: 'from which in 1846, we are told, seven human skeletons were unearthed, each body laid with feet to the east. Fragments of military accoutrements in the mound would seem to point to a skirmish in this district....' In 1901, another writer recorded the same find,[54] giving the year of discovery as 1847, and referring to 'the buckle of a sword belt and other articles which are supposed to have belonged to some of the followers of the Young Pretender'. Earlier, in 1823, Whitaker made a record of a comparable find not far away:[55] 'At Crakepot ... several pieces of iron armour, together with several battle axes (I presume of the same metal) ...' These sound quite likely to have been 'Anglian' burials, and they probably had counterparts in Wensleydale – at East Witton, Leyburn, Wensley and perhaps Askrigg.[56] In the central part of Swaledale, there are several artificial mounds, most of them low on the daleside; they may well be burial mounds, and they are not necessarily all prehistoric (Fig. 8.4).

This chapter has travelled a long way. As an archaeologist, I would like to be able to identify more remains from this absorbing early medieval period, and to excavate those likely to help us to fill in more details and develop a more precise dating framework. But landscape archaeology has been very useful in one respect; redating the Grinton-Fremington dykes set off a train of thought which has led to a new view of early medieval territories in Swaledale. Now that the deeply rooted distinction between Lower Swaledale and Upper Swaledale has been established, we have a framework for studying the development of early settlements and communities.

Notes

1. Clay 1935, vol. IV, 32.
2. Fleming 2008.
3. King 1970.
4. Rivet and Smith 1979, 278–9.
5. Raistrick 1968, 64.
6. Wheeler 1954.
7. North Yorkshire County Record Office (NYCRO) Grinton Tithe Map (1841).
8. Guilbert and Taylor 1992; G. Guilbert, pers. comm.
9. Gelling 1974.
10. Faull and Stinson 1986, 311a.
11. Gelling 1984, 169.
12. Gelling 1984, 169, 183.

13. Raistrick 1926.
14. Ekwall 1960, 414.
15. Lancaster 1912, 1,2,12,210,251,430.
16. NYCRO ZBO(L)1/1.
17. Faull and Stinson 1986, 311a.
18. Fieldhouse and Jennings 1978, 37.
19. Harrison 1879; Ashcroft 1984.
20. See especially Ashcroft 1984.
21. Harrison 1879, 255.
22. NYCRO ZLK.
23. NYCRO ZKU X5.
24. Raistrick and Jennings 1965, 21.
25. Smith 1967, vol. II, 231.
26. Phillips 1984a, 31.
27. Williamson 1993, 56.
28. Bassett 1989, 23–7.
29. Smith 1928, 273.
30. Harrison 1879, 228.
31. NYCRO ZLK; Z 186/2.
32. VCH vol. I, 239–40.
33. Roebuck 1980, 32.
34. VCH vol. I, 239.
35. VCH vol. I, 239–40.
36. Fleming 1994.
37. Wood 1996.
38. Faull and Moorhouse 1981, vol. 1, 173–4, and vol. 4, map 10.
39. Bogg 1908, 165; VCH vol. I, 73.
40. Higham 1986, 250–6.
41. Clarkson 1993.
42. Pennar 1988, 70.
43. Short 1994, 83.
44. O'Sullivan 1985.
45. Williams 1975, xlii–xliii.
46. Alcock 1987, 250–4.
47. Smith 1928, 270.
48. Harrison 1879, 204.
49. Ekwall 1960, 309.
50. For the place-names mentioned in this paragraph, see Gelling 1984.
51. Ekwall 1960, 455.
52. Lancaster 1912, 432; Smith 1967, 312.
53. Bogg 1908, 243.
54. Spencer 1901, 44.
55. Whitaker 1823, 315.
56. Faull 1974.

CHAPTER THREE

Decoding the
Pattern of Townships

One of the landscape historian's major tasks is to try to work out early patterns of settlement and land-holding. This is quite a complicated business. The schoolbook picture of medieval England – a neat little planned village at the centre of a territory which is at once the manor, the parish and the land of a community – is a considerable over-simplification. The parish, the manor and the land of the face-to-face community – known in northern England as a township – do not necessarily have the same boundaries. For instance, the Dartmoor parish of Widecombe in the Moor was just that – a priest's district, a ramshackle territory containing seven different manors of greatly varying size; some of those manors contained more than one township, and the parish boundary picks its way from point to point, suggesting piecemeal agreements with townships in neighbouring parishes.[1] In Lower Swaledale, East Applegarth is in Richmond parish, whilst West Applegarth, 500 yards (c.500m) away, is in Marske. The pattern is not only variable, it could change; new manors, parishes and townships were regularly being created. But the creators of new administrative units rarely worked in a complete vacuum; whether they split existing units up or cobbled them together, the configuration of the boundaries and/or the character of the names will usually give the game away.

The kingdom of the Swale took the name Swaldal under the influence of Norse settlers, probably in the tenth century. By that time it would have lost most of whatever political independence it had once possessed. Swaldal later became both the manor of Healaugh and the parish of Grinton (which included Fremington, a different manor). The enormous parish of Grinton stayed intact for a long time. Muker did not become a separate parish until 1719, Melbecks eventually following in 1838. Likewise, the manors of Grinton and Muker were not created until the sixteenth century; they were formed from lands previously held by Bridlington Priory and Rievaulx Abbey respectively.[2]

For the landscape historian, the most useful units of analysis are the townships and the main settlements within them. A township was a definable area of land, but it was also a community, the self-organising, workaday, face-to-face theatre of action and experience for generations of people. The inhabitants of the townships crop up in documents as individuals, when they pay their rents, or get married, or fall foul of the law; but we also have to picture their existence as social beings, as members of communities. The history and character of the township as an institution is not very well documented. How early in the Middle Ages were township communities in existence in forms which would be recognisable to their later inhabitants? How far was their existence acknowledged and respected by other administrative and political authorities? In the period leading up to the legal constitution of the civil parish as the smallest administrative unit in England, townships were granted increasing recognition. The names and boundaries of the Swaledale townships were marked on the First Edition of the Six-Inch Ordnance Survey map (1857). As you enter Swaledale from Westmorland, the inscription on the first boundary stone proclaims that you are entering the Township of Birkdale. And Gunnerside was described as a 'town' in the court records of 1624, when there was a proposal to establish a constable for 'Gonnersett, Mewkarr and the other towns upwards and downwards to Gonnersett' and to get the township to swear him in and provide 'a paire of Stockes for the punishing of rogues &c'.[3]

For the landscape historian, the township is the primary territorial unit to be reckoned with, for the last few hundred years at least. This is because the pattern of land use was once determined by the township community, not by families or individuals. The moors which are marked on the map, such as Reeth High Moor or Whitaside Moor, have not been labelled casually; they were well-defined traditional summer grazing zones, the common land of the townships whose names they bear. On some moors, the name itself makes this clear, as in the case of Thwaite Common or Muker Common. In 1963, a published survey of common lands listed over 45,000 acres (18,000 hectares) in Swaledale subject to common rights.[4] These figures included one or two common cow pastures, located below the common moors. For the northern side of Upper Swaledale, the pattern of township moors and cow pastures was well shown on a map drawn by Richard Richardson in 1770.[5]

Common moors and cow pastures were mentioned in sixteenth-century documents, and marked on maps from the late seventeenth century onwards – or occasionally earlier. In post-medieval documents, their names are also the labels for the places where particular parcels of land were located or from which people came. Thus it is possible to produce a map of the townships of Old Swaledale and Arkengarthdale, as they would have existed from about the late sixteenth century onwards. After the judgements recorded in the vigorously fought court cases of the mid-sixteenth century,[6] which were all about traditional Swaledale rights, it would have been virtually impossible for new townships to be created.

The township boundaries interlock like pieces in a jigsaw puzzle. But they differ considerably in size, shape and character. Given the varying quality of land in Swaledale, it would be unrealistic to expect all the township territories to be units of much the same size and population density. The more fertile parts of the dale should have relatively small, populous townships, the land having been more frequently divided between claimant communities, whilst the less valued land, at the western end of the dale for example, should contain fewer, larger territories with low population densities. But, even allowing for this, there are anomalies on the map which suggest change – the insertion of new townships into an older pattern, and the division of large territorial units into smaller ones. Why does Healaugh, which gave its name to the only medieval manor in Upper Swaledale, not have its own named moor? Why do Feetham, Low Row and Lodge Green each have a common cow pasture, but apparently have to share a single upland pasture called Melbecks Moor? Why are the neighbouring townships of Keld, Thwaite and Angram so different in size, and why do their boundaries meet so intricately, in contrast to the simple, direct courses normally taken by township boundaries? Some places behave like townships as far as maps and documents are concerned, yet they are unexpectedly small, considering the average size of their neighbours. Keld has a cow pasture but no moor. Cogden and Summer Lodge are independent in that each has a (small) moor, but they seem never to have been substantial 'communities' (Fig. 3.1).

It seems that Grinton parish and Healaugh manor are not the only territorial entities to have had alternative names. Reeth High Moor is also known as Healaugh Side; Feetham Pasture is sometimes called Kearton Pasture, sometimes 'Feetham or Kearton Pasture', and Lodge Green Pasture is marked on the tithe map of 1843 as 'Lodge Green or Little Rowleth Pasture'. Kisdon is now a hill, and a farm high on its southern flank; but why are 'High Kisdon', 'Low Kisdon' and 'Kisdon Scar' on the other side of the Swale, in Ivelet Cow Pasture? Evidently the people who talked to nineteenth-century mapmakers insisted upon the preservation and recording of alternative names, double names and various other oddities, and the mapmakers respected their wishes. A significant influence here may have been the knowledge of an early nineteenth-century land surveyor who lived locally – Anthony Clarkson from Smithy Holme, in the wilder part of the dale to the west of Keld. Clarkson produced several maps of Swaledale, from high-quality tithe maps to rather sketchier productions.

Is it conceivable that these alternative names provide keys to the earlier history of Swaledale communities, before the later pattern of townships was firmly fixed? Working with *individual* place-names and their interpretation can be tricky; but *patterns* are rather different. It may be possible to reconstruct a kind of township history, a sequence for early Swaledale communities, by comparing place-names, the sites chosen for settlements, and the size, shape and character of township boundaries. The general expectation, derived from quite a number of studies elsewhere, is that territories in the post-Roman period were initially large, a good deal bigger than the typical late medieval parish or manor. Later, these large early units of land were subdivided and broken up. Landscape historians have reached this conclusion for various reasons. Some, like Steve Bassett, have argued that early Anglo-Saxon 'kingdoms' much the same size as the kingdom of the Swale were widespread.[7] For Devon, W. G. Hoskins made the case, on the basis of place-name patterns and boundary configurations, for large early 'estates' based on river-valleys.[8] Alan Everitt, using much the same kind of evidence, showed that in Kent such river estates were later subdivided according to a recurring series of steps.[9] Scholars who put forward these ideas

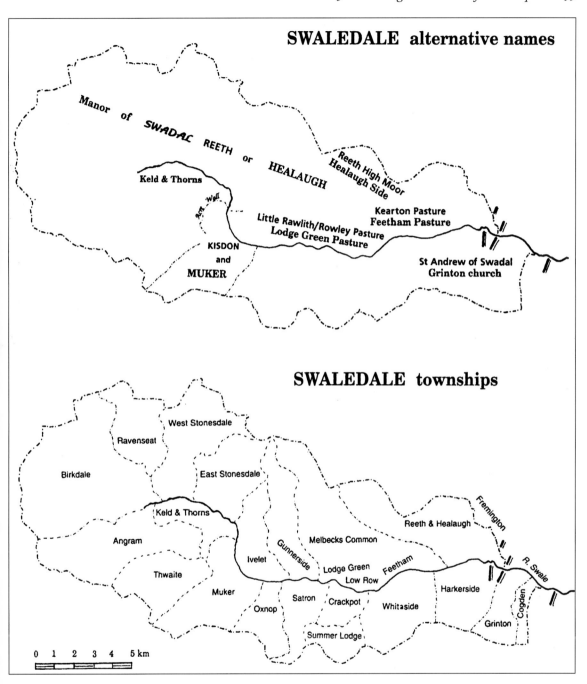

SWALEDALE alternative names

SWALEDALE townships

FIGURE 3.1. Map of Old Swaledale to show alternative names and township boundaries; both reflect medieval settlement history.

also have to take account of summer grazing zones, which were sometimes established within individual territories, and sometimes located at a distance on common pastures shared by people from a broad region – as in the case of Sherwood, the 'shire wood'.

Some time ago, Professor Glanville Jones put forward the concept of the

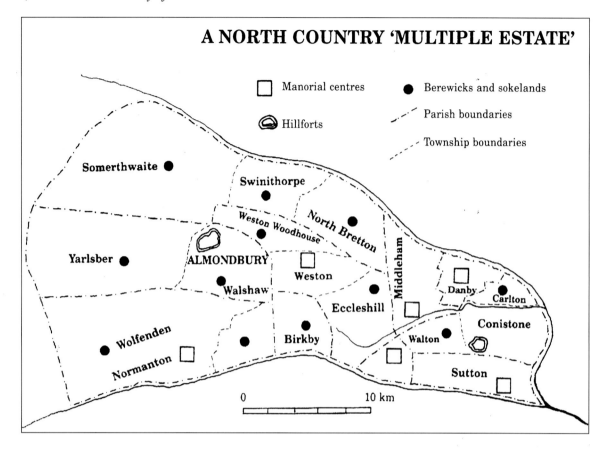

A NORTH COUNTRY 'MULTIPLE ESTATE'

□ Manorial centres   ● Berewicks and sokelands

◎ Hillforts   ⌐·⌐ Parish boundaries

⌐ · ⌐ Township boundaries

Somerthwaite ●

Swinithorpe ●

Weston Woodhouse   *North Bretton* ●

Yarlsber ●   ◎ ALMONDBURY   □ Weston   Middleham   □ Danby   □ Carlton

Walshaw   Eccleshill   □ Walton   Conistone

● Wolfenden   ● Birkby   ◎   Sutton

Normanton □   0   10 km

FIGURE 3.2. Glanville Jones' model of the ideal 'multiple estate' in northern England, with representative place-names (redrawn after Jones, (see note 11) with slight modifications).

'multiple estate' to describe a form of early medieval territorial organisation which operated at this kind of scale.[10] He suggested that the basic form of the multiple estate was still embedded in the manorial arrangements of later medieval England and Wales, and could be picked up by the alert historian; he believed that multiple estates probably originated in the pre-Roman period. Jones suggested that some places within the 'estate' would have reflected its history, while others would have specialised in particular productive roles within the greater whole. He drew a map of the 'ideal' multiple estate in northern England (Fig. 3.2).[11] The places marked on this map would mostly have become parishes, townships and/or subsidiary manors by the thirteenth century. Their easily translatable names express the role of each part of the original 'estate' within the whole, as well as the influx of various human groups. The different symbols show the status of the places represented, within the manorial hierarchy. Thus in the lowland part of the estate, the centrally located 'king's *tūn*' contrasts with the '*by*' of the Danes, and the '*tūn*' of the Welsh. The 'ceorls' *tūn*' represents a low-status community of bondmen. The 'south *tūn*' and the 'middle homestead' reflect the extensive mental map which went with the multiple estate. The hill country also has a complex history; we find the wood of the Welsh, the northmen's tun, and the north tun of the Britons. It is a well-wooded, part-wilderness zone, where a game reserve known as a Forest might well have been created in the later Middle Ages; as expected, as we travel further into the hills, parishes and townships get larger. There is a valley of the wolves, a summer clearing, a pig farm and a place with a wood house. The name Almondbury means 'the burg of all the men'; in choosing this name (which, as it happens, is the name of a real Iron Age hill-fort near Huddersfield) Jones was trying to emphasise the former unity of the large-scale terrain and the role of the big, centrally-located hill-fort in this scenario.

Tom Williamson is one scholar for whom the multiple estate has worked out on the ground. Writing about Norfolk, he has suggested that there were early 'river-estates' here, the territories of small tribal groups, some of whose names may be preserved in the names of hundreds; and that later 'the great estates of the Middle Saxon period ... seem to have contained economically specialised sub-units, farms or hamlets which produced some specialised commodity, or provided some particular service, for the estate centre'.[12] These arguments are based on place-names and on the historical status of the place at the estate centre. Names in *ham* tend to be estate centres, whilst names in *tūn* indicate outlying places. *Tūns* may be named in terms of their geographical relationship with the estate centre, but some of them carry the names of particular specialisms – there might be a herdsman's *tūn,* a summer *tūn,* a meadow *tūn,* a leek-growing *tūn* and so on. Personally, I would prefer to describe the numerous early medieval 'estates' or small 'kingdoms' whose existence has been recognised in England and Wales over the past few decades as 'folk territories'. They are large by later standards, and they often lie in naturally defined pockets of land such as river basins. Some of these folk territories formed a clear enough identity for historians to be able to pick them up several hundred years later. The existence of others is more shadowy. What was the early territorial pattern in Lower Swaledale, for instance?

It's quite clear from old maps, and from what can be seen on the ground, that in the Middle Ages cultivation of cereals, and perhaps other crops such as flax, was much more important here than in Upper Swaledale. Much of the area around Downholme, Stainton and Walburn Hall is covered in ridge and furrow, and long strip lynchets or terraces along the contour, once ploughed by oxen or horses. This is particularly noticeable when the sun is low in the sky, or when snow has partially melted; the ploughmen have worked high on the slopes above Stainton, on the top of How Hill at Downholme (wrecking most of an Iron Age hill-fort in the process), and high on the hillside where Downholme Park was later established in the late fourteenth century.[13] The extent of medieval ploughing in this part of Lower Swaledale makes it impossible to find much of the Romano-British landscape here.

It is hard to conjure up this densely occupied medieval landscape now, to imagine the substantial village which once existed at Walburn – its buildings, barns, gardens and crofts still well preserved as grassy banks in two fields to the east of Walburn Bridge. Then there is Stainton, once quite a large hamlet, and Ellerton, its main 'street' visible from the modern road. It ran along the only south-facing slope in the entire township, from behind the nineteenth-century house called Ellerton Abbey in a WSW direction, across the Richmond-Grinton road and on to Swale Farm. Judging by the layout of these old roads, when it was first founded Ellerton probably lay at the end of a road leading out from Grinton, to a badly drained land full of alder thickets, as the name suggests.

If there was a large early medieval 'territory' in Lower Swaledale – whatever name we choose to describe it – Downholme looks like an obvious centre, with places like Walburn, Stainton and Ellerton as the outlying *tūns*. In historical times these were townships within the ancient parish of Downholme; the early church was located at the centre of the most productive area of Lower Swaledale, and just below the hill-fort whose prestige may still have been celebrated in local oral traditions. It is likely that land on the north side of the Swale was also included in the territory centred on Downholme. Marske, with its hall and its church, looks at first sight like an autonomous, old-established settlement. But if this is the case, it is odd it was not mentioned in Domesday Book – was it included under another heading, such as Downholme? The name, which means 'the marshes',[14] hardly suggests a spot for an early, primary, settlement. The early settlement in this area is more likely to have been Skelton. It is another *tūn*; the name is alleged to mean 'shelf-tūn', the settlement on a shoulder of land,[15] but it might easily be 'scale-tūn', referring to a shieling or summer pasture station. Further out was Feldom, another deserted medieval hamlet whose name means 'at the fields',[16] implying the existence of arable land.

Before the building of Downholme Bridge (or its predecessor?) Downholme and Marske were in fact linked by a route shown on old maps, which ran north past Downholme church, across what is now the main road, and down to the River Swale (Fig. 5.2). Why is Downholme church so isolated, 500 yards (c. 500m) away from the present village? It's tempting to argue that the original Downholme lay along this road, perhaps just south of the church, and that its remains have been obliterated by ploughing, after the village moved to its present location. In terms of the early medieval multiple estate, the area north of the river may have been the equivalent of the upland pasture zone of Glanville Jones's model, a mixture of woodland pasture and moorland – a wilderness zone used at first for distant pasture. It was also available for more permanent colonisation and expansion, which eventually took place, with the establishment of places like Feldom and Marske.

Much of the present hamlet of Downholme has been built along a road which has come over the moor from Hudswell, and continues further west towards Ellerton, in the form of Stop Bridge Lane, an unmetalled track. But the western end of this lane meets what is clearly another very old road which can be traced on the map, running south from here, mostly along modern roads and tracks, all the way to Ulshaw Bridge on the River Ure, in Wensleydale. North of its junction with Stopbridge Lane, it shares the same course as the old Downholme-Ellerton road already mentioned; the modern road here has a hollow way beside it, deepened by running water. And it cannot be a

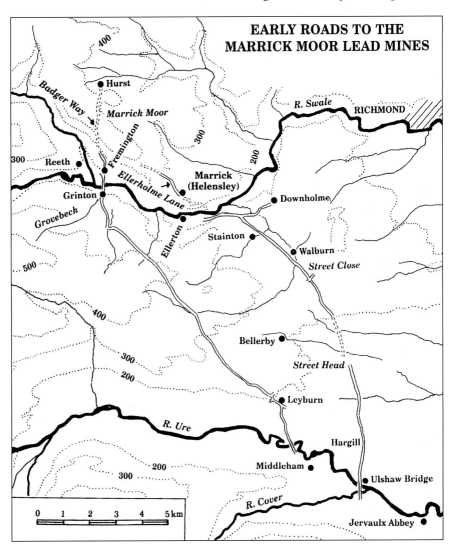

EARLY ROADS TO THE MARRICK MOOR LEAD MINES

FIGURE 3.3. Map showing Roman and medieval roads to and from the Marrick Moor lead-mines. The Roman route (which may also have been used in the Middle Ages) is the eastern one.

coincidence that, on the north bank of the Swale, Ellerholme Lane comes down the hillside from Marrick as a deep hollow way, heading south-east; there was a ford across the river here, marked on a map of 1782 as Ellerholme Wath (Fig. 3.3).[17] The Ulshaw-Marrick road is older than the Downholme-Ellerton road, despite appearances on the map at the place where they meet. A late seventeenth-century map (Fig. 5.3) shows that the junction between the two roads was different then;[18] at the point where the road from Ulshaw bent sharply to the east towards the road from Downholme, a hedge continued its line, so that there was then a little triangular enclosure here. Road junctions have often been changed and realigned, especially in recent centuries, and one cannot always take maps at face value. I know more than one place where a road junction has been replanned in such a way that a nineteenth-century road appears to be earlier than a Roman road!

A good reason for believing that the Marrick-Ulshaw road existed in the Middle Ages is that the main axis of the medieval village of Walburn – that is, the road which runs past the front of Walburn Hall – came off it at right angles, at the junction where, at the present day, the road running past the Wath Gill army base meets the main Leyburn-Richmond road (Fig. 7.4). Another sign of the road's antiquity is that, further south, it forms part of the boundary between the ancient parishes of Spennithorne and Hauxwell.

In fact, this road is probably much older. An early eighteenth-century map of Walburn marks a significant field name – Street Close – about one kilometre south-east of Walburn, near Halfpenny House, and there is also a 'Street Head' name on the route, further south (Fig. 3.3).[19] These names suggest that our route was probably a Roman road. East of Marrick village, not far from the route, is St Ellen's Well, which was recorded as Sainte Elinkell in 1664.[20] This is significant, I think, because a distinctive feature of Roman roads in West Yorkshire is that many of them are associated with wells or springs dedicated to St Ellen, or St Helen.[21] These are normally just off the road rather than right beside it. In west Wales, near where I live, there is a Roman road called Sarn Helen. What lies behind this pattern is not very well understood; the Christian link is with Helena, mother of the emperor Constantine, but it is likely that the cult of Helen was assimilated into that of an earlier goddess with a Celtic name, who protected travellers.[22]

But it is not just the names which suggest that this road was established in Roman times. Its course is very direct, and it has an obvious purpose, in Roman terms – to reach Marrick from the River Ure by the best route. And given the nineteenth-century discovery of a Roman pig of lead at Hurst, on Marrick Moor,[23] the conclusion seems irresistible that the road was constructed in order to transport the products of the Marrick Moor lead-mines to the Ure, down the river to the cantonal capital of Isurium, at Aldborough, near Boroughbridge, and, then, if necessary, onward by road or river. In the Middle Ages the Ure was navigable as far as Jervaulx,[24] and there seems no good reason why lead could not have been transported by boat in Roman times; after the investment involved in mining and smelting, waiting for the river to rise would hardly be a problem. The island at Ulshaw Bridge is called 'The Batts'; according to the dictionary, *bat* means a pack-saddle or an obsolete form of 'boat'. Either interpretation would fit!

The former Roman road ran through the Downholme territory. Downholme itself was set away from the road, with its potential for bringing trouble. If the early Downholme *was* near the present church, on the north-east side of How Hill, it would not have been visible from the road. The axis established by the road suggests that Marrick might have been part of the Downholme estate. But perhaps the most interesting point about Marrick is that, as I mentioned before, the old, pre-Conquest name for Marrick village was something like 'Hellensley'. English-speaking settlers, then, named this place "Helen's clearing", a pretty clear indication that they knew of the sacred spring and its name. Perhaps this symbolises what really happened in Swaledale on the arrival of English-speaking settlers – underneath the change of language, a good deal of continuity.

The position of Hellensley in what now seems rather an exposed position, gives us a hint that English settlements may have been located high on the daleside. Is it possible to find evidence for this preference further west, in Old Swaledale? Kearton, which has another English name, is now a quiet place – a few buildings, a footpath running through an informal green. The cow pasture above had alternative names – Kearton or Feetham Pasture. Feetham is *below* Kearton, on a terrace above the river; it has a Norse name, meaning 'at the meadows'.[25] I interpret the twin names for the cow pasture as preserving a record of the sequence of settlement here. Could it be that earlier pre-Conquest settlements like Kearton and Hellensley were located high on the daleside, and later ones – perhaps those with predominantly Norse names – just above the river meadows? In many areas, a group of settlers would have had to choose between a site high on the dale-side – perhaps where the erosion of a band of softer sedimentary rock, a long time ago, had created a shoulder – and a position on a natural terrace just above the flood plain of the river. There is a flavour of the choices to be made in the pairs of 'High' and 'Low' names – High and Low Oxnop, High and Low Fremington, High and Low Whita (although the old name was Nether Whita, which has the same meaning).

According to Margaret Gelling, names in *tūn* and *lēah* (clearing, or stretch of wood pasture) date mostly to the period 750–950.[26] Grinton, Fremington and Ellerton were all in place by 1066. Names in *ingtun* often denote blocks of land carved out of larger territories, usually round about this period.[27] Fremington is a classic case. It was a separate vill by 1066, and one can see on the map that it must have been cut out of Hellensley/Marrick, which was originally a block of land defined mostly by water-courses – the Swale, Marske Beck and Slei Gill (Fig. 2.3). The very fact that there is no Fremington Moor must raise the possibility that, as an independent township, Fremington was a late interloper. Documentary research might establish whether Fremington people had common rights on Marrick Moor, or whether they relied entirely on pastures below Fremington Edge.

On this basis, it seems that we have Skelton, Hellensley, Kearton and perhaps High Fremington as evidence for high-level pre-Conquest English settlements (Fig. 3.4). But what about Healaugh, which also has a *lēah* name, meaning 'high clearing or wood pasture',[28] but is a low-level settlement? Healaugh has an interesting history. When I first started to try to work out the location of each township's woodland zone (of which more later), I became convinced that Reeth's woods must have been in the Healaugh area. So it was interesting to read shortly afterwards of a statement made in 1303 that Healaugh 'was neither village, borough or hamlet, but a certain site of the manor of Reeth'.[29] It looks as if, around the time of Domesday, Healaugh was simply in a clearing in a woodland pasture belonging to the vill of Reeth. A large pasture just east of the village was once called Scale Ing, which may imply the former presence of a pastoral out-station.

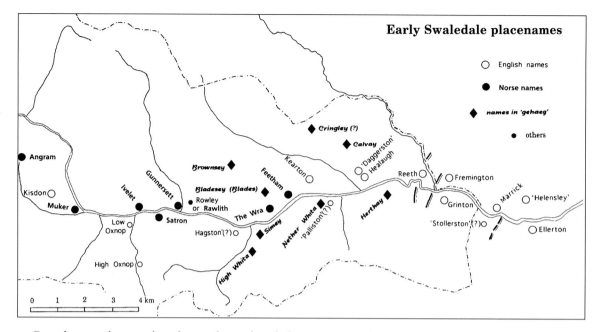

FIGURE 3.4. Map of Old Swaledale, showing place-names relating to early medieval settlement history.

But this is where archaeology takes a hand, because it is clear that there *was* once a high-level settlement here, which we might call Old Healaugh, with buildings strung out along the contour (Fig. 3.5). There is still a public footpath running from the late nineteenth-century Thiernswood Hall, behind Dagger Stones Farm (formerly in front of it) and past the ruined Bank House, a dwelling which was here in the seventeenth century, as we know both from parish registers and from the (mostly reused) stonework of the house itself. A 'Bernard of the Bank' was mentioned in the Healaugh Lay Subsidy list for 1301.[30] East of Bank House, if you ignore the footpath's sharp kink to the north (to join the metalled road which leads on to the moor), and project its line eastwards along the contour, a glance through a nearby gateway shows that it continued across the field as a hollow-way; in good light conditions one can see one or two platforms where buildings have stood. From here, the axis of Old Healaugh continued across the deep notch of Shaw Gill, through which the road up from the present-day hamlet runs. In the fields further east, there are various building platforms (and one or two fairly recent field-barns) along this line. On the moor, immediately above and outside the enclosed land, there are hollow tracks, which are coming down off the moor and heading for points along the 'main street' of Old Healaugh. So most of Healaugh has migrated downhill; Dagger Stones Farm is all that remains today.

But was this old high-level settlement originally called Healaugh? I must turn here to the name Dagger Stones, which has never been satisfactorily explained. There are indeed many stones behind the farm. But if the name refers to the stones, it should be pronounced 'Daggersteeans' or 'Daggerstanes', whereas the actual pronunciation is 'Daggerstuns'. Nor was this once 'Daggerston's Farm'; there is no evidence that 'Daggerston' has ever been a surname here. When I

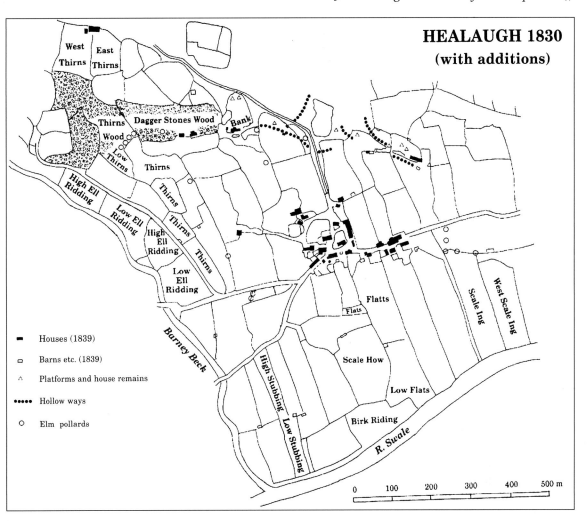

FIGURE 3.5. Map of Healaugh based on the 1830 Tithe Map, showing field names relating to woodland, clearance and medieval land use, elm pollards, and the location of 'Old Healaugh' (above the modern village, and east of Bank).

was a schoolboy, I helped with the excavation of a deserted late medieval moated manor house in south Herefordshire. The site was called Wallingstones, and we assumed at first that it was named after the old masonry on the site. It was only when I was looking through the archives in Hereford that I discovered that the place was called Waldyngeston in the Middle Ages.

Probably the name 'Dagger Stones' has a similar history, and the original high-level settlement here was once called Daggerston, or something very similar – another *tūn* name. As I suggested above, it looks as if this was a well-wooded zone at around the time of the Norman Conquest, so perhaps Daggerston was a small settlement, or its size was later reduced. At any rate, it seems to have suffered the same fate as Hellensley, having its name changed – to Healaugh ('high clearing or wood pasture'), a name which fits the location. Curiously enough, there are other unexplained names in Swaledale which end in *ston* or *stone*. There is Stallerstone or Stollerston Stile, between Cogden and Ellerton, and Pallistone, near Low Whita, and perhaps Hagston, which was also on the south bank of the Swale, north-west of Crackpot.[31] These *ston* names may refer to early settlements now lost, or places which have changed their names.

In this part of Swaledale, attention has to focus on the early role of Reeth. Apparently the name is English, and means 'rough place'.[32] In fact Reeth is a prime site for settlement, on a low shelf between the main valley and that of the Arkle Beck, with plenty of riverside pasture and easy access to the moors above. If the site's arable potential was not as good as Downholme's, it was good by Upper Swaledale standards. The land immediately west of Reeth was well farmed in the Roman period; there were fields defined by walls, perhaps with hedges growing on top of them, on both sides of the valley. There may have been something of a recession here in the post-Roman period. Elizabeth Livett's unpublished pollen diagram from Ellerton Moor suggests some regrowth of trees at this time. The behaviour of the Grinton-Fremington dykes in relation to the Roman field boundaries suggests that they were constructed in farmland which was at least partly abandoned. But this may be a strictly local phenomenon. For incoming Anglians, it would have been well worth taking over the land of people numerous and well organised enough to build these earthworks.

Reeth is like Downholme, set in a prime location, with an old hill-fort (in this case Maiden Castle) not far off. Like Downholme, it has an old English 'topographic' name, and had outlying *tūns* – Daggerston and Grinton, with Kearton further to the west. There is a case for seeing Reeth too as the well-chosen core settlement of a large territory, perhaps the principal settlement in Old Swaledale, with its outlying zones developing as subsidiary settlements at a later stage.

Further west is Muker, Swaledale's number two settlement in terms of importance (Fig. 3.6). Like Reeth, Muker is in a prime position at the meeting of two sizeable streams, the Swale and Straw (formerly Trow) Beck, with plenty of good meadow land around. Muker is a Norse name, meaning 'the narrow acre';[33] any cultivation here is likely to have been undertaken on the narrow shelf to the west of the village. This is a zone of Norse names; yet on the shoulder above Muker is a place with an English name, Kisdon. Is this a candidate for a high level English settlement, effectively Muker's ancestor? It might be argued that the farm has simply taken its name from Kisdon Hill. But on the other hand Kisdon is sometimes spelt 'Keston', so it might have been a *tūn* originally. What is more interesting is the presence of three or four 'Kisdon' names quite a long way from Kisdon Farm, in Ivelet Cow Pasture, on the other side of the Swale – High Kisdon, Low Kisdon, Kisdon Scar and Kisdon Bottom. Is it possible that Kisdon was once a large territory on both sides of the Swale, taking in a good deal of land to the west of what is now Ivelet?

Archaeological evidence may support this idea. Above Kisdon Farm is a wall in use today, running over Kisdon Hill. It does not look particularly old, but it probably follows an old boundary line. It is called the Acre Wall, presumably because it once marked the limits of Muker's land. It can be followed down the steep slope above the Swale, before it gets lost in a conifer plantation. But running

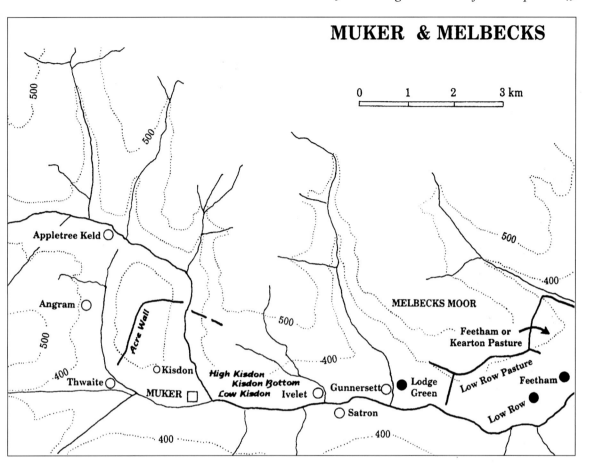

FIGURE 3.6. Map of boundaries and place-names around Muker and Melbecks, to illustrate the development of townships from larger territorial units (for details, see text).

straight up the steep slope opposite, across the river, is a part-ruined, part-robbed wall, which kinks north at its lower end as if to cross the river and continue up the opposite hillside, which it does. It runs up to a sheepfold on the top wall of Ivelet Cow Pasture, and eventually dies out on the moor above. Before Ivelet Cow Pasture was established, an early version of the Acre Wall evidently crossed the Swale, taking in an area which included all the 'Kisdon' place-names.

This wall may be medieval in origin. At Preston Richard in Cumbria the 'Ekergart' (Acre-garth) is mentioned as early as the late twelfth century.[34] At Muker, it does look as if the wall's ruined eastern section dates from a time when Muker (inheriting Kisdon's old land?) stretched across the river, but before Ivelet had become established as a township on this part of the daleside. On these arguments, then, Kisdon fits the emerging pattern, as a high-level English predecessor of Muker. And there is a late eighteenth-century documentary reference to 'the territories of Kisdon and Muker' – another Anglo/Norse twin name, like Kearton and Feetham.[35]

Muker, in fact, looks like a large Norse territory, with its outlying lands becoming established settlements at a late stage. If Muker's eastern neighbour, Ivelet, trespassed on Muker's original Acre Wall, so did its neighbour to the west, Thwaite; the western end of the Acre Wall is interrupted by the central portion of Thwaite's land. Further out were outlying grazing zones – Angram ('at the pastures'), Satron (meaning much the same thing), and Gunnersett (modern Gunnerside), which meant Gunnar's *saetr* or summer, pasture.[36] According to Margaret Gelling, these names in the dative ('at…'), like Feetham ('at the meadows'), make it clear that Old Norse was actually spoken in Upper Swaledale; it is not a case of Norse names being brought in from outside, later on. These places come into the literature as post-Conquest *vaccaries* (dairy farms),[37] but this linguistic evidence suggests that these *vaccaries* were based on pre-Conquest Norse shielings, or perhaps farms which had started life as shielings.

This may seem odd, because a glance at the map shows that most of the Upper Swaledale 'seat' *(saetr)* names are out on the hills – Lovely Seat, Rogan's Seat, Alderson's Seat, and so on. But shielings were not always on the moors, especially in the earlier Middle Ages. We have seen already that there was once a 'scale' at Healaugh; and on Whitaside, there was once a Dowley Seat only half-way up the daleside, near what is now Drover's House. Was 'Dowley' once an English settlement, or should we think in dialect terms and translate it simply as 'gloomy seat'? Anyway, the important point seems to be that, as the population grew in the later Middle Ages, there were no longer any of these shielings in the dale itself; all the summer pastures were much further out, on the moors.

Muker (and Kisdon before it?) is at the heart of a territory large enough to contain a range of resources, where the outlying shielings and settlements were linked with the centre, as in the multiple estate model. There was enough land for the the outliers to become independent townships, eventually, and this is what seems to have happened here. As we have seen, the twin name 'Kisdon and Muker' crops up sometimes in the documents; around 1700, the Muker Manor Court records refer to 'Angram in Meucar', 'Keld in Meucar' and 'Thwaite in Meucar', illustrating the old relationship between Muker and its outliers.[38]

Between Reeth and Muker is a zone which illustrates very well how a large territorial entity is subdivided (Fig. 3.6). There were three cow pastures here – Feetham, Low Row (the name comes from the Norse The Wra, meaning a nook) and to the west 'Lodge Green or Little Rowleth Pasture'. Here again we encounter the link between an early name and a position high on the daleside, coupled with a later name for a place located on the edge of the river plain. The name Rowley, Rowleth, or Rawlith does not seem to have any early recorded forms – the first element might mean a row (of houses) or the roe deer, the second a clearing or a slope. If the name means 'roe deer clearing' it would be similar to Hindrelagh, 'hinds' clearing', the pre-Norman name for Richmond.[39] 'Little Rowley' may have been another example of a place with a *lēah* name located high on the daleside. It is on the shoulder of the hill, well above Lodge Green which is apparently a much later settlement;[40] the ruined remains of one or two rectangular buildings suggest that there was indeed some kind of medieval settlement here.

But the interesting thing about these three townships is that they do not have separate moorland commons; above their top wall there is simply Melbecks Common, which they share. As far as we know, there was never a settlement called Melbecks; it seems to have been the name for a territory. The name means 'between the becks' and we have documentary evidence that the zone between Bernopbeck (now Barney Beck) and Mossdale Beck (now Gunnerside Gill) was a single common in the fourteenth century.[41] Occasional sixteenth-century references to Melbeckside suggest that a single undivided cow pasture may once have served Feetham, Low Row and Little Rowleth.[42] The genesis of the name Melbecks is intriguing. Although the name is apparently Norse it may have English origins.[43] There is a Mellbeck in Westfalia, about 20 miles (32km) east of Düsseldorf, and a Melbeck about 10 miles (16km) south of Lüneburg, in the old homeland of the Angles in north Germany. One can imagine that after an influx of Norse settlers, an easily translatable English name would survive well. It is interesting that the old name persisted, to be given to the new parish created here in 1838, long after Low Row and Kearton or Feetham had developed as separate townships.

What of early high-level settlements in Melbecks? I have already mentioned Kearton, with its English name. There was Smarber, apparently a Norse name translated by A. H. Smith as 'butter hill' (but perhaps 'small burial mound' is more likely;[44] Tim Laurie discovered the convincing remains of such a mound on the limestone pavement just above Smarber). Blades was 'Bladesey' in 1300[45] – the *gehaeg* or hedged enclosure of Blades. Did Blades originally have the English name *blaec-dūn,* the black hill (like Blaydon) or *bleo-dūn,* the coloured hill, like Bleadon in Somerset? Eilert Ekwall says that the latter name refers to 'the variegated appearance of the hill-side, green parts interchanging with white, where the limestone comes to the surface'.[46] This is a good description of the area above Blades; and Blea Barf is the name of a hill just across the dale. 'Bleadonsgehaeg' could easily have become 'Bladesey', and then just 'Blades'.

Gehaeg – meaning 'a hedged enclosure' – is the most noticeable English place-name element in Upper Swaledale, and it gives us a third phase of settlement which is identifiable from place-names and choices of location. According to Margaret Gelling, this is the word which gave us all or most of the names ending in 'ey' or 'ay' (also 'er' or 'a', occasionally). These names are not distributed at random; they are found around Reeth and Melbecks, north and south of the river, and they tend to relate to areas *above* the daleside. Above Reeth is Calver or Calvay Hill, and further along is Cringley, plausibly interpreted as *kringla + gehaeg. Kringla* means 'ring', clearly a reference to the almost circular prehistoric enclosure on the saddle between Calver Hill and Cringley Hill; it is marked on the 1:25000 map. Further west is Brownsey (and at one time Bladesey). Across the dale, two large townships have *gehaeg* names – Whitaside and Harkerside, which was once Hercay, and before that Herthay, the deer enclosure. This is a good example of how names change over time, showing why we should try to find early forms of present-day place-names.

If a *gehaeg* was normally in woodland, the 'ey' and 'ay' names would fit the idea of *late* clearance (and occupation?) very well, because of the kinds of land where they occur. They are found *above* primary settlement land, on moors or hill shoulders rather than the upper dale-sides; on the disadvantaged north-facing side of the dale; and in association with the third-best settlement zone, where Swaledale becomes relatively narrow and steep-sided, squeezed between the more favoured territories of Reeth and Muker.

Let me summarise. What was happening in terms of land occupation in the earlier post-Roman centuries is not at all clear. Place-name studies have their limitations, and in any case not many place-names have survived from this era. To make much sense of this period, we will need the results of skilfully targeted (or lucky!) archaeological excavations. The place-names which apparently relate to the period from perhaps 800 to 1066 do seem to make a pattern, with English names high on the daleside and Norse ones lower down. But the significance of this pattern is debatable. If some English names seem early – such as Hellensley, or Oxnop – others may be later than the Conquest; we have seen that Healaugh is probably a late English name, and how Hellensley was supplanted by Marrick. Low Whita (formerly Nether Whita) was once called Whealsay (the twelfth-century dairy farm of 'Whallesheved'[47]) and before that it may have been Palliston. Furthermore, some of the settlements with Norse names could have been 'English' settlements taken over and renamed. It is possible to work out sequences of names, and sometimes pick out the really old ones – but only up to a point. In Lower Swaledale, the late-settled outlying parts of the large Downholme territory were partly or wholly deserted in the later Middle Ages – Walburn, Ellerton, Feldom, though not Stainton, which still had fourteen houses in 1694 (Fig. 5.3).[48] In Old Swaledale, there were three major territories – Reeth, Kisdon and Melbecks, in descending order of importance and access to good land. Gradually, especially in the Muker area, more permanent settlements were created where there were once woodland shielings. Further clearance of *hays* continued after the Conquest, especially on the disadvantaged south bank of the river, which must still have been very wooded then. Over the centuries, the old, large territories were subdivided. Sometimes new, intrusive territories were established – Healaugh in Reeth, or Thwaite in Muker. Summer Lodge is another late and intrusive development, and so, in all probability, was Keld (formerly Apple Tree Keld), which does not possess its own named moor.

In the early twelfth century, when Walter de Gaunt established (or re-established?) the game reserve known as the Forest of Swaledale, which took in all the old land of Swale, there would still have been plenty of woodland around – dense woods, perhaps, on uncleared valley sides and bottoms well away from settlements; old-established wood pastures with not much in the way of undergrowth; scrubby birches, alders and rowans further out on the moorlands and in the far west. As well as taking advantage of the hunting, the de Gaunts derived income from the manor, including their *vaccaries* or dairy farms, and they made land grants to Bridlington Priory and Rievaulx Abbey, which were also involved in dairy farming.[49] Land grants, rents and taxation are the principle themes of the documentary record. But there are also references to rights: behind the documents were communities of people whose ancestors had been in the dale long before the onset of feudalism. Later, when these communities are better documented, they emerge as relatively small townships, with complex systems of duties, rights, regulations and financial transactions. What happened within individual townships in the post-medieval centuries, as communities fragmented under various social and economic pressures, would make an interesting study.

The three large 'territories' which seem to have formed within the folk territory of Swale in the earlier Middle Ages formed the framework for the development of the later townships, and even later parishes; a similar pattern seems to be visible in Lower Swaledale, centred on Downholme. The pattern of a core area and outliers which started out as shielings is most easily seen in the Muker area, where Norse place-names and changing boundary relationships pick it up quite well. More than one line of evidence suggests the development of small townships from a large, early Melbecks. The idea that Reeth lay at the core of one of these larger territories is more problematic; it is based mainly on the natural advantages of the place. In Lower Swaledale, Downholme had rather similar advantages. It is not very clear how these large early territories 'worked'. We have only the place-names to guide us and they have their limitations; in the Muker area, for instance, the Norse place-names do seem to suggest a central settlement area, with outlying grazing stations, but this place-name pattern must have been imposed upon an earlier pattern of 'English' settlements which may have organised themselves on different principles. It seems that we can identify 'central places', such as Muker, Reeth and Downholme, but that is not to say that they were like the centres of the more elaborate 'multiple estates' in other parts of England. This was a thinly populated upland valley, after all. But isolated settlements can never be completely independent. Dispersed as they were, the inhabitants of the early medieval settlements of Swaledale were members of larger communities, on which several important aspects of their lives must have been focused. We can guess that these communities must have been very different from the later medieval townships, though precisely how they differed is very hard to determine at this distance. Ironically, we are using names written down in documents to pick up communities which, for all we know about them, might as well be prehistoric!

Notes

1. Gawne, 1970.
2. Fieldhouse and Jennings 1978, 114.
3. Atkinson 1894, vol. III, 223.
4. Hoskins and Stamp 1963, 340–1.
5. North Yorkshire County Record Office (NYCRO) ZQX 5/4.
6. Fieldhouse and Jennings 1978, 115–30.
7. Bassett 1989, 23–7.
8. Hoskins 1952.

9. Everitt 1986.
10. For a list of Glanville Jones's papers, see Gregson 1985. For a reply to Gregson's critique, see Jones 1985.
11. Jones 1971.
12 Williamson 1993, 85.
13. NYCRO ZBO.
14. Smith 1928, 154, 293.
15. For a possible derivation, see Smith 1928, 293.
16. Ibid.
17. NYCRO ZPT 26/15.
18. NYCRO ZHP.
19. NYCRO ZAZ (M) 1. For the Roman road hypothesis, see Fleming 1996.
20. NYCRO ZHP – MIC 1324 0028.
21. Faull, 1981, 155–6, 176–7 and map 10; Hey 1979, 75, 84–5.
22. Jones 1986.
23. Speight 1897, 207.
24. Edwards and Hindle 1991, 126.
25. Smith 1928, 271.
26. Gelling 1974 and pers. comm.
27. Gelling 1978, 177–84.
28. Smith 1928, 273.
29. VCH 1914, vol. I, 242.
30. Brown 1896, 8.
31. 'Stallerstane' in 1409 (Lancaster 1912, 248); 'Stallerstone' in 1533 (NYCRO CRONT I/Peacock); 'Stolerston' in 1632 (NYCRO Z683). A close called Pallistone in 1711 (NYCRO ZIF, 359; location, see Grinton Tithe Map (1841, in NYCRO)); Hagsten or Hagstone Holme in 1703 (NYCRO MIC 144 (Muker Manor Court Records; for location, see Grinton Tithe Map (1841, in NYCRO).
32. Gelling, pers. comm., 5.11.92.
33. Smith 1928, 272.
34. Winchester 1987, 60.
35. NYCRO ZQ5/7.
36. For Norse names in Upper Swaledale, see Smith 1928, 270–3.
37. McDonnell 1990.
38. NYCRO MIC 144.
39. Watts 1982.
40. McDonnell 1990, 35.
41. Harrison 1879, 252.
42. Ashcroft 1984.
43. cf. Smith 1967, 9.
44. Smith 1928, 272.
45. McDonnell 1990, 25.
46. Ekwall 1960, 48.
47. Fieldhouse and Jennings 1978, 38. See also Fleming 1999.
48. NYCRO ZPT 26/15.
49. Fieldhouse and Jennings 1978, chapter 3; McDonnell 1990.

CHAPTER FOUR

Conflict and
Common Sense

....

The study of past territories and settlement patterns is mostly about pattern recognition. The end product is usually a map, or maps, covered in lines and dots. However, drawing lines and dots on a map is one thing; reconstructing the actions and ways of life of the people responsible for them is quite another. Once I had gained some understanding of the medieval territorial pattern in Swaledale, I wanted to try to find out about the townships as communities managing their own land. I was encouraged by the persistence and partial survival of common rights, and the evidence from maps and the landscape itself – ridge and furrow, identifiable common cow pastures, meadows once shared and so on.

Nowadays, we are not very accustomed to thinking about the management of common land, because many communities have been deprived of the common rights which they once enjoyed. The process is said to have started with the Statute of Merton in 1236, which gave parliamentary sanction to the enclosure of wastes by a lord of the manor; from this time onwards there were frequent legal disputes between lords and commoners over enclosures and common rights.[1] As T. E. Scrutton put it in 1881:

> All legal rights of common originate in the lord's grant or in his permission or sufferance, and this is the essence of the legal view … the historical fact that freemen had rights of common independent of any lord, before the Conquest, cannot affect the legal position of manorial rights after the Conquest or today; nor can the legal theories of Norman lawyers or of today detract from whatever truth lies in the early history of the Free Village Community.[2]

In other words, statute law, passed by an undemocratic parliament, triumphed over customary law, in a process that may be compared with the 'legal' take-over of the lands of the natives of North America. Much later, in fact, those who advocated enclosure did actually complain that commons such as Hounslow Heath and Finchley Common were 'a disgrace to the country' and were 'as if they belonged to Cherokees'.[3]

Landlords were keen to raise rents, make more money, and develop more productive farming. But it was not only the actions of landlords which led to the decline of the commons. The commoners themselves often enclosed land 'by agreement', a phrase which disguises a range of political circumstances, including pressure or financial incentives applied by wealthier or more powerful neighbours. As F. W. Maitland pointed out, 'in England every right is apt to become vendible'.[4] In Swaledale, during the sixteenth and seventeenth centuries,

the commons were in decline, at least in the sense that they were diminishing in area, as more and more common land was enclosed. The process was already under way in the later Middle Ages. The enclosures took a variety of forms, which can be seen in the landscape today. Sometimes their small size and rather irregular outline suggest the actions of individual families, clearing brushwood or woodland. Sometimes they take the form of broad rectangular strips, side by side, displaying their origins as shares or *dales* in a common arable field or meadow. Later, enclosure mostly took place after the passing of an Act of Parliament. In Swaledale, as one might expect, it was the poorest land, often on north-facing slopes, which survived the early phase of piecemeal, small-scale enclosure, eventually to be subdivided by parliamentary enclosure in the early nineteenth century. In a great belt on the southern side of the dale, stretching all the way from Keld to Low Whita, the upper slopes of the daleside are subdivided by ruler-straight walls laid out by surveyors. Mostly, it was the old common cow pastures which were subdivided, and their top walls, snaking along the contour, were incorporated into the new layout (Fig. 4.1).

Fieldhouse and Jennings have documented the complicated legal and financial manoeuvres which were taking place in these post-medieval centuries.[5] In a time of inflation, landlords were trying to increase their incomes by attempting to replace various forms of customary tenure, associated with fixed rents, by short-term leases, so that they might raise the rents when the leases expired. They tried

FIGURE 4.1. Straight walls typical of the period of parliamentary enclosure in the early nineteenth century.

to do this directly, or through the courts, or by buying up the freeholds, as at Walburn for instance. If they met with too many obstructions, they tried another method – seeking to increase the *gressoms,* the various one-off payments made by new tenants, or to new landlords. If they were really desperate they would sell the estate. The tenants for their part sometimes resisted very stubbornly, and sometimes won their court battles; but sometimes they reached a settlement, in or out of court. Other complicating factors included confusion (actual or feigned) about the precise nature of customary rights and obligations; the poverty of some of the tenants, who sometimes simply could not pay; the attitudes of the landlords, which ranged from rapacity to paternalism; the fact that landlords usually lived outside the dale, which gave their stewards some interesting responsibilities (and opportunities); the differences between different estates, which led to invidious comparisons; and the effect on various different kinds of tenancy of Swaledale's traditional partible inheritance – rights and property being divided among all the sons, and sometimes the daughters as well.

Reading Fieldhouse and Jennings on this topic is a sobering experience for anyone with an orderly mind! It makes one wonder how far the situation on the ground is really reflected in the surviving legal and financial documents. It also leaves one under no illusion that past communities were necessarily harmonious, or single-minded. One wonders how well the remaining common lands were being managed at a time when the commoners were exerting and suffering all these conflicting pressures. Yet at the same time, given the evidence for commons management systems in the literature and in the landscape, both before these turbulent centuries and after them, it is worth standing back from some of these struggles, and looking at land-use and political organisation from the point of view of the township community, which may itself have originated and developed partly in order to defend the commons, their amenities and organisational structure.

In recent years, more insight has been brought to bear on these questions by human geographers and social scientists, and by economists who are interested in the management of common property resources, such as fisheries, in the modern world. In the late 1960s, the idea of the Tragedy of the Commons was introduced.[6] It was suggested that collectively used resources were always in danger of overexploitation, for a reason which sounds all too familiar – users of the common would not allow the long-term interests of the community to stand in the way of their own short-term gains. However, as the author of the Tragedy idea recognised, there may be ways of managing the commons to avoid catastrophe. In fact, most known commons are not open access, but have been carefully managed, with quite complex systems of rules and regulations, which specify that rights of common are restricted to a well-defined group of users. Furthermore, it seems to be difficult to find examples of commons which have failed because of overexploitation. Elinor Östrom has made a close analysis of self-governing commons which have stood the test of time, and published her conclusions in her book *Governing the Commons.*[7]

Successful commons have several key features. The boundaries of the common, and the qualifications of those entitled to use it, must be clearly defined. The rules which govern the exploitation of the common must be determined with reference to local conditions. Commoners should be able to participate in changing the rules if necessary; there have to be regulations about the procedures for changing the regulations. Observance of the rules has to be monitored by officials responsible to the body of commoners as a whole; they must be properly compensated for their work, and will usually be commoners themselves. An individual who breaks the rules must be penalised, with sanctions on a sliding scale according to the gravity of the offence. There must be a cost-effective, locally available form of arbitration to resolve conflicts between commoners, or between commoners and officials. The right of commoners to self-government, which after all is based on their local knowledge and experience, must be respected by external agencies of government.

Much of this seems like common sense, as it were. So why should any well-managed commons system fail? The answers to this question are quite complex. Commons management systems are not always proof against the effects of population growth within the group, or the growth of conditions which favour production for exchange (cash crops) as the importance of a money economy increases. Ultimately, however, we cannot blame disembodied social trends and economic forces. Commons systems are usually subverted from within, as some families and households come to believe that their own interests are detachable from those of the wider community. They start to build political coalitions for furthering their economic and social self-interest, at first working within the rules or just outside them. Sooner or later they develop the political muscle or bargaining skills to outflank the system's ability to defend itself. It is easy to imagine the outcome. Frequently, the attitudes of individuals and households outside the dominant group are part of the problem. Should they take action to defend and increase the safeguards against this kind of behaviour, or should they cut their losses and make haste to join the winners? The defence of systems of government which are relatively just, egalitarian and democratic requires regular hard work and attention to detail; it demands considerable political wisdom and skill. It is all too easy to forget what is at stake in the longer term, and to sell out – sometimes literally.

We might think about this in a bit more detail. Let us start by supposing that, once upon a time, the commoners were not diehards fighting a stubborn rearguard action against the forces of progress, but rather close-knit communities for whom sensible commons management was part of normal farming practice. I would argue that in most places the medieval commons would have gone through a sequence of change which can be broken down into three stages. In the first stage, which I call the co-operative phase, commoners have relatively free access to the resources of the common; the emphasis is more on access than on rights, and more on rights than on restrictions. Rights are *exercised*: they rarely have to be asserted. Population density may be quite low, and it may be important to build links between scattered communities, to create collaborative institutions, organise work gangs, put all the household flocks under the care of a community shepherd and so on.

This is a far cry from stage three, the competitive phase, when the rules are much more complex. Now there is perpetual conflict between those who try to circumvent the system and the officials charged with policing it; and also between relatively powerful groups who are manipulating the system to their advantage and the smaller commoners, the importance of whose stake is out of all proportion to its size. Sharp practice and political manoeuvres become more effective courses of action than attempts to stick to the rules, or to change them by argument and consent. The impartiality of arbitrators and officials can no longer be taken for granted, and the communal ethos itself may be called into question. The commons system in its competitive stage may have to change rapidly and drastically if it is not to break down altogether, destabilised by forces which it has been unable to control. Change on that scale may be too much to expect.

How does the system move from the cooperative stage to the competitive? Phase two is critical; this is the time when the system flips over from one to the other. I call this the 'regulated' phase, since the move from stage one to stage three must have involved more effective management, with the creation and enforcement of more regulations. The whole sequence, of course, assumes that the system is coming under steadily increasing pressure – from a rising population, or incentives for higher agricultural production (including higher taxation), or both.

This description of a system passing through a series of stages sounds very abstract and mechanical. That doesn't mean that it is 'wrong'. But we need to bring human action and emotion into the picture. Loyalty to the commonwealth is not necessarily a matter of calculation and cost-benefit analysis; in some societies, the way of thinking which makes the commons work is part and parcel of the commoners' ethical values and their beliefs about the nature of the world. Recent theoretical studies have suggested that there are three mainstream attitudes.[8] First, there are 'individualists', who seek equality of opportunity and open competition, and believe that nature is bountiful and open to exploitation. Second, there are 'egalitarians', who are strongly group-centred, and who seek an equal distribution of resources, because for them nature is not inexhaustible. Third, there are 'hierarchs', who favour institutionalised authority and organised inequality, believing that social and economic class systems are 'natural', and thus beneficial to social harmony and good government. Each of these attitudes has its problems. The individualists run the risk of selfishly destroying the world's resources, the egalitarians may hold back innovation and individual initiative, and the system perpetuated by the hierarchists may be too rigid to accommodate necessary change. In some societies, one or other of these attitudes may be dominant, or at least extremely widespread. In others, such as our own, they are found side by side, part and parcel of a historic struggle for power and an ongoing political argument.

If we are to consider how such ethical and political questions relate to the history of the commons in places like Swaledale, we also have to think about the structure of the family and the household, how common rights were handed down, and how co-operation and competition worked in the townships – and before the townships emerged.

In Swaledale, partible inheritance meant that property holdings or cattle-gates were usually divided equally among the sons of the deceased (the number of cattle-gates held determined how many animals could be kept on the commons). This custom survived into the eighteenth century. In 1694, a tenant at Ravenseat paid for 'the fifth part of a messuage and tenement the whole into 5 parts being equally divided. And also to the fifteenth part of the same messuage and tenement, the whole into 15 parts being equally divided … 'In 1704, Michael Peacock of Angram was 'admitted tenant of a two and ffortieth part of a house and several parcels of ground'.[9]

One forty-secondth of a property sounds like the product of two or three generations of partible inheritance, a bit like one-fortieth of a cattle-gate (which is also recorded). Commentators worry about these matters, claiming that partible inheritance would have been an inefficient system, splitting up individual holdings to the point where they became unviable, leading people to make strategic marriages in order to reunite their holdings.[10] But rules of inheritance are one thing; how they work out in the real world is quite another. In 1974, J. W. Cole and E. R. Wolf published *The Hidden Frontier,* a fascinating study of two neighbouring communities in the Tyrolean Alps. Their description of the area in the Middle Ages is quite reminiscent of Swaledale:[11]

> The total rents to be derived from a single high valley were rarely sufficient to support its own nobleman. Therefore, many were simply included within the domain of a lord whose home continued to be a castle in the lowlands. Low productivity, a dispersed settlement pattern, restricted size and remote location all contributed to the erosion of feudal patterns of managerial supervision in favour of peasant management . . . The overlord . . . was forced to make do with the collection of a fixed, hereditary rent from each estate.

One of these communities, St Felix, was German-speaking, and was governed by impartible inheritance; the integrity of the farm holding was to be preserved, and normally inherited by the eldest son. Romance-speaking Tret, like Swaledale, had partible inheritance; here, it was the *family* which was to be kept together. The implication should be that the number of farms in St Felix was permanently fixed, whereas in Tret holdings would be continually split up, and their numbers would vary from generation to generation. But in fact, the number of holdings in St Felix went up from 23 to 62 over the period of recorded history, whilst in Tret: 'the total of land holdings is fifty, and none is so small that it cannot provide a meaningful portion of a family's support; many have shown little change in composition for several generations'.[12]

Apparently the inheritance rules were honoured more in the breach than in the observance. Householders had to try to balance two objectives – to manage coherent farms, and to provide for all their children. In St Felix, estates sometimes had to be divided, or have distant parcels of land added to them, and in Tret heirs were disinherited or accepted compensation in exchange for their portion of land. In Tret, the process of subdivision stopped somewhere near the threshold of viability, or very slightly below it:

> often enough, holdings have been divided a bit too far – the division produced two or more holdings which, while obviously too small, were still large enough to tempt the peasant to make a go of it. Three results are possible from such divisions: a man might survive if able to supplement his farm income by engaging in a trade or craft; he might earn enough money to buy more land by working outside the village, or he might enlarge his holding through marriage to a land-holding woman…,[13]

Different inheritance 'rules' had much the same outcome; each community ended up with an elite core of land-holders, and a fringe of labourers and tradespeople, with or without certain rights of common, who remained within the community to take advantage of kinship ties; a few left to seek work elsewhere.

In Swaledale, the same sort of distinction between rules and reality must have applied. Partible inheritance was originally about sharing rights to land among members of groups of kin; that is what its popular name, *gavelkind*, meant, and we can understand that sort of scenario. In 1539 virtually all the monastic tenants in Birkdale, Keld and Angram were called Alderson.[14] Among some families the principles of *gavelkind* remained intact, and the heirs shared the obligation to pay the heriot and the rent for a given property. But this was just the legal position, recorded in the documents; reality was probably rather different. It's obvious that in normal circumstances individuals were not literally making use of a fifteenth part of a house or field-barn in their daily lives; presumably one-eighth of a beast-gate would usually have been rented out to someone with serious livestock interests. Closes do not display numerous subdivisions; where they do, the internal walls usually define *dales,* shares available for reallocation. Nowadays, some farm boundary walls in the Muker area still include *ekes,* the vertical breaks in the stonework which marked the boundaries of different maintenance sectors (Fig. 4.2) – a practice probably derived from an older system of share-farming among groups maintaining the *gavelkind* principle.[15] The old kin-based land-holding system declined slowly. Perhaps the commons system came to be dominated by larger families, with more political leverage.

The Swaledale commons go back a long way. For Downholme, common pasture was mentioned in 1201, and again in 1309.[16] In 1383 a document recorded

> common between Mosdalbek [= Gunnerside Beck] and Bernopbek [= Barney Beck] for the whole year for all cattle and animals which the said enclosures aforesaid of Gunnerset park and Folyng in winter could reasonably sustain, and also to take, cut and pull down branches of trees sufficient within all the woods of Swaledale [= Upper Swaledale], as well as for the structure of Mosdalhegge within the bounds aforesaid between Mosdalbeck and Bernopbeck, as for the sustenance of whatsoever animals and cattle in winter.[17]

FIGURE 4.2. Ekes – vertical joins in walling indicating that maintenance responsibilities were shared. *Above*: top wall of Ivelet Pasture. *Below*: painted and carved initials, Gunnerside Pasture.

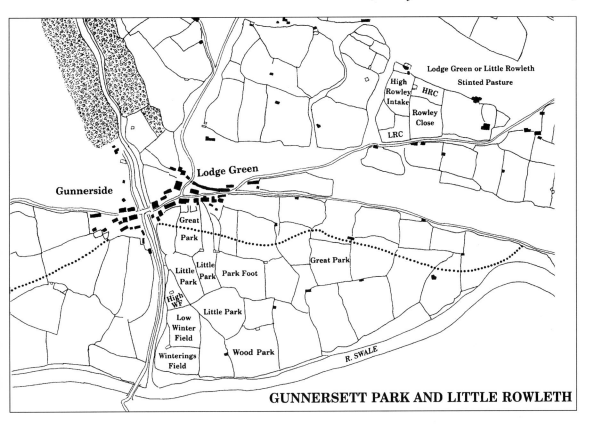

Labels on map: Gunnerside; Lodge Green; Lodge Green or Little Rowleth; Stinted Pasture; High Rowley Intake; HRC; Rowley Close; LRC; Great Park; Great Park; Little Park; Little Park; Park Foot; High WF; Little Park; Low Winter Field; Wood Park; Winterings Field; R. SWALE; **GUNNERSETT PARK AND LITTLE ROWLETH**

FIGURE 4.3. The Gunnerside/Lodge Green area, based on the tithe map. Some of the field-names indicate the location of the medieval 'winter park' in Gunnerside Bottoms. Note the relationship between Gunnerside and the footpath and road approaching from the east. The Rowley/Rowleth names were those of a medieval settlement, the high-level predecessor of Lodge Green. The medieval 'Mossdale Hagg' probably covered the area of woodland and irregular field boundaries on the east bank of Gunnerside Beck.

This is an early mention of Melbecks Common. But it also refers to a rule found widely on the commons – that no-one should keep more livestock on the summer pastures than can be overwintered. Foal Ing is located in Low Row, between the modern road and the river. We can work out from a cluster of nineteenth-century field-names ending in 'Park' that Gunnersett Park was in Gunnerside Bottoms (the classic 'walls and field-barns' landscape south of Lodge Green) (Fig. 4.3). The document also refers to the right to pollard the trees. In other words, Upper Swaledale had a good deal of wood pasture – a classic dual-purpose use of land frequently practised on the commons of Scandinavia and Germany as well as in other parts of Britain. 'Mossdale Hagg', as it would be called today, must have been on the eastern side of Gunnerside Gill, and it probably included the steep slopes below Potting and Winterings, where the irregular patchwise pattern of field-walls suggests parcels of land hewn gradually from woodland. 'Hagg' often refers to a coppice, and this wood may well have included some coppice stools, protected from browsing at critical times during the coppice cycle to allow the stems to grow.

If we take the right to lop trees – the right of greenhew – as evidence for common wood pasture, we can trace the commons further back. In 1274 more than half the total value of the manor of Healaugh was derived from 'vaccaries and pastures of the forest', and in the early thirteenth century Gilbert de

Gaunt granted unlimited and exclusive pasture rights over a large tract of land to Rievaulx Abbey, including the right to cut evergreen branches for winter fodder.[18] In the late twelfth century, the canons of Bridlington Priory, who had pasture land between Harkerside and Haverdale Beck, 'were allowed to take from the woods, *without felling trees,* [my italics] building materials for two vaccaries'.[19]

We know very little about the management of Swaledale's medieval commons. But there is one interesting possibility. As I have already mentioned, well-organised commoners need to appoint officials, who combine practical, managerial and judicial roles. There are just one or two possible glimpses of such individuals from Swaledale surnames – such as Pounder (the man who looks after the pound or pinfold), Barnward (the warden of the barns), Midwood (which is Medward, the warden of the meadows), Calvert (which means 'calf-herd') and Wetherhird. We know these surnames from various sources. 'Wetherhird' occurs in a medieval document;[20] Calvert is a common surname today. Barnward and Midwood have not been recent surnames in the dale (though Upper Swaledale's present vicar is called Midwood); they occur as 'Barnward Close' and 'Midwood Close' on tithe maps. A twelfth-century document renders Haverdale as 'hawardesdale', the hayward's dale.[21] It's unlikely, for fairly obvious reasons, that the name actually *means* 'the hayward's dale', but it looks as if the scribe thought he recognised a familiar word. These names probably go back a long way, if only because neither the surnames nor the roles which they represent are likely to have been invented in post-medieval times. Of course, it is a moot point whether these were commons or manorial officials, and such surnames might have originated outside Swaledale. It's impossible to use this evidence to *prove* that there were commons officials in medieval Swaledale. But as we shall soon see, Swaledale's 'decadent' post-medieval commons certainly did have officials.

Nowadays, Swaledale commons are not open-access commons; they are stinted. A number of individuals own so many 'gates', or 'cattle-gates'; the number of gates determines the number of animals which they may graze on the moor, and there is an agreed formula for working out how many sheep are equivalent to one cow and so on. At Low Row in 1847, for instance, there were 124 cattle-gates shared between 35 owners;[22] one person had 26 gates, but many others had only 1, 2 or 3. Partly as a result of Swaledale's lingering tradition of partible inheritance – according to which all sons were joint heirs, and sometimes daughters as well – some individuals had odd numbers of gates, like $2\frac{1}{2}$ + $\frac{9}{30}$; and one person in Little Rowleth had $8\frac{3}{5}$ + $\frac{1}{30}$ + $\frac{1}{40}$ + $\frac{1}{8}$. The distribution of gates among quite a number of commoners was usual in the nineteenth century; at this time there were 36 commoners in Feetham, 26 in Great Rowleth and 20 in Little Rowleth.

Various regulations have been preserved in writing. On Reeth Low Moor, a hundred years ago, there was a summer stint from 5 May to 11 October, followed immediately by a winter stint (presumably at lower stocking densities) which lasted until 1 April, after which all stock had to be removed, allowing about seven weeks for the vegetation to recover in time for the next grazing cycle. Reeth High Moor, on the other hand, which was further out, was open all the year round.[23] On the other common moors, the grazing seasons were regulated, often with specific dates for driving stock on to the moor ('dogging and driving' them, as the phrase went in the sixteenth century) and for bringing them back in the autumn. There is normally only one narrow gate in the wall which separates cow pasture from moor, allowing livestock to be counted through and their movements to be carefully controlled. These gates have names, such as Fore Gill Gate, North Gate, Sun Gate and Greenseat Gate. Keeping the gates in good repair was one of the responsibilities of the elected commons officials. Maintaining the top wall of the cow pasture was the responsibility of the community, and the wall-builders left numerous *ekes* in order to create short stretches of wall which different individuals or families were required to keep in good repair (in proportion to the numbers of gates which they held?). To this day, the *ekes* on the outer face of the top wall of Gunnerside Pasture are marked with sets of initials in white paint, and in one or two places initials have been professionally carved on the stones (Fig. 4.2).

It is hard to tell the age of these top walls. In some places, above Lodge Green and Rowleth Wood for instance, they look as if they have been built by professionals, with carefully chosen quarried stones, probably in the early years of the nineteenth century; they have not needed much repair. But there are also more ramshackle walls, like those above Blades, where there has been so much patching-up that it is hard to work out what the original 'style' (if any) was like. Many of the original *ekes* survive only to a height of three or four courses of stone, and some of them may have vanished altogether. According to T. D. Whitaker, writing in 1823, the 'common or stinted pastures' were fenced off from the commons 'in the reign of Henry VIII',[24] and considering the momentous legal struggles between landlords and tenants in the sixteenth century, it does seem likely that the older-looking walls date from this period. Looking at larger stones or blocks incorporated in the bases of these walls, it is hard to tell whether one is seeing earlier phases of walling or simply rough foundation courses. Walls may not have been absolutely necessary in the Middle Ages; livestock might have been hobbled, or simply kept together on their pasture by close herding.

There are places, however, where the top wall once took a different course. I have already mentioned that the Acre Wall at Muker pre-dates the top wall of Ivelet Cow Pasture, and there is evidence that the Ivelet top wall itself was once located slightly lower down the hillside. At Summer Lodge, the ruins of a top wall can be seen running along the contour through the north-facing enclosed land labelled Summer Lodge Pasture, and out on to the open moor, below West Greena Hill. From its length and position this looks like the former top wall for Whitaside. Only one short stretch of it has continued in use. It is unlikely that this wall would have gone out of use in recent centuries, given the pressures on property; so it is tempting to suggest that it is medieval.

Documents from the Northallerton record office tell us more about how local self-governing communities regulated the commons. The late eighteenth-century 'Byelaw Book of Muker', where some 245 'gates' were administered, indicates that every year two 'byelaw men' were normally chosen.[25] In 1818 there were three – Alexander Cottingham, James Calvert and Edward Reynoldson – who were appointed 'By laws of Muker Pasture for the Rising Year and to have one Cattle Gate for their office'. Another office-holder in Muker was the Master of the Bulls. To convey something of the flavour of commons regulations, it is worth quoting from an agreement made in 1790 between one Richard Guy and 'the Inhabitants of the Town of Muker'.

> Richard Guy in consideration of his having and receiving the Rents and Profits of the Bull Pasture, and the sum of forty shillings a year, to furnish and supply the aforesaid inhabitants with two good and sufficient bulls to be approved of by James Clarkson of Satron, James Grime of Muker, and Christopher Peacock of Appletreethwaite during the time that the cows are upon the Pasture, and one Bull as aforesaid for the remainder of the year. All persons not Inhabitants [this word is crossed out, and the word 'Land-owners' inserted] of Muker who stock the Pasture with Cows or Queys, to pay one Shilling each for such Cow or Quey. All persons who change their stock after the 26th day of May annually to pay half a crown each for such cow or quey, one half to the Master of the Bulls, and the other moiety to go towards the payment of the aforesaid forty Shillings. All cows which are kept to graze in the inclosed pastures belonging to the Town, to be allowed to be bulled with the Pasture Bulls, as they can agree with the Master of the Bulls…

The book contains numerous records of fines paid for abuse of the stinting regulations. It also lists expenses paid to officials – for mending a gate on Muker pasture, for the use of the bull, for seeking and fetching bulls, for repairing the pinfold at Kisdon Gate, for repairing the Pound Fold door, for viewing and repairing fences, for keeping the bull for sixteen days and so on. The good governance of the bull – or in this case bulls – was obviously of critical importance, and is commemorated by the fact that the field-name 'Bull Park' recurs in various parts of the dale. A Derbyshire farmer once asked me if these 'bull parks' were on sloping ground, since this would apparently have helped the bull to get a purchase while fulfilling his duties. Knowing the Swaledale terrain, I was able to reassure him on that score!

It would be good to know more about other systems of organisation and administration in Swaledale. Between township and lordship there are many areas of silence. But there are one or two clues. In the Grinton parish registers for the year 1661 there is a list of the names 'of those who were chosen to be the foure & twenty according to the ancient custome for the parish of Grinton'. This Council of Twenty-Four was evidently still in being in 1752, when it had four 'divisions' with six members each. Members for Grinton, Reeth and Melbecks were listed, but there is a blank where the names of members of the fourth division should be. This division must have been Muker, which may have stopped participating after it was refounded as a separate parish in 1743.[26] These councils of Twenty-Four were known elsewhere. Bedale had one, and so did Richmond in the late sixteenth century, when new local government reforms had to accommodate the old council of Twenty-Four.[27] In fact, councils of Twenty-Four are recorded from quite a number of places in England.[28] They sat in rural communities such as Monyash in Derbyshire (where they were mentioned in 1345) as well as cities like Winchester (first mentioned in 1280). These bodies often met in the local church, and they dealt with both civil and church business; sometimes, the Four-and-Twenty appointed the priest, as at Alnwick in Northumberland. In Derbyshire, the Barmote councils of the lead-miners, which go back to at least the thirteenth century were composed of twenty-four members.[29] Twenty-four seems to have been a number of ancient significance (although four, twelve, sixteen and forty-eight also crop up quite frequently in the history of local self-government). Of course the number 24 is a useful one for a council representing several districts, because it is divisible in six different ways.

It would be good to know how old the mysterious Council of Twenty-Four was, and what business it dealt with. Such a council may have concerned itself with local weights and measures, such as the Swaledale perch which was presumably used in the upper dale.[30] There may also have been guilds in Swaledale in the later Middle Ages – bodies involved in religious observances and perhaps craft organisation. Around 1200 there was a Gildhusbec and a Gildhuswad ('guild house ford') somewhere between Downholme and Ellerton;[31] the name is probably preserved by the modern 'Gill Beck', a name which makes little sense literally translated.

We know that Old Swaledale had a pillory and ducking-stool in the late thirteenth century; it also had a gallows, one of ninety-four in Yorkshire alone which were revealed by a royal enquiry to discover 'who usurped the rights of the king by holding their own courts, issuing their own writs, and hanging offenders up on their own gallows'.[32] People were also hanged at Richmond, where one of the streets is called 'Gallowgate' and one of its open fields, to the north of the town, was called Gallow Field. Possibly the 'Gallow' or 'Gallows' marked on nineteenth-century maps on the daleside above Feetham tell us where the Swaledale gallows was located.

The history of the Swaledale commons in the later Middle Ages must have been as turbulent as the river itself. For Swaledale was a contested landscape. No doubt there were distinctions of power and status in pre-Conquest Swaledale, and they were probably intensified by the incursions of various groups of newcomers. Families trying to make a living here had to cope with the exactions and transactions of pre-Conquest lords, and then with their feudal successors. The de Gaunt family, who held the manor of Healaugh until 1298, imposed Forest Law on Swaledale; Arkengarthdale was also a Forest, and then there was New Forest, to the north-east, located in what looks much more like hunting country. At least five deer parks were enclosed in the Middle Ages, too, doubtless often at the expense of wood pasture rights, and people were not above breaking into them and taking the deer, as Christopher and William Tiplady were accused of doing at Marrick Park in 1439.[33]

The de Gaunts gave land in Swaledale to monastic institutions, notably Bridlington Priory and Rievaulx Abbey, far away to the east; it is interesting that they chose land on the well-wooded south bank of the Swale and at the western end of the dale, rather than on the more populous north bank. The nunneries at Ellerton and Marrick were given land, and so were Jervaulx, Easby and Bardney (Lincolnshire). As Fieldhouse and Jennings' notes explain, these grants of land involved certain rights, privileges and restrictions, all of which had to be fitted into the existing scheme of things, individuals and families holding their land on the basis of various legal and financial rights and obligations.[34] No doubt in practice what actually happened sometimes diverged markedly from the stipulations of the law!

Certain local surnames, such as Wensley or Teesdale, remind us that we must also envisage the arrival of newcomers who wanted work as lead-miners or lead-smelters, or to practise a trade, perhaps serving the mining industry. These people were not necessarily unwelcome; on the contrary, their labour and skill, developed in other lead-fields, may sometimes have made all the difference. Some of them would have married into Swaledale families; some may have wanted to buffer themselves against the uncertainties and dangers of lead-mining by investing in a small farm. This was the approach of the irritatingly virtuous hero of *Adam Brunskill*, Thomas Armstrong's delightfully old-fashioned novel about Swaledale (published only a couple of years before *Lucky Jim* and *Room at the Top!*). In certain circumstances a few may have been permitted to make intakes on the common cow pastures, whilst others may have continued for several generations as families of landless labourers. There must have been an increasing distinction between the core land-holding families and those on the margins of the community.

I have already emphasised the need for self-managing commons to be adaptable in accommodating change. It is not always obvious that they were; after all, given the weight attached in common law to precedent, anyone called to give evidence in court would have had every incentive to claim that their current practices had operated for time out of mind – and to make sure that their testimony was written down. But one does come across evidence for organised change. At Downholme, in 1730, there were 'gates' on How Hill; it was a stinted pasture.[35] Yet on the ground it is clear that in the Middle Ages there were arable strips here. After the fourteenth-century recession, it seems that the rather exposed How Hill was converted into a common pasture. And sometimes a community changed the layout of its arable land, turning the axis of the arable strips through 90 degrees; I have seen evidence for this just below Riddings Farm, near Reeth, and in Walburn, just off the road to Downholme, where melting snow produces a gridiron pattern of green and white stripes (Fig. 5.4).

So the history of the commons in a place like Swaledale was probably as much about change, competition and power struggles, as about calm, 'democratic' decision-making. Eventually, as happened all over England, the hierarchs and the individualists won out over the egalitarians. In the long term, of course, we are all commoners of the earth and in this light the position of the 'egalitarians' makes more sense than that of the 'individualists' or that of the 'hierarchists'. The history of the commons is a sobering reminder of just how tough-minded, clear-sighted and well-organised egalitarians need to be.

Notes

1. Scrutton 1887, 56–68.
2. Ibid., 41.
3. Ibid.,140.
4. Quoted in Britton 1977, 16.
5. Fieldhouse and Jennings 1978, 111–35.
6. Hardin 1968.
7. Östrom 1990.
8. Buck 1989.
9. North Yorkshire County Record Office (NYCRO) CRONT 2: MUKER (Muker Manorial Court Records 1686–1743).
10. Fieldhouse and Jennings 1978, 135–40.
11. Cole and Wolf 1974, 72.
12. Ibid., 179.
13. Ibid., 182.
14. Fieldhouse and Jennings 1978, 60.
15. Phillips 1984b.
16. Farrer 1942, vol V, 29; Harrison 1879, 101.
17. Harrison 1879, 252.
18. Fieldhouse and Jennings 1978, 39.
19. Ibid., 38.
20. Brown 1896, 26.
21. Lancaster 1912, 249.
22. NYCRO ZQS (MIC 1478).
23. Ibid.
24. Whitaker 1823, 310.
25. NYCRO ZRD2.
26. Slingsby 1905.
27. Bogg 1908, 493; Lewis 1975, 24; Clarkson 1821, 100–1.
28. Addy 1913, 255–81, 472.
29. Kirkham 1968, 44.
30. Lancaster 1912, 250.
31. Farrer 1942, 29.
32. Smith 1889, new series vol 1, 45, 54.
33. Harrison 1879, 218.
34. Fieldhouse and Jennings 1978, chapter 3.
35. NYCRO MIC 1822.

CHAPTER FIVE

Reconstructing Community Landscapes

Swaledale's common lands now look mostly like the grouse moors which they are. But *former* common lands are all over the place; as well as the daleside cow pastures, there was common arable land, common wood pasture and common meadowland. Nowadays, access to land is severely restricted by farmers and landowners who tend to demand as much freedom as possible to pursue their own economic interests;[1] in Swaledale, a landowner may feel free to forbid his gamekeepers to drink in the local pub, in case they become too friendly with poachers. It is hard, now, to imagine a landscape controlled and managed by the local community. The traces of this vanished world are still visible, however, in particular patterns of field boundaries, and in the ridge and furrow which still creates dramatic green and white stripes when the snow is melting.

In the later Middle Ages, and probably earlier, Lower Swaledale had much more arable land than the upper dale, and it is here that we can find most evidence for what the open fields were like, on the ground and on old maps. The lines of walls first put up in the sixteenth or seventeenth century have sometimes followed the sinuous, 'reverse S' curve of ridge and furrow, the result, it is said, of the long process of turning teams of plough oxen round on the headlands. In Lower Swaledale, the classic case is Hudswell, whose narrow, strip-like fields include several whose boundaries incorporate this 'reverse S' plough-curve; they are obvious on the map, or when seen from the other side of the dale.

Had the burghers of Richmond held on to their open fields a couple of generations longer, we might have had photographs of them. But they did survive to be mapped in the early years of the nineteenth century – a great arc of land including much of modern Richmond, from the Skeeby road to the Reeth road. On the north side was the great Gallow Field, almost a mile from end to end, and separated from the West Field by the Hurgill to Reeth – *hageil* in Old Norse, meaning the highway. These fields each contained almost 150 acres (60 hectares). They were 'fields' in the old sense of the word – that is, open fields; what *we* would call fields used to be called closes. The 1766 plan of West Field is fascinating (Fig. 5.1); it shows one or two faithfully mapped 'reverse S' strip edges and some traces of the old 'furlongs' (smaller blocks of strips which were subdivisions of the great fields). Some of the old strips have been consolidated into larger parcels of land, but we can see that some strip parcels were still very narrow, perhaps 10m or a little less (a chain is 22 yards or about 20m). (In the Gallow Field, the strips in the most intensely subdivided zones average something like 7–9 yards (c.7–9m) in width, so the narrowest ones were

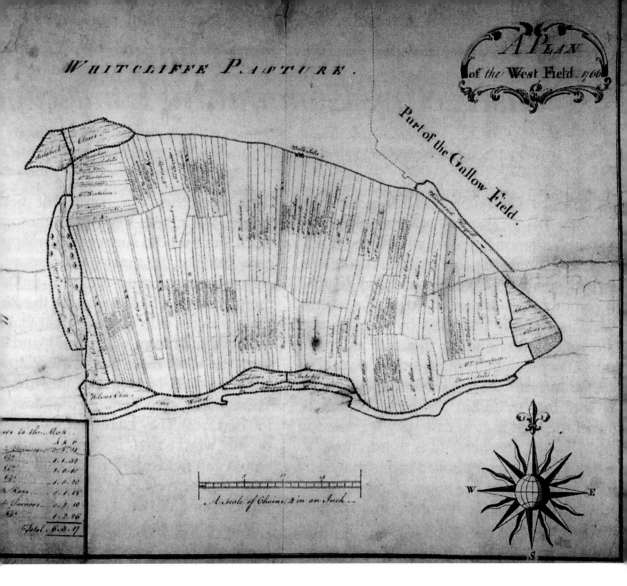

WHITCLIFFE PASTURE.

A PLAN of the West Field. 1766

Part of the Gallow Field.

A Scale of Chains. 4 in an Inch.

W   E

S

FIGURE 5.1. Plan of the West Field, Richmond (1766) (reproduced by permission of the North Yorkshire County Record Office).

probably still one or two ridges wide). We can see how individuals – Wilson, Topham and Chaytor – have nibbled away at the edges of the West Field, making their closes, presumably by agreement; and at the bottom of the field, we can see what an old-fashioned, pre-turnpike road looked like, negotiating its way through occupied land. Some of the strips are labelled 'townsland' and these were still presumably common land.[2]

The map of Downholme, produced for the Duke of Bolton in 1730, shows what the landscape looked like when the enclosure process had gone further (Fig. 5.2).[3] Just west of the church, in Church or Kirk Field, the land was still in narrow strips – the narrowest ones round about 10 yards (c.10m) in width – with four different tenants. The old name for an allotment in the common field was a *dale*. The word means share; it is the same word *as dole*. 'Wandills' on the Downholme map is supposed to refer to *dales* measured out or marked by wands or poles set along the headlands.[4] At Wandills, the ridges have clearly been consolidated into narrow parcels, probably divided by hedges. In other parts of the township (or

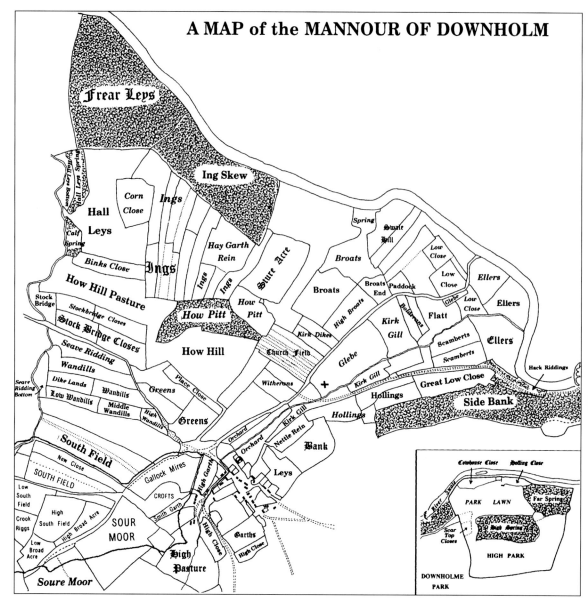

A MAP of the MANNOUR OF DOWNHOLM

lordship, as the mapmakers usually chose to call it), hedged closes cut across the strip layout – Corn Close, or Low Close, for example.

Strip-fields were also called *ranes* – and the map marks Bolderans and Witherans, as well as Nettle Rein and Haygarth Rein.[5] *Dale* and *rane* are Old English words; *flatt,* which is Old Norse, has the same meaning, and so do names in *lands* (as in Dike Lands, on this map). *Broats* comes from Old English *brot,* meaning a small plot;[6] *Scamberts* should mean 'short plots'. As well as South Field and Kirk Field, it looks as if Downholme had a subdivided meadow – Ings – and a hay garth where hay ricks might be built. There was permanent pasture in Frear Leys and Hall Leys – and, in the 18th century, also

FIGURE 5.2 *(left).* Downholme in the eighteenth century; a simplified copy of a map of c.1730, with the missing area at bottom left completed from a map of 1778. A good deal of the medieval land-used pattern can still be picked up in the names and boundaries (reproduced by permission of the North Yorkshire County Record Office).

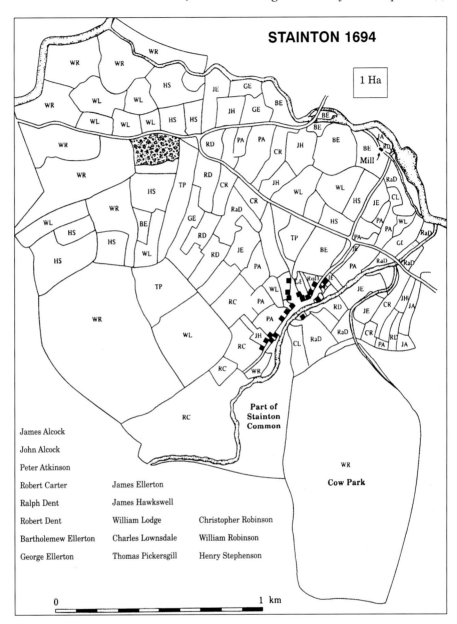

FIGURE 5.3. Stainton in 1694, redrawn from a contemporary map, showing the medieval-derived pattern of scattered and intermixed closes of the tenants denoted by their initials and listed at the bottom. The very large enclosure at bottom right was the Cow Park (formerly common). The old Roman road from Ulshaw Bridge runs past the village, and the mill – with its leat and tail-race – is to the north-east.

STAINTON 1694

1 Ha

Mill

Part of Stainton Common

WR

Cow Park

James Alcock

John Alcock

Peter Atkinson

Robert Carter   James Ellerton

Ralph Dent   James Hawkswell

Robert Dent   William Lodge   Christopher Robinson

Bartholemew Ellerton   Charles Lownsdale   William Robinson

George Ellerton   Thomas Pickersgill   Henry Stephenson

0   1 km

on How Hill itself, though there is archaeological evidence that the hill was used as arable land in the Middle Ages. Downholme's wood pasture was originally in Side Bank and on the steep slopes further east, before Downholme Park was created in the late fourteenth century. 'Hollings' may refer to an area where hollies were grown as emergency winter fodder. Downholme Moor provided summer *grazing*, as well as heather for thatching and probably a certain amount of game. This eighteenth-century Downholme map still provides a good general picture of medieval land use in Lower Swaledale.

The map of the small township of Stainton is earlier, dating from 1694

(Fig. 5.3).[7] At this stage in the life of the township, there were 15 tenants, sharing about 835 acres (338 hectares); leaving aside William Robinson's 266 acres (107 hectares), and two holdings of 4 or 5 acres (1.5–2 hectares), there were 12 other farmers, with an average holding size of 38 acres (15 hectares). All the farmers lived in the village; the map shows how scattered were the holdings of each tenant, especially in the areas of the old arable fields, to the north of the village and to the south-east, towards the area of the modern Wathgill army camp.

There were sizeable arable fields at Walburn, Marske, Ellerton, Marrick, Reeth and – in proportion to township size – at Grinton, Fremington, Healaugh and Hercay (Harkerside). The strip lynchets to the west of Reeth are particularly magnificent, but it is also worth looking down from the path which leads up to Fremington Edge. From here one can see parallel lines of walls and hedges sweeping over the land above the village – preserving the outlines of the old North Field. In this central part of Swaledale, more recent ploughing has flattened quite a lot of the medieval pattern – but when the sun is low in the sky, and as the snow thaws, it is possible to pick out quite a lot. Further west there was some arable land of the recognisable medieval type at Booze in Arkengarthdale and also in Gunnerside township, around Dyke Heads. In some places it is possible to see that the direction of the ridge and furrow has been switched through 90 degrees – for example at Reeth (just below Riddings Farm) and at Walburn (Fig. 5.4). Elsewhere in Upper Swaledale and Arkengarthdale, there seems to be little evidence of ridge and furrow, or of the characteristic field-shapes and field-names found further east, although it is unlikely that cultivation was unknown in these areas in the Middle Ages – after all, Muker means 'the narrow cultivated ground'. On tithe maps, the field-name 'Corn Close' does crop up from time to time, which ought to indicate that growing

FIGURE 5.4. Walburn; melting snow shows how the orientation of medieval ridge and furrow has been changed through 90 degrees.

cereals was not very common in the post-medieval period – perhaps confirming John Leland's description of the area in the earlier part of the sixteenth century: Arkengarth dale ... bereth some bygge [barley] and otys, litle or no woodde Suadale [note the pronunciation] litle corne and much gresse, no wodd, but linge and sum nutte trees'.[8] But one can think of several reasons why it might be wrong to make too much of this kind of thumb-nail sketch.

The presence of so much medieval arable land in central and Lower Swaledale raises an interesting question: where were the corn-mills? In fact, water-mills were present in almost all of the townships involved. Some are mentioned in post-medieval documents. Grinton Mill was in existence in 1580, Satron in 1602, Reeth in 1623.[9] The evidence takes various forms. Fremington Mill is still a standing building, with a water-wheel still in place. A charming picture in Speight's *Romantic Richmondshire* shows the mill at Marske in the nineteenth century, before it was destroyed; it stood in the area which is now the water garden of Marske Hall, and appears to have been overshot, fed by a wooden launder approaching from somewhere near the Hall.[10] The mill at Stainton was operational in 1694; the map marks it clearly, with the leat, the mill-building and the tail race, and a large mill-pond. Robert Dent had the mill, along with 22 acres (9 hectares) of land; he lived in the village. It is still possible to make out the course of the leat, and to work out where the mill stood.

In Walburn and Ellerton, townships which were probably largely deserted by the late fourteenth century, mill-names do not survive on post-medieval maps. At Ellerton, high up on the course of the only beck which could be utilised, flowing north towards the deserted village, are the remains of a broken earthen dam. At Walburn (Fig. 7.4), the stream which flowed through the green at the north end of the old village has one or two suspiciously straight bits, the remains of a building near the side of the beck and earthworks which just might be all that is left of dams. But the best evidence is quite near the bridge to the north of Walburn Hall, where it is possible to make out the remains of a building, a leat, a funnel-shaped pond and perhaps also a corn-drying kiln. It may be that the mill at Walburn was moved downstream at some stage. Perhaps one of the most awkward mills to get to was the one at Marrick; it must have stood near the priory, where the dam is still well preserved. The need to get pack-animals from the village to the mill and back may have been the main reason for the construction of the flight of stone steps on the southern edge of Steps Wood, which was certainly in place by the late sixteenth century, as we know from the earliest of the Swaledale maps.[11]

In the upper dale, where there is apparently not very much evidence for cereal-growing, there were also water-mills. There was one at Haverdale, and another further up Summer Lodge Beck, where it is still possible to make out the dam. And there was one at Gunnerside, where the building is still standing. Further west still was Satron Mill, which was just south of Ivelet Bridge (Mill Bridge is still marked on the map).

Many of these water-mills were probably first established in the Middle Ages, and most were still in being in later centuries. The Grinton parish registers occasionally remind us that they were dangerous places: George Blades was drowned at Satron Mill in 1649, and young Bartholemew Ellerton was drowned in the mill dam at Fremington in 1755 ('and was carried into the Swale'). Of course, the survival of the mills doesn't necessarily mean that large quantities of corn were being grown locally. Presumably much of the grain was imported and milled in the dale itself.

In Swaledale, it was essential to grow enough winter fodder to support livestock over the winter. The primary hay-making areas were the *ings,* valuable meadows often located in well-drained zones beside the Swale and the Arkle Beck and their tributaries, and often close to the main settlements. The *ings* are marked on the tithe maps, which give us a comprehensive coverage of Upper Swaledale in the period 1830–43. In the Middle Ages, this meadow land was divided into unfenced *dales.* When the *dales* were converted into narrow walled closes, their names incorporated the name of the original common meadow. Thus at Muker, a series of neighbouring closes beside the Swale have names like Little Long Ing, Hawes Long Ing, Ned's Long Ing, Taylor Mary Long Ing and Long Ing End; and just to the south, at the confluence of the Swale and Straw Beck, are Foal Ing, High Foal Ing, Low Foal Ing and Bess Neddy's Foal Ing.

The names of these original large meadows are usually simple enough – Keld (= spring) Ing, Summer Ing, Foal Ing, Ox Ing, Long Ing, Scale Ing, sometimes just Ing or Ings. Gun Ing, in Muker, must be named after someone with a Scandinavian name beginning with 'Gun' – Gunnar, perhaps, or Gunnildr. Sometimes a meadow was a *holm* – a piece of land partially surrounded by water, like the meadow to the south of Reeth, which lies between the Swale and the Arkle Beck (Fig. 5.5). Here, the nineteenth-century closes formed a 'family' of names – Great Mill Holme, Low Mill Holme, Ralph Mill Holme and so on – showing that the whole area was once Mill Holme, or possibly 'Mel' Holme, the holm *between* the Swale and the Arkle Beck. The other meadow was some way to the north of the village; it too has a family of names, all ending in Sleets. It is possible that this name comes from Old English *slaeget,* meaning a sheep pasture, but in Old Norse terms the name means level ground, and I prefer this, if only because it sounds like an example of the sardonic humour which is so familiar in Swaledale today; this land, just above the Arkle Beck, is anything but flat. Both Mill Holme and Sleets were subdivided coaxially, with long boundaries running parallel to one another from one side of the meadow to the other. Originally, these long strips would have been periodically reallocated. Later they became part of fixed farm-holdings. Something of the original character of the commons system has survived in the pattern of the modern fields.

The pattern is also visible further west (Fig. 5.6). The nineteenth-century map of Crackpot shows that there was a small *ing,* Warr Ing, just north of the settlement, but the original *ing* (Old Ing) lay to the south. This too was coaxially subdivided, and had a subdivision called Broad Dale – that is, broad share. At Ravenseat, the old *ing* was also identified by name, and two of the subdivisions

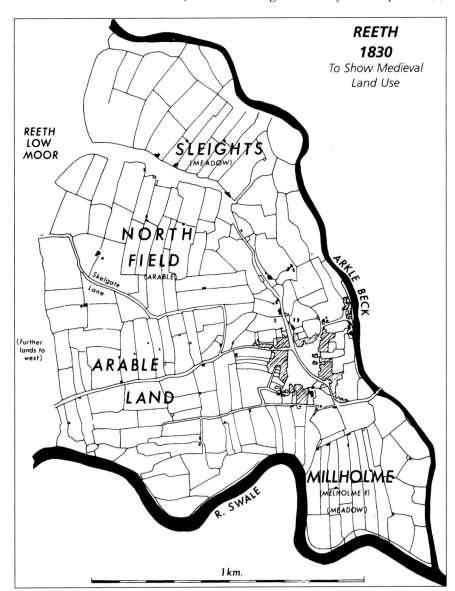

**REETH
1830**
*To Show Medieval
Land Use*

REETH
LOW
MOOR

SLEIGHTS
(MEADOW)

NORTH
FIELD
(ARABLE)

Skelgate
Lane

(Further
lands to
west)

ARABLE

LAND

ARKLE BECK

R. SWALE

MILLHOLME
(MELHOLME ?)
(MEADOW)

1 km.

FIGURE 5.5. Medieval land-use zones at Reeth, as deduced from the names and boundaries on the 1830 Tithe Map. The strip lynchets which divided much of the arable land to the west of the village can be seen on Figure 1.3. In Mill Holme and Sleights the original *dales* (allotments), laid out coaxially, have been enclosed.

also had names in *dale* in the nineteenth century. Just below Low Row was quite a large meadow called Foal Ing, which included a *dale* called Wardale.

In Lower Swaledale, it is possible that people took hay crops from the arable lands, using the system of regular fallows built into the open field system. Even when a field was in cultivation it may have been possible for individuals to protect their own strips with temporary fencing. At Downholme, as we have seen, there seems to have been a *haygarth* near the Ings. Stephen Moorhouse, who works on the medieval landscapes of Wensleydale, has suggested that hay made on strip lynchets was sometimes stacked on terraced platforms built on the ends of the lynchets.

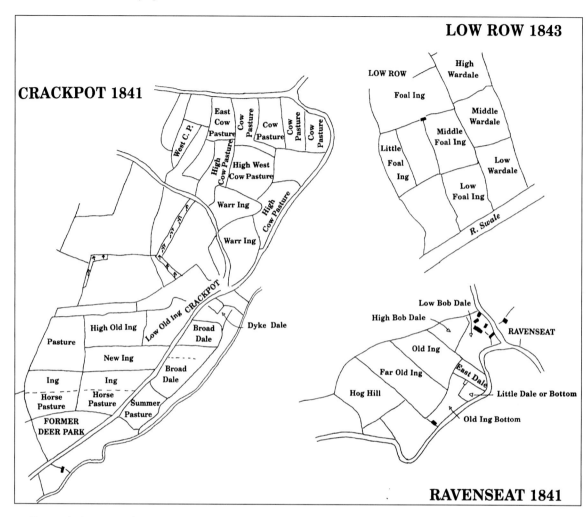

FIGURE 5.6. Crackpot, Low Row and Ravenseat: field-names on the tithe maps show how former common fields have been subdivided, often coaxially, and how their names and a few of the old *dale* (allotment) names have survived.

Beyond the *ings,* there were common pastures. Around Reeth, Harkerside and Healaugh the daleside was largely taken up with strip parcels of arable and meadow, often fitted in among the old Roman field boundaries. But further west, above and beyond the *ings* and the *garths* around the settlement areas, the dalesides were mostly occupied by large cow pastures. In early times these would have been wood pastures, providing browsing, grazing and supplies of timber and leaf fodder, and their presence must have been a major reason why the de Gaunts designated Swaldal as a hunting preserve, the Forest of Swaledale. The woods on these commons were gradually eaten away (literally, to some extent) but they survived in some places, especially on steep slopes and in deep gills. Grazing on these pastures was largely reserved for the period from late autumn to early spring, after the livestock had been brought down from the moors. Ivelet Pasture was labelled on a 1769 map as 'common from the middle of September to the middle of April'.[12] Where the daleside was already reserved for other uses, the common pasture had to take in higher, less productive areas.

Gunnerside Pasture is mostly moorland, and so is quite a lot of Feetham Pasture, although grazing quality may have been higher in the past under a different system of management. The commoners of Reeth eventually had to use the exposed flanks of Calver Hill as their near pasture – Reeth Low Moor. Their summer grazing, Reeth High Moor, was considerably further away. Walburn and Stainton had large cow pastures well separated from their arable ground – on the rougher land in the area where Wathgill army base is now situated.

The common pastures were not divided into *dales*. They seem to have been used more flexibly; eventually, it was possible to create and enclose *riddings* or *intakes* there, presumably with the agreement of the other commoners. The lower part of Lodge Green Pasture is packed with intakes, separated by a maze of lanes and open funnel-like areas which preserved access to the common. On these commons we also come across charcoal-burners' platforms, and bale hills – large mounds in locations deliberately exposed to the wind, where lead was smelted in the Middle Ages. Often, rabbits have tunnelled into the bale hills, and brought up many bits of slag and charcoal.

There are one or two elements which do not quite fit into this pattern of *ings,* moors and cow pastures. They may help us to understand more about the landscape of Upper Swaledale when the population was lower and the woods were thicker – around the twelfth century or so, and perhaps earlier. My curiosity was first aroused when I read Harrison's *History of Yorkshire,* volume I, published in 1879. Harrison or, to give him his full name, George Henry Strabolgie Neville Plantagenet-Harrison, must have been quite a character. He devised a genealogy which demonstrated that he was the last of the Plantagenets ('all his ancestors in the direct line stood upwards of seventy-five inches'); the tangled branches of his family tree encompassed many an illustrious ancestor, going all the way back to 'Odin, King of Asgardia' sometime before the birth of Christ. He claimed to have been barred from the British Museum Reading Room 'because I claimed to be Duke of Lancaster'.[13]

Despite all this, some of Harrison's gleanings from the medieval records are quite interesting. In 1383 there is a documentary record of 'common between Mosdalbek [= Gunnerside Beck] and Bernopbek [= Barney Beck] for the whole year for all cattle and animals which the said enclosures aforesaid of Gunnerset park and Folyng in winter could reasonably sustain ...'[14] The whereabouts of 'Gunnersett Park' is not a mystery; on the tithe map, field-names incorporating the word 'park' make it clear that it was in Gunnerside Bottoms, to the south of Lodge Green (Fig. 4.3). In view of the remark about winter use, it's also interesting to find the names 'Winterings Field', High Winter Field, and 'Low Winter Field' in the same area. Is it possible that when the dale was more wooded, livestock overwintered not in a large daleside cow pasture, but in a fenced-off 'park' close to the settlement? In such an enclosure, livestock would have had access to hay or leaves as winter fodder, and they would have been prevented from straying; deer and wolves would have been excluded, and the stock would have manured the land. Hay meadows *(ings)* could have been located within such a park, or nearby. The other wintering place mentioned in the 1383 document was Foal Ing (at Low Row), which was certainly meadow land, to judge by the name.

The 170–acre 'Cow Park' marked on the 1694 map of Stainton looks quite like this kind of setup (note the name) and so does the Cow Pasture at Walburn not far away. I think we can identify another of these early enclosed winter pastures much further west, where there is a series of 'park' field-names in the rather hollow, sheltered valley to the west of Keld. If there *were* winter cattle parks in Swaledale in the twelfth and thirteenth centuries, and perhaps earlier, they might well have been surrounded by hedges, or timber fences; this was the time when *hay* or *gehaeg* was becoming a common place-name in the eastern part of Old Swaledale. Harkerside gets its name ultimately from 'Herthay' (which means deer park). But the big semicircular walled enclosure not far away, marked 'Deer Park' on the map, is 'Swale Intake' on other maps – evidently this was one of Sir Solomon Swale's grandiose projects, in the late seventeenth century. In Arkengarthdale, the early written form of 'Whaw' shows that the place-name derives from Old Norse *kvi*, meaning an enclosure.[15]

The word 'park' tends to conjure up images of deer, and the activities of the aristocracy, so that it's tempting to assume that the word comes from the French *parc*. But *pearroc* is an English word; in recent centuries it has been quite a common field-name element in various parts of the country. Around the time of the Norman Conquest and afterwards, there were probably both 'cow parks' and 'deer parks' in Swaledale. Given that both deer and cattle would have spent most of their summers browsing in the woods, and that both may have been given supplementary rations of hay and leaves in winter, we may be looking at similar management practices. In the Pennines, controlling livestock with fences goes back seven or eight thousand years, if we accept Christine Williams' interpretation of her pollen diagrams from Soyland Edge, near Halifax.[16]

The word 'lodge' for a park-keeper's house also sounds aristocratic, and there was certainly a Park Lodge in Downholme Park, which was licensed in the late fourteenth century. But the 'lodge' at Lodge Green probably related to the cow park of the commoners of Melbeckside in the fourteenth century. And what about Summer Lodge, where it is possible to trace a large enclosure on the north side of the beck, as a line on the map and as an earthwork on the ground? And then there is the large, very oval earthwork enclosure on Birks Edge, above Whitaside, which seems to have no name or legend attached to it. Either this one, or Summer Lodge, might have been Bridlington Priory's Whitaside deer park.[17]

Probably the management of deer and cattle in winter was associated with enclosed parks, looked after by commons, manorial or forest officials as appropriate. Where the park was some way away from a main settlement, such an official would doubtless live in a lodge. But what would the management pattern look like in summer, when livestock might browse further afield, in the daleside woods and out on the open moors? As I have mentioned already it looks as if some pastoral out-stations lay within the main valley, in the earlier Middle Ages, with places like Gunnersett, Angram and Satron being outstations or *saetr* for the community at Muker. Further east, 'Summer Lodge' may have referred originally to a seasonally used shieling. The field name 'Scale Ing' just east of Healaugh may reflect the former existence of a distant shieling for Reeth. But most of the names in 'seat' are out on the moors, as a glance at the map makes clear. As the population increased, and farming and lead-mining intensified, the dalesides must have gradually lost their tree cover, becoming more and more open, with winter commons and some areas of wood pasture. At the same time, the use of moorland shielings must have increased – a movement towards the pattern with which we are more familiar. Communities with pastures distant from the main settlements had outstations, seats or scales where livestock could be given shelter or brought under cover or into pens for various purposes – milking, clipping, castration, sorting into different groups and so on.

Most of the 'seat' names are at the 'Norse' end of the dale: Pinseat, Lovely Seat, Ray Seat, Jewel Seat, Crook Seat, High Seat; and several named after individuals – Rogan's Seat, Robert's Seat and Ravenseat (Hrafn's Seat), for example. This emphasis on perpetuating the names of ancestral figures is a distinctive and apparently Scandinavian custom, perhaps going with surnames in 'son' – Hodgson, Clarkson, Alderson, Reynoldson, for instance – in suggesting that people at the 'Norse' end of the dale emphasised descent and kinship. This contrasts with the custom in the more 'English' part of the dale, where quite a number of surnames – Kearton, Harker, Blades, Feetham, Raw and Ellerton, for example – were derived from places.

These common moors were more than simply grazing grounds. Here, lead was mined and smelted, coal was dug (this was certainly happening in the Middle Ages[18]) and stone was quarried. From quite early times, the commoners were attempting to improve the heathland pasture; Leland, writing in the early sixteenth century, pointed out that 'in places where they cutte down linge [heather], good grasse springith for the catel for a yere or ii until the ling overgrow hit'.[19] In 1620 a Whitaside man found himself in court for moor-burning on May 11th, which was later than allowed.[20] But there must also have been areas where the heather was allowed to grow tall, since it was widely used for thatching. So was juniper, probably; it was apparently much more widespread in the seventeenth century, with several hundred acres in Reeth, Healaugh and Muker.[21] Doubtless the moors were also used for hunting. The practice of grouse-shooting on these moors is older than most people imagine. According to Whitaker, there were deer on the moors to the north of Muker, conserved for hunting by the Wharton family, until 1725, when the effects of lead-smelting finally caught up with them: 'after the warm and sheltered gills were stripped of their clothing, the stags pined for want of their accustomed winter food, of which many died, while the rest fell an easy prey to poachers'. But keen hunters soon adapted to the new situation: 'after the nobler pursuit had ceased, hawking and netting for grouse was in use to the year 1725, when shooting flying was introduced, to the great astonishment of the dalesmen'.[22] The shooting lodge at Grinton – now a very popular youth hostel – was already in existence by the late eighteenth century.[23]

A few of the moors were apparently unstinted, which allowed some of the bigger farmers to build up larger flocks and herds (depending, of course, on their ability to feed them in winter).[24] In the early sixteenth century, evidence given in relation to disputes between the townships of Marske and Marrick provided a lively account of the kind of thing which went on in the hill pastures:

> hathe sene the Askes and Bulmers, owners of the manors of Marrigge, cutt downe, carrye awaye, and burne at theire leade bales such wodde as grewe apon the saide growndes of Heselhowe and Hawethornes, and hadde the brakens, ling and thornes growing apon the same, and cariyed awaye the same ... hath sene the tenants buyld lockes and shepe fooldes apon the said two groundes, and have hay stackes standing apon the same. Helmsley hymself hath had hay standing at the foote of Hawthornes and therwith foddered his cattells sondrye years together ... hath sene Master Aske, owner of the lordship of Marryck, have a stak of hay uppon Heselhowe, and there used to fodder his shepe, and spaned lambs and mylked ewes uppon the sayd ground.[25]

A *lock* is a temporary sheep-fold, probably made of hurdles. One of Swaledale's unidentified medieval places was called 'Frithloc' ('the fold in the wood');[26] it was probably on the daleside across the river from Low Row.[1]

Over the years, numerous temporary folds and shelters must have been built out here. The 'Tan' element in Tan Hill and Tackan Tan (which is just north-west of Tan Hill) relates to the Scots dialect word *tan*, meaning a temporary hut. And Beldi Hill, which gave its name to a well-known lead-mine just east of Keld, comes from the Middle English word for a shelter, which is also rendered as *bield*. Most of the visible standing structures seem to be quite recent. For instance, Robert's Seat House, on a hill just north-east of Ravenseat, is represented by a small roofless rectangular building, which can hardly be more than about 150 years old; according to Ella Pontefract it was a 'watching house' used by gamekeepers on the lookout for poachers. I have seen the remains of two small rectangular structures in the heather just east of Calver Hill, on Reeth Low Moor; from their appearance they could easily be medieval 'seat houses' or 'scales', as could others on Harkerside Moor. Their walls are likely to have been built of turf and thatched with heather. Harrison described the old village of Aske, on the road from Richmond to Ravensworth, as consisting of 'a few very ancient haggs' (houses built of turf, and thatched with straw) which were pulled down and replaced by stone-built cottages in the 1820s. Where the turf walls rested on low stone footings, traces of such structures should survive to be spotted by the archaeologist.

These seat-houses were essential shelters and equipment stores, but they would also have played more active roles, as visible reminders that certain parts of the common were habitually used by the flocks and herds of particular families or communities. As the population increased, the wooded dalesides would have looked more and more like woody cow pastures. Increasingly, it would have made sense to create some enclosed meadowland in these pastures, complete with seat-houses for storing the hay and sometimes sheltering the stock, with facilities for milking in the dry if necessary.' 'Seat-house' seems to have been one word for the ancestors of the field-barns (laithes) which are so common in Swaledale. Most of the standing buildings now on view are unlikely to be older than the late eighteenth century. One wonders what their distribution would have been like when there were open cow pastures on the dalesides, and to what extent the early field-barns stood in the same places as those standing today.

Almost all these buildings would have been thatched. But from the late eighteenth century onwards, most of them were rebuilt or re-roofed with stone slates, derived from local quarries on the moors. Stone roofs have a shallower pitch than thatched roofs, which were associated with a variety of gable end profiles, some shaped like tall isosceles triangles rising from the tops of the walls, others with more rounded or sinuous profiles. One or two ruined buildings which were never roofed in stone still display these end profiles very well (Fig. 5.8). And occasionally, when a roof was raised, the original gable end profile was incorporated into the modified building, and can still be seen (Fig. 5.7); there is a magnificent example on the right-hand side of the road just as one enters Angram from the south. It may also be possible to see how the quoins with the triangular or near-triangular profiles appropriate to the earlier types of gable end have been turned round and reused in the later structure. These field-barns deserve serious archaeological study. There are pitfalls for the unwary, however. There are various reasons why the few primitive-looking structures may not be much older than the finest examples, and stones with dates carved on them may not be all they seem. There is a fine example on a barn just south of the footpath from Keld to Kisdon Force (Fig 5.9). The large lintel-stone has three sets of initials – all Aldersons, presumably – a reminder, also seen on the lintel-stones of various Swaledale houses, of the local custom of partible inheritance. But this wasn't necessarily a shared barn. On closer examination, it's clear from the way the stone has been cut that it has been removed from somewhere else – a dwelling-house in Keld, presumably. The style of the barn looks nineteenth century.

It may be possible to pick up other indications of early commons management practices, dating from times when communities were smaller and more homogeneous, and they needed to create links between families and localities rather than emphasise their differences – the early, 'co-operative' stage of commons development. When livestock from a group of households could be kept together, it was possible to designate and manage particular areas in different ways. We have already come across Bull Parks, and meadows called 'Ox Ing' and 'Foal Ing' (where horses were kept, presumably after the hay crop had been taken off); there are also Horse Pastures. Walburn and Kexwith each

FIGURE 5.7. Gable end of field-barn at Crackpot, showing how it has incorporated the earlier profile built for a thatched roof, perhaps supported by crucks.

FIGURE 5.8. Remains of a formerly thatched house.

FIGURE 5.9. Field-barn near Keld, with a datestone over the window which does *not* date the building.

had a Cow Pasture and a Horse Pasture. Muker had two daleside pastures – a small one on Kisdon and a much larger one on the north-facing daleside. In both 1617 and in 1686 there are records of individuals having cattle-gates in Keld Cow Pasture and sheep-gates on Kisdon, and the distinction between the two kinds of pasture probably goes back a long way. 'Calver', the hill just west of Reeth, probably means 'the calves' hedged enclosure'. Calvert Houses was formerly called something variously written as Cawenerd House ('cowherd house'), Coverley or Calverley House ('the house in the calves' or calf-herd's clearing') or even Calsett ('the calves' fold'). 'Yaudhope', the earlier name for Ewelop between Fremington and Marrick, means 'horses' clearing'. The thirteenth-century form of Storthwaite suggests that the name meant 'bullock field' originally.[33] Some place-names – which should be relatively early in date – link animals and enclosures in much the same way, especially in Arkengarthdale. So the first element of Faggergill means 'sheep enclosure'.[34] Words for enclosures crop up quite regularly; Whaw, which was spelt 'Kiwawe' in the thirteenth century, was made up of two Old Norse words, both meaning 'enclosure'.[35] Medieval Arkengarthdale had a place called 'Lokehous' (the house at the fold).[36] In the Middle Ages, there must have been a considerable contrast between the landscape around Downholme, with its great blocks of ranes and flatts, and the dalesides in Upper Swaledale, where stretches of wood pasture were interrupted by clearings and hedged enclosures, and parks for cattle and deer. There must have been wild places, out among the seat-houses, where the moor was already pock-marked by coal and lead-mines, and the smoke from moor-burning and lead-smelting rose into the sky. In some places, this landscape of woodland farming must have looked quite like a scene from the Neolithic, several thousand years earlier. But down by the river, the common *ings* and *holms* were probably just as carefully subdivided as the fields further east; these were also the landscapes of communities.

Notes

1. Godwin 1990.
2. North Yorkshire County Record Office (NYCRO) ZAZ (M) 4/1. 4/4; DC/RMB.
3. NYCRO ZBO (M) 1/5.
4. Armstrong *et al.* 1952, part 3, p. 497.
5. NYCRO ZAZ (M) 1.
6. Smith 1956, part 1, 53.
7. NYCRO ZPT 26/15.
8. Toulmin Smith 1906–10, vol. IV, 32.
9. NYCRO CRONT2/GRINTON; ZQH2 10/57; ZLKMIG1744.
10. Speight 1908, 196.
11. University of Leeds, Brotherton Collection.
12. NYCRO XQH 6/42.
13. Harrison, 1879, viii.
14. Ibid., 252.
15. Smith 1928, 296.
16. Williams 1985.
17. Fieldhouse and Jennings 1978, 48.
18. Ibid., 160.
19. Toulmin Smith 1906–10, 32.
20. Atkinson 1894, 243.
21. Speight 1908, 239.
22. Whitaker 1823, 309.
23. NYCRO ZQT 2/3.
24. Fieldhouse and Jennings 1978, 141.
25. Raine 1881, 39.
26. See Fleming 1999 for an identification of this place.
27. Smith 1967, part 2, p. 292.
28. Pontefract 1934, 46–7.
29. Harrison 1879, 68.
30. NYCRO MIC 2001/70; New Forest Tithe Map (1839).
31. NYCRO CRONT 2: MUKER; ZJV. 21.
32. Harrison 1879, 231; NYCRO ZQX 5/4.
33. Smith 1928, 296.
34. Ibid., 295.
35. Ibid., 296.
36. S. Moorhouse, pers. comm.

CHAPTER SIX

In Search of Old
Wood Pastures

....

In the middle ages, there were three designated hunting reserves in the Swaledale area – the Forest of Swaledale, the Forest of Arkengarthdale and the New Forest, out in the wilds midway between Reeth and Barningham. 'Forest' is primarily a legal term, implying control and management. At the time of the Norman Conquest, these 'forests' may actually have been quite heavily wooded, at any rate enough to provide cover for deer and other game. It was clearings which were the distinctive landmarks, and were given names – such as *lēah, thwaite, hay,* and *ridding.* We do not know much about the history of these forests, from the huntsman's point of view. To most of the people of Swaledale they were mainly woodland pastures. And they were under pressure. As the population expanded, the number of summer out-stations and winter parks would have increased. As the more valuable land in the dale was opened up, browsed by deer and cattle or cleared by felling or ring-barking, summer grazing-stations would have been transferred to moorland locations. Individual families or groups made *hays* or *riddings,* presumably with the agreement or tacit consent of their neighbours. Sooner or later, it would have been necessary to control and manage what woodland was left, within the boundaries of each emergent township. Rights would have to be clearly defined, and some kind of conservation strategy would have to be developed. The solution to this problem, for many medieval communities, was the development of a *wood pasture,* a dual-purpose regulated woodland where commoners could both graze their livestock and have access to supplies of firewood and possibly timber.[1] In quite a number of places, the old wood pasture carries the name of the community which had rights in it, and the main access route is often still visible on the map. Frequently, the former wood pasture is on poor soil, near the parish boundary.

In Swaledale, it is still often possible to work out where zones of wood pasture have been – or survived longest – and to pick up traces of woodland management practices which go back to the Middle Ages and beyond. In a landscape where stone is now more noticeable than wood, this may seem surprising, and indeed it was quite a long time before the pieces of this particular jigsaw puzzle came together. It all started one July evening. Early in our work together, Tim Laurie and I were on our way to look at an ancient settlement site in the pastures to the east of Fremington. Suddenly I stopped, rooted to the spot. In front of me were two elm trees, about ten yards (c.10m) apart, incorporated in the wall which ran beside the footpath. Although the trees were in leaf, I could see that these were not like the elm trees which I had enjoyed climbing as a boy. From

the size of their trunks, one would have expected them to be tall trees, with several main stems rising to high canopies of leaves. But here, the main stems looked younger than they should have been. Something had inhibited their growth; six or seven feet above the ground, the trunk of each tree expanded into a gnarled and knotted mass of wood, a crown from which the tree's upper stems all sprang. As a keen student of Oliver Rackham's work on the management of ancient woodland,[2] I realised that these trees were pollards; they had been systematically lopped just above head height (Fig. 6.1).

We started to look out for more elm pollards. It turned out that there were quite a few of them, including some which looked quite old (Fig. 6.2). Many of them were dead or dying, victims of the recent epidemic of Dutch elm disease, and then of the chainsaw. Most of the trees were on field boundaries, or very close to them, though we also spotted some from the roadside, in the woods – notably in Rowleth Wood (between Low Row and Gunnerside) and in Side Bank Wood opposite Downholme Bridge. In these steeply sloping woods, the elms were cut closer to the ground – 'stubs', as Rackham calls them, rather than pollards in the strict sense. As far as we could tell, the trunks of the trees were usually hollow. And pollarding as a regular practice had clearly stopped a long time ago. Quite frequently, the gnarled and knotty crowns of the trees had enfolded themselves around stones, which must have been chucked in from

FIGURE 6.1. Two elm pollards. *Left*: a pollard near Reeth which is still alive. *Right*: a long-dead example from Fremington.

FIGURE 6.2. A very old-looking elm pollard, now sawn up, from the upper side of the former wood pasture at Low Whita (its position is indicated on Figure 6.8).

the fields or dislodged from adjacent walls. Many of the elm pollards were in central Swaledale, around Fremington, Marrick, Reeth, Grinton and Healaugh. There was a row of them along the big linear earthwork just west of Grinton, and one or two very old-looking trees along the eastern boundary of Marrick Priory, beside the deep hollow-way leading down to the old ford across the river, which Turner, the celebrated painter, crossed on the 29th of July 1816, just before he made a sketch of the priory.[3]

These are wych elms, which predominate in the north country. Several of the pollards had had their upper branches sawn up, allowing us to count the annual rings, and to work out when the thickest of the stems had started to grow, and thus when pollarding had stopped – some time during the first half of the nineteenth century, for the most part. Local farmers were rather taken aback when their attention was drawn to these trees; no-one could really tell us why the trees had been lopped. After I had given a lecture in Reeth, an old man came up and told me that 'prods' of elm were used to tie down bundles of thatch on the roofs of field-barns; pollarding died out when the barns got their stone slate roofs. 'Are you suggesting this, or telling me?' I asked. 'I'm telling you', he replied. His story certainly makes sense, in terms of the chronology of barn roofs, stone quarries and tree-rings. But it was hard to believe that the original reason for pollarding was to produce thatching-prods.

FIGURE 6.3. Ash pollards at Watendlath, Cumbria. Wood pastures in Swaledale probably looked rather like this in their heyday.

I persuaded Oliver Rackham to visit Swaledale. He was cautious about estimating the age of the trees – though he was prepared to regard the most venerable elm at Marrick Priory as five or six hundred years old. He also spotted some hawthorn pollards, some of them perhaps three hundred years old, on sloping ground to the north-east of Reeth. (The trick is to notice the distinctive kink in stems otherwise growing fairly straight up). Rackham also confirmed what we suspected – that trees which are periodically lopped grow very slowly. The oldest trees in England are pollards.

In terms of the general history of the English countryside, there is nothing necessarily unusual about these elms. Oliver Rackham has explained how trees on boundaries were sometimes pollarded (despite prohibitions in tenancy agreements) and how the fashion for pollarding died out in the early nineteenth century.[4] In spite of this, however, I felt that there was something about these trees which we had yet to understand. We could not age them in the normal way, by finding the stumps of the ones which had been felled and counting the annual rings; apparently they were all hollow. I suspected that our age guesstimates were probably overcautious, and that the pollards might be older than we were prepared to think. Another thing was that they were not distributed evenly, but clustered in certain areas. And I was aware that in some parts of England, pollards used to be characteristic trees of common wood pasture, where grazing and the harvesting of wood were practised side by side.

In parts of the Lake District, there are ash pollards which until quite recently were lopped to supply sheep with leaves as supplementary winter food;[5] apparently the leaf fodder also makes their meat taste good. The sheep nibble the bark as well. (In the Cévennes, on the eastern side of the Massif Central in France, I have seen sheep make very short work of a bundle of ash stems

FIGURE 6.4. A fragment of old wood pasture: alder pollards at West Arngill Wood.

deliberately cut for them and left on their pasture. They enjoyed both the leaves and the bark). There are some fine examples of ash pollards around the National Trust's farm at Watendlath, just south of Derwentwater (Fig. 6.3). The tradition goes back a long way, as Winchester points out:[6]

> sales of branches formed a regular part of the lordly income from Derwentfells in the later thirteenth century, while c.1281, the monks of Calder Abbey were granted leave to cut down the branches of trees in Copeland Forest to feed their stock in the winter and spring. In the forest of Kendale in the mid-fifteenth century holly and ash were the species from which 'croppynges' and 'shreddings' were harvested.

Leaf fodder and sheep went together on an old-fashioned early twentieth-century farm at the head of Bilsdale, in north-east Yorkshire, where 60 or 70 ewes were kept in the old Ingleby Greenhowe deer-park, fattening extremely well through the summer on ash and elder leaves; at the end of the summer the lambs were sent off fat, while the ewes survived much of the winter on 'fallen leaves, and the bit of grass and heather higher up'.[7]

But how could I link old pollards, standing on field boundaries in enclosed land, with wood pasture or leaf foddering? The breakthrough came several years later; I had started research in the County Record Office at Northallerton, and came across a map of the manor of Healaugh in 1770, made by Richard Richardson of Darlington.[8] What was striking on this map was the pattern of common moors and pastures in Upper Swaledale. A good deal of the land was defined as either the moor or the common cow pasture of a named township. For example, the name of the open stretch of hillside on the east bank of the Swale, reached by a narrow footbridge from Muker, was Ivelet Cow Pasture, and it has had a wall at the top since at least the late eighteenth century. Not long after seeing Richardson's map, I was walking through Ivelet Cow Pasture towards Keld, on a well-used footpath.

I crossed Arn Gill – which is 'eagle gill', and probably got its name before there were cow pastures here – and passed over West Arn Gill.

And once again, I stopped abruptly. Beside the path were two obvious pollards – not elms this time, but alders (Fig. 6.4). And just ahead, a little upslope, were about a dozen more, within a rectangular enclosure defined by a wire fence, which enclosed an area of bracken optimistically labelled 'West Arngill Wood' on the map. Here, for the first time, I was able to identify old pollards, not on field boundaries, but out in the open, *on a common*. This, surely, must be a remnant of wood pasture; there was even one little cluster of alder pollards where the regular spacing between the trees and the well-grazed woodland floor beneath them allowed me to imagine what an old Swaledale wood pasture might have looked like. Seeds from other trees had long ago lodged in the crowns of one or two of them, and propagated themselves, so that birch, rowan and alder were commingled in a mass of stems just above head height.

Walking back from West Arngill Wood, I spotted another obvious alder pollard, all by itself, high up on the other side of the river. Ivelet Pasture has other pollards scattered around, with one or two elms further along, near Swinnergill, and at least one birch pollard to the south of West Arngill, on the shoulder of the daleside.

This was exciting. I returned to the archives and tried to gather some documentary evidence. It turned out that there were one or two references to lopping trees in Fieldhouse and Jennings' *History of Richmond and Swaledale*. Some of the most useful accounts come from outside Swaledale. In the fifteenth century, at Braithwaite, in Wensleydale, it was permitted to cut underwood but 'saving evermore, abiding and standing still there, all okes, almes, esshes, holyns and crabtrees without any felling or hewing down, or cropping or twisting of them'. A document dating from 1584, referring to the Ravensworth/Whashton area, refers to 600 horseloads of 'toppes and graynes of oaks, hollies and underwood'. *(Grains,* I think, means the cluster of stems making up the crown of a pollard. In the north country, this term is the name for the place where rivulets at the headwaters of a beck converge – like Grains in the Water, in Derbyshire. The word was also used in Swaledale to refer to the prongs of a fork).[10]

For Swaledale itself, there are references in 1592 to 'an underwooded pasture land' and 'wooded pasture land' in Grinton, and records of the Muker manor court from 1618 and 1669 refer to payments made by tenants for *greenhew,* the right to cut pollards for leaf fodder. The 1618 record refers to the tenants' obligation to pay their 'greenhewe' 'as at all tymes heretofore they have usually and accustomably done'.[11] And the lease for a tenancy at Walburn, drawn up in 1726, forbade the lopping of trees.[12]

But there was also the landscape to work on. Supposing that every township's common cow pasture had once carried woodland – a vital resource, after all – it made sense to work methodically, township by township, trying to deduce where the woodland had been. The plan worked (Fig. 6.5). So what were the clues which helped me to identify the locations of former wood pastures?

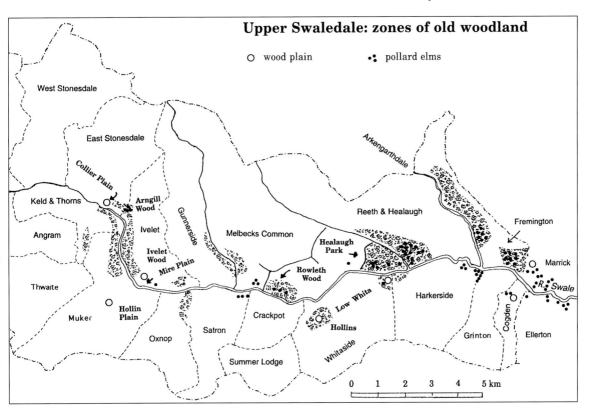

Upper Swaledale: zones of old woodland

○ wood plain   •: pollard elms

FIGURE 6.5. Long-term woodland and wood pasture zones in Upper Swaledale, showing locations of surviving elm pollards and 'wood plains'.

In the first place, the tithe maps of the 1830s and 1840s had schedules which specified how each parcel of land was used – and they show that, at that time, many of Swaledale's woods were also pastures. The labels vary – pasture and wood, pasture wood, grass and wood, woody pasture; in the parish of Muker about 120 acres (roughly 50 hectares) came into this category. To an extent, the tradition survives to this day. Some hillside pastures carry trees and bushes, giving them a park-like, almost African appearance, especially when thorn bushes are dominant, as they frequently are. This must be the result of relaxed grazing pressures, some years ago. Rowleth Wood is perhaps the best example in Swaledale of a wood which is pastured nowadays; the muddy footpath running through it is pitted with deep hoof-prints. Rowleth is not enclosed like a conventional wood; it has developed as woodland on a common. Above the trees, one comes straight out on to the open grassland of Low Row Pasture. The modern road runs without a fence through the lower part of the wood; in May, the remaining elm stubs and pollards stand among glorious spreads of wood anemones and bluebells – as they do in the wood opposite Downholme Bridge. The road through Rowleth Wood was once barred by a gate in the wall which separated Rowleth Pasture from Little Rowleth Pasture (alias Lodge Green Pasture). Just west of Strands, the stone stoop (gatepost) is still visible, with no less than eight successive holes drilled for the hinges (Fig. 10.3).

So the tradition of animals browsing and grazing in woodland continued into the nineteenth century, and is still just about alive today. Names on old maps, including the tithe maps, also reveal the presence of the glades which were called 'lawns' or 'launds' in other English wood pastures. In Swaledale they were called 'plains' or 'wood plains' and sometimes they had specific names; for instance, east of Keld, on the north bank of the Swale below the waterfalls, was one called 'Collier Plain'. Evidently it was used by charcoal-burners, who also made quite a few platforms further along the river, in Ivelet Pasture and Ivelet Wood. I know of thirteen locations of former wood plains in Swaledale, distributed all the way from Keld to within a couple of miles of Richmond. By the time they were named on eighteenth- or nineteenth-century maps, most of them were no longer in the woods; they simply gave their names to walled closes. They were quite small, and of various different shapes; most of them eventually had walls built round them. Mire Plain, across the Swale from Muker, is still a rectangular walled close, isolated in pasture land. Most other wood plains were incorporated into local field patterns; they stand out as roughly oval or kidney-shaped parcels of land, usually on a flattish shelf on the daleside, with the walls of other fields radiating from them. Some wood plains were beside the river.

In the Middle Ages, the wood plains may have looked rather like the openings in the leaf-meadows on the Swedish island of Gotland, in the Baltic Sea. Several of these leaf-meadows have been preserved and maintained as nature reserves and fragments of an older countryside; thanks to the kindness of two Swedish friends who helped on the Swaledale project, Pår Connelid and Catharina Mascher, I was able to visit those leaf-meadows in May 1993, when they looked idyllically beautiful. The Gotland leaf-meadows are on level ground. They are looked after carefully, dead leaves being carefully gathered up and burnt. Over the years, the locations of the plains in which the hay is made are shifted. Another place which conveys some impression of what wood pastures might have looked like is Watendlath in the Lake District. One area just outside the ring-garth (the boundary of the farm's enclosed land) contains numerous ash pollards, distributed at fairly regular intervals like the trees in an old orchard (Fig. 6.3).

Ivelet Common had two recorded wood plains – Mire Plain, which was mentioned in 1702,[13] and Swinnergill Plain. As well as the alder pollards, there have been elm pollards here, though only one or two survive. Ivelet Wood looks like a coppice, but the multiple-stemmed hazel 'stools' here probably result from the depredations of livestock. This wood in its present form is not particularly old; Tom Gledhill has excavated a seventeenth-century charcoal-burners' platform here, and discovered that most of the charcoal came from slow-growing ash trees (pollards?). Interestingly, the ash is not well represented here today. It would be good to know whether commoners had the right to burn charcoal on the common; or did charcoal burners simply pay for the wood and the right to process it?

Nearer to Ivelet, the daleside is enclosed. But just south-east of Calvert Houses there are quite a few ash trees on the field boundaries. Their ages vary; several quite old trees have grotesque and sometimes rather massive limbs which have obviously been trained along the boundaries on which they stand.

From the opposite side of the dale, these trees stand out clearly, and one can see from the boundary pattern that they once stood on the edge of a wood – a wood which had gone by the 1850s, since it was not marked as such on the First Edition Six Inch Ordnance Survey map. It looks as if this land was enclosed piecemeal, the boundaries including lengths of stone wall and fences, with stretches of hedge which incorporated any available young trees and saplings.

What of Muker's wood pasture? To the south of the village there is a Hollin Plain, and a couple of kidney-shaped parcels of land which probably started out as wood plains; they obviously pre-date the Enclosure period walls which run up to them. Hollin Plain was described as having 'a cowhouse thereon standing' in 1700.[14] Probably a clump of hollies was maintained and encouraged here, to provide a supply of evergreen winter fodder. This was a well-known practice in the Pennines, where the name 'Holly Garth' survives in some places; in the

FIGURE 6.6. *Above*: clump of old hollies at Marrick Woodhouse. These hollies were probably used for emergency winter fodder. *Below*: an ancient holly stool at Eskeleth.

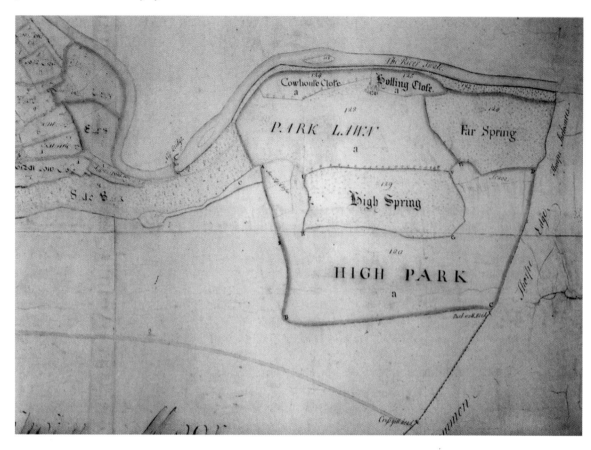

Lake District, groups of hollies which were used in this way can still sometimes be seen just outside the ring-garth. Just west of Rash, not very far from Hollin Plain, there is in fact a group of very old hollies in exactly this position, beside a footpath. There are also suspicious-looking clumps close to farms in some places – for example at Oxnop, Usha Gap and Woodhouse Farm, Marrick (Fig. 6.6). At Satron in 1700 there were two closes called Cow Hollins.[15]

The oldest holly I have come across is at Eskeleth in Arkengarthdale, beside the road to Seal Houses, just east of Yealand House (Fig. 6.6). A dozen massive stems spring from an underground stool covering an oval area about 9 feet by 6 feet (3m by 2m); seen at ground level they look like the legs of an elephant. This ancient tree is a stupendous sight. It must be the sole survivor of its generation, preserved by the happy accident of finding itself, in its old age, on a roadside verge. There must once have been others; the existence of only one 95-year-old in Swaledale does not mean that only one person was born here ninety-five years ago!

In Downholme Park in the late eighteenth century, there were two closes beside the river. One was Cowhouse Close, and its neighbour was called Holling Close, which probably once contained the emergency winter fodder for the cattle of the park keeper, who lived at Park Lodge. But not a trace of holly is visible here today (Fig. 6.7).[16]

FIGURE 6.7. Downholme Park in 1730. Note the presence of springs (coppices), the provision for cattle ('Cowhouse Close' and probably Holling close) and the open area or lawn. Nowadays the main Richmond-Leyburn road runs east to west through the northern fringe of the park (reproduced by permission of North Yorkshire County Record Office).

Muker's longest-surviving wood pasture zone lay to the north of the village. Here, the irregular edges of the closes marked on the map show that they have been cut out of woodland. Clearly, there was once a zone of daleside wood pasture here which stretched almost all the way to Keld. The upper pastures on the daleside still carry numerous trees. From the footpath on the east side of the Swale a single alder pollard can be seen high on the daleside in North Side Pasture. Names on the map, such as 'Old Springs' and 'Spring Brow', show that coppicing was practised here *(spring* means coppice). Was this done by commoners, or by individual tenants after the land was enclosed? Another classic feature on the map is the lane to the wood pasture, running north out of Muker. Just beyond the gate at the north end of this lane are two old ash pollards, beside a field boundary.

Where was Feetham's wood pasture? Feetham Wood is on a small, narrow, precipitous sling of land immediately above the Swale; it hardly looks fit to carry the name of the township. The nearby house, 'Wood End', does not seem to be well named; it has been well to the west of the present wood since at least the mid-nineteenth century. But there is a way of explaining these oddities. Just east of this area is Healaugh Park, with Park Hall at its centre. Healaugh Park is consistently marked on seventeenth- and eighteenth-century maps by one of those picturesque little palisades designed to help the gentry to locate the places that mattered. The park was in existence by the fourteenth century, and later became the headquarters of the steward of Healaugh Manor. In its heyday, there was apparently a chapel here, and a hunting-tower, complete with lead roof, from which spectators could watch deer-coursing; its location remains to be found.[17] The old park boundary is clearly visible on the map, a wall crossing the watershed between the Swale and Barney Beck, to make a roughly triangular park whose other sides were defined by these watercourses. The map marks two 'gates' in the former park wall – Robin Gate, on the present Feetham–Healaugh road, and the gate at Hilltop which is still maintained.

It looks very much as if the park was cut out of Feetham's wood pasture, which of course must have been larger then. This would account for the attenuated 'Feetham Wood' – as so often, the locals saw no reason to change the name – and the location of Wood End. The western boundary of the park may originally have been a palisade or a hedge; if there was an old boundary-wall, it must have collapsed and then been rebuilt. Four nineteenth-century field-names in *spring* show that there was once a substantial coppice in the park. Perhaps the boundaries of the four *spring* parcels included those of compartments cut in rotation.

It is not known whether the Feetham commoners retained any rights in the park – but there were certainly rights of way across it. The modern road from Healaugh to Surrender Bridge takes a sharp bend just after crossing Barney Beck. The nineteenth-century tithe map, which marks footpaths, shows that its course has diverged from that of the original route, which split into two – the

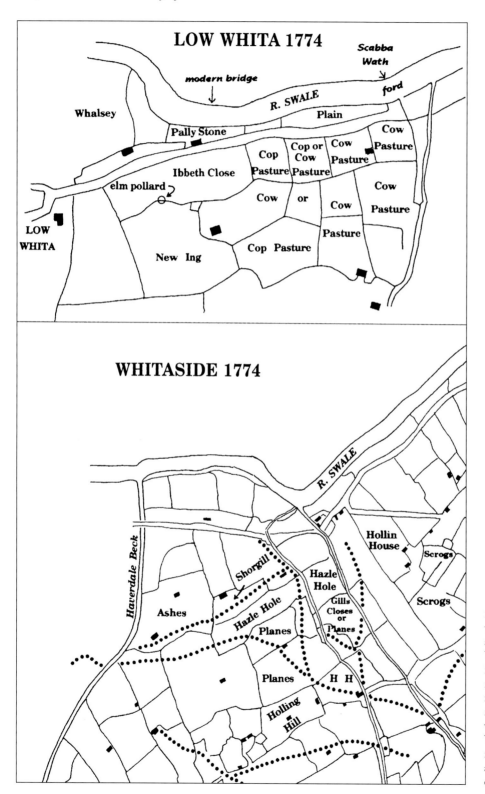

LOW WHITA 1774

Scabba Wath

modern bridge

R. SWALE

ford

Whalsey

Plain

Pally Stone

Cow Pasture

Cop Pasture

Cop or Cow Pasture

Cow Pasture

Ibbeth Close

elm pollard

Cow Pasture

LOW WHITA

Cow   or   Cow Pasture

Cow Pasture

Pasture

New Ing

Cop Pasture

WHITASIDE 1774

R. SWALE

Haverdale Beck

Hollin House

Scrogs

Shorgill

Hazle Hole

Ashes

Hazle Hole

Gills Closes or Planes

Scrogs

Planes

Planes

H H

Holling Hill

FIGURE 6.8. Areas of where wood pasture survived longest, at Low Whita and Whitaside, illustrated from a redrawn map of 1774 and field-names for the tithe map. Note the numerous woodland names at Whitaside and the 'plain' names in both areas, with a high density of rights of way at Whitaside.

upper road towards Kearton, which linked settlements on the upper daleside, and the low road, heading for Feetham and beyond via Robin Gate. The upper road, which ran through the park, has been supplanted by the metalled road just to the north; it is no longer in use as a public right of way, although the line of the medieval route continues west of the park as a footpath through Kearton. So when Feetham's wood pasture was taken over and turned into a park, it looks as if the existing routes were maintained in use.

On the other side of the dale, two zones of former wood pasture can be detected on Whitaside (Fig. 6.8). One of them can still be picked out from the other side of the dale. The zone around Hollin's Farm is the only part of the daleside where the pattern of stone walls is obscured by a scatter of trees and woody vegetation (plantations excepted). Work with a couple of old maps provides a historical explanation. There is a 1774 map of Grinton, made by a surveyor whose employer was mostly interested in the lead workings on the moors above; but he showed the field boundaries in the enclosed land.[18] By adding field-names from the tithe map, drawn sixty-seven years later, one can get a fair picture of the local landscape before the 'Improvement' phase of the early nineteenth century. The field-names were not suddenly invented for the tithe map! The results are instructive. Three fields were called 'plains', and no less than four footpaths crossed these plains in the eighteenth century. Around here are several names indicating former woodland. 'Shorgill' is of course Shaw Gill, and 'Scrogs' also means woodland. Ash, hazel and holly are all mentioned. Evidently there was plenty of evergreen winter fodder here. The Ordnance Survey has misunderstood the situation, and put an apostrophe in, to produce 'Hollin's'. But this was not the house of someone called Hollin or Hollins; it is the house at the hollies. A few of the closes here display the irregular edges which show that they have been cut out of woodland.

There was also wood pasture further east, at Low Whita – formerly Nether Whithay. There were common rights on the daleside here in 1624, when a document mentioned cattle-gates on Whithay West Cow Close; twenty-five years later there was a 'Woddie Cow Pasture' here.[19] Again, it is illuminating to put the 1841 field-names on to the 1774 map, and look at the area immediately east of Low Whita (Fig. 6.8). The modern bridge is some way upstream from the ford which it replaced, which was called Scabba Wath. Between the bridge and the site of the earlier ford was a small, narrow close beside the river; it was called, simply, Plain.

The names for the closes immediately to the south, across the road, show that there was once a large cow pasture here. What is more, the pasture had an alternative name, Cop Pasture – perhaps a survival from earlier times. In Cumbria, *cop* meant a pollard.[20] Is it possible that what were once 'cop pastures' became 'cow pastures' once they had lost most of their trees, the transition being mirrored by an almost imperceptible change in the word used to describe them? Did the person who copied the field names onto the Low Whita portion of the tithe map's schedule have this explained to him by the tenant farmer? Or was he influenced by a certain ambiguity in the way the latter pronounced the names? Just a stone's throw to the west of the closes labelled 'cow pasture' stood one of the most venerable of the elm pollards (Fig. 6.2). It was only cut down recently. It stood on the bank at the upper edge of the field, immediately above a platform cut into the hillside for an ancient settlement site. The prominent front edge of this platform, and the banks which define the fields which went with it, can be clearly seen from Scabba Wath Bridge. Probably the old 'cop pasture' once contained clusters of pollard elms – or would they have been quite regularly spaced, like the trees at Watendlath?

In north-east Yorkshire, the old word for a pollard was *dotterel* or *dotterd*; it is recorded for Bilsdale in the seventeenth century. The Furness Fells had numerous *dotered* oaks in the mid-sixteenth century[21] I have never heard of the use of this word in Swaledale. But we do find the names 'Doctor Wood' or 'Daughter Close'. Did these names originally refer to *dotterds*?

At Healaugh, the nineteenth-century fieldnames which I have marked on the map suggest that the wood pasture lay not far away to the west of the settlement; it was called Thirns ('thorns') Wood (Fig. 3.5). Evidently this wood once extended all the way from the level of present-day Healaugh to the edge of the moor, and presumably along the steep slopes above Barney Beck. The Healaugh area happens to be one of Swaledale's best zones for surviving elm pollards. In the late 1990s, three of them were still just about living – one beside the road just to the east of Healaugh, and two which stand side by side on a field boundary about 100 yards (c.100m) west of the village, just below the road to Park Hall. The beauty of their summer foliage is a poignant reminder of what we have lost to Dutch elm disease.

There are several dead elm pollards around Healaugh, and some very large tree-stumps which may well represent cut-down pollards. One or two massive standing pollards can be seen by taking the public footpath which runs behind Dagger Stones Farm and past Thiernswood Hall. The pollards are mostly on the edges of woods, fields and routeways. When did they first become pollards? Is it possible to estimate the age of these hollow trees? In 1966 Mitchell estimated that a tree growing in the open gains one inch (2.5cm) in girth every year; and a tree growing within a wood, half an inch. According to Oliver Rackham, this formula works well for maiden trees of middle age.[22] Probably it is about right for the Yorkshire Dales. Not far away, in Wensley – which gave its name to the valley which was previously called Yoredale – a much-loved maiden elm used to stand on the green. There is a photograph of it in Speight's *Romantic Richmondshire,* which was published in 1897. According to Speight, its girth was 18 feet (5.5m), and it was planted in 1690, to celebrate the accession of William and Mary, like a couple of elms which were planted at the same time at Spring End in Swaledale.[23] If these figures are accurate, the estimated age of this tree in 1897 would have been 216 years; its actual age was 207. But what about pollards?

Two members of our team, Tom Gledhill and Ros Nichol, have made an inventory of the elm pollards in the zone between Healaugh and Marrick; Tom later gained a doctorate for his studies on the history of North Yorkshire woodland. Tom and Ros took girth measurements, which varied for the most part between about 10 feet and 23 feet (3.5m and 7.5m). Considering how we might estimate the age of pollards – whose growth will have been slowed down by regular lopping – Tom and I thought that 0.75 inch (19mm), a compromise between the woodland growth rate and the open country rate, might be about right. But this turns out to be too fast – it produces trees too young for their own management history! If we take the stresses and long-term consequences of regular pollarding to be roughly equivalent to the constraints of competing in a wood, and modify the rate to 0.5 inch (13mm), most of our trees will be between three hundred and six hundred years old.

This seems about right for those old-looking pollards which interrupt the courses of boundary-walls, and must surely have been incorporated into them, rather than inserted later. The younger pollards would then date from the seventeenth century, and would have been planted or promoted on boundaries. This might be understood as the tree management policy of people who were enclosing land piecemeal at the time. But in this central part of Swaledale, the distribution of elm pollards is not uniform, or random. The pollards do not occur in zones of medieval arable land – around Reeth, for instance. Nor has this pattern resulted from recent selective felling of elms in some areas rather than others; one can check with the meticulously crafted First Edition of the Six Inch Ordnance Survey map, produced in the mid-nineteenth century, which depicts all major trees in their correct positions. The tree coverage was not very different from that of the present day. I would argue, then, that the distribution of the elm pollards in general reflects the distribution of former wood pasture zones; the really old ones may be survivors of actual wood pastures, whilst the younger pollards should reflect local perpetuation of old wood pasture practice.

If anything, the thickest trees should be older than the 13mm growth rate suggests, because they will have spent a greater proportion of their lives with the disadvantages of being middle-aged or elderly pollards. It seems possible, then, that the very oldest trees go back before the period of the Black Death. The wood pasture tradition in which these trees had their origins is a good deal older than that. James Raine, the nineteenth-century historian of Marske, quotes a document of 1213 dealing with a grant of a parcel of land 'in Marsk Field' called 'Side Bank' with woodland which included 'a big tree-trunk called the Almestock' (my translation). This sounds very like an elm pollard.

It looks as if Reeth lost its wood pasture zone around Healaugh at quite an early stage. Probably the people of Reeth had to obtain quite a lot of their timber and firewood from outside the township, and the same may have been true for Grinton, where land shortage may also have resulted in an early loss of wood pasture. But not far away was Fremington, which must always have had plenty of woodland, on the steep and unstable hillside below Fremington

Edge, and spreading along the slopes above the Arkle Beck. Across the river from Reeth are quite a few elm and thorn pollards, and the old lane running west from Fremington to its distant woodlands is obvious on the map.

Ellerton's wood pasture must have been on the steep, north-facing side of the dale. The village street ran west from behind what is now a nineteenth-century house called Ellerton Abbey, in a curvilinear course taking it through Swale Farm, to Nanny Pasture and Dolly Pasture and a series of woods whose names are marked on the map – Stollerston Wood, Acre Wood, Scar Spring Wood (Stollerston is probably a lost early settlement). The route to summer pasture on Ellerton Moor must have gone up Juniper Gill. The juniper which once grew here, as it did on other north-facing slopes in the townships of Harkerside, Whitaside and Muker, was probably encouraged, and used as animal bedding and in the construction of the walls and roofs of sheds. In parts of Norway, there are juniper groves, with groups of magnificent trees shaped like dark pillars; juniper was until recent times very much part of the farm economy there.

The oldest elm pollards in Marrick are the ones at the Priory. They were planted just inside the precinct wall of the nunnery, on the eastern and southern sides. The elms on the eastern side survive, just; Oliver Rackham estimated the age of one of them as five or six hundred years. The nuns must have walked beneath them when they were quite young trees. They must have been planted for their beauty, and for the shade and seclusion which they offered. There have been elm pollards in the general area around the nunnery too, especially between Marrick and Fremington in the zone at the base of the steep slopes of the daleside. There is still a lot of woodland – as well as signs of former woodland – on this hillside. Many of the trees are apparently self-sown elms, probably the descendants of local elm pollards.

Judging by what has survived, this part of Swaledale, from Marrick and Ellerton upstream as far as about Healaugh, must once have had many more elm pollards. With the encouragement of the old British stream-name, the Lemon ('elm stream'), on the moor above Grinton, it is tempting to believe that the elm was a dominant tree in the prehistoric wildwood of this part of the dale. The name of Elmet, the old British kingdom which covered a good deal of West and South Yorkshire, meant 'elm wood', so there may have been other parts of the Pennines where the elm was widespread. But we should remember that in the Roman period, much of the daleside and the land immediately above it was subdivided into fields. It is quite likely that the low field-walls which date from this period were originally topped by hedges, and possible that it was elms in these hedges which spread to become the dominant trees of the regenerating woodland of the early post-Roman period. We do not know when the custom of pollarding started. In Bilsdale, in the North York Moors, 'old dotterd okes' and 'dodderell okes' were recorded in a survey of 1642; they must have started life around the time of the Crusades, perhaps before. If elm pollards had useful lives of four or five hundred years, a few of those which are being cut up at present may be only the third or fourth generation since late Roman times – if pollarding started as early as that. The history of hedges in Swaledale is not at all well documented, but they are likely to have figured in the *gehaeg* enclosures of the period around the Norman Conquest, and in 1251 over one hundred persons were accused of pulling down a hedge in Fremington.

There must once have been more ash pollards in Swaledale. Because of the early demise of pollarding here, we cannot expect to see young pollards, like the ones in Cumbria, and it is hard to identify old ones. Ash trees have a habit of 'self-pollarding'; once the main stems reach a certain weight they tend to split and break off, producing a false 'pollard' effect. Ash makes much better firewood than elm, so redundant ash pollards would have been more vulnerable to the axe. Nevertheless there are a few old ash pollards in Swaledale. The remote settlements in the deep valleys to the north of Marske probably had numerous pollarded ash trees, quite a few of them on the boundary of the enclosed land, like the ones at Watendlath, in Cumbria. One can still see one or two convincing examples at Kexwith, for instance.

One old area of wood pasture was probably enclosed to make Marrick Park, which certainly existed in 1388 (when William of Marrick was accused of hunting in it without leave); and in 1439 the same charge was brought against two other defendants. As shown on a sixteenth-century map, the park once extended a little further west; the position of its former boundary can still be worked out on the map. Labels on the map drawn in 1592 tell us that the 'old park' lies within the 'parke newe encloside out of the towne fieldes ... and convertide from tillage and medowe to pasture'. The lane linking the wood pasture to the village is still in use, along with the public right of way through the park, which was the subject of a lawsuit in 1889; the dispute was all about the breaking down of the 'Plain Gate', located to the east of the house.

Downholme Park was established in 1377. It looks as if inroads had been made into the wood pasture before the park was made; there are medieval strip lynchets, terraces for cultivation, running through High Spring Wood, and traces of a medieval farm not far away. There are good eighteenth-century maps of the park,which make it clear that deer were not its only product (Fig. 6.7). The names in *spring* refer to coppices; as in the park at Healaugh, these must have been a significant source of income. There are still some large old coppice stools in the woods in and around Downholme Park, as well as much younger ones (Fig. 6.9). Other field-names show that cattle were grazed here, probably with a clump of hollies for emergency winter rations. The *lawn,* the open area within the park woodland, is a classic parkland feature, recreating and domesticating the beauty of a woodland glade, with echoes of both wildwood and wood pasture. If we can fully trust the maps, which is debatable, Park Lodge made its appearance sometime between 1730 and 1778. The modern road, its turnpike ancestor constructed in the 1830s, has made the park a less secluded place. From this road, near Downholme Bridge, it is not difficult to see evidence for old woodland management practices, with several old elm stubs, pollards and coppice stools. Over the years, wood must have been a more important source of revenue than venison. The old maps show that the course of the modern main road into Downholme has also obscured the old, broad track from the village to the old wood pasture zone (Fig. 5.2). The modern road also provides a good view of the park wall, running beside the Swale; this may well be the original medieval wall, at least in part.

These medieval parks form an interesting commentary on their times. At one level, they represent the arrogance of a landowning elite, intent on perpetuating their taste for hunting and eating venison at the expense of many of the rights which local communities had enjoyed in their wood pastures. The aristocracy's need for parks was an indirect reflection of the vigour of people of humbler stock, who had steadily and remorselessly opened up the woods to create ploughlands, meadows and pastures, and to smelt lead from the surrounding moors; a new mine was opened not far from Downholme in 1398, for instance. Over the later Middle Ages, pastured woodland gave way to township wood pastures, and these in turn came under threat, from landowners wanting to empark them, from the needs of a growing number of commoners and from the demands of the lead-smelting industry. By the sixteenth century, local supplies were inadequate for the smelt-mills, as Leland reported: 'the wodde that they brenne their leade is brought owte of the shire, and out of Dirhamshire'. At much the same time, in the New World, native Americans, noting how enthusiastically their camp fires were appreciated by the recently arrived English colonists, shrewdly suggested that it must have been a shortage of wood which led them to leave their homes across the ocean.

FIGURE 6.9. Old oak coppice stool at White Scar Wood, Downholme.

The parks concentrated and captured a debased form of the hunting experience which must have been increasingly hard to come by in many parts of England. As we have seen, they were also contested. Gangs broke into them, apparently more as an insult and a provocation and for fun rather than for the sake of the game – like the much later night raids of young men from Swaledale on the rabbit warren between Carperby and Woodhall, in Wensleydale. The Miners' Hunt, in the 1870s, was another opportunity for fun. But park ownership implied a command of a certain high-status way of life. When Sir Solomon Swale tried to establish himself in the dale, he apparently tried to set up a deer park – just before grouse-shooting came in; and his coat of arms, which can still be made out on one or two of the boundary stones on the watershed further south, was 'three harts' heads cabossed'. Parks also captured landscape – the kind of landscape which the gentry later chose to put in place around their homes. And yet, in the context of Swaledale, these parks were not particularly exotic; they must in fact have been quite like the 'winter parks' which we can just discern, albeit rather faintly, as features of the older Swaledale landscape, and they go back to a much older tradition, prehistoric in origin, of trying to control game by manipulating their habitat.

Between the coming of Norse settlers and the creation of parks such as Downholme and Marrick, the relationship between woodland and open country must have shifted dramatically. Like the English, the Norse at first named some places after natural features; but these 'topographic' names soon became 'habitative' names which reflected their own sense of ownership and land-winning. Thus 'Hváll' ('round-topped hill'), just along the beck from Muker, became Thwaite ('clearing'), and another 'Hváll' became 'hváll-gehaeg' (the hedged enclosure at Hváll), which became Whealsay. But the place was soon renamed Nether Whitay; it is now called Low Whita, and a single field-name on the tithe map provides the key to the story.

At first, there would have been winter parks, and outlying summer 'seats' or *scales* in the woods; this was the phase of pastured woodland. Then, as numbers grew, more land was cleared, and pressures intensified, the *scales* in the dale were replaced by permanent settlements, and summer pastures were now relocated out on the moors. More and more hay for winter keep was grown in the riverside *ings,* supplemented by leaf fodder from the woods, which now contained an increasing number of pollards. These woods also contained open glades (wood plains). As pressures intensified, the wood pastures must have come more and more to resemble 'leaf-meadows' – that is, pastures containing smaller numbers of lopped trees or pollards, isolated or in small clusters – with some of the plains being enclosed by individual families, with or without the agreement of fellow commoners. Eventually, all that was left of the wood pasture tradition, in most places, was the practice of pollarding.

This was the general sequence, but of course there must have been a good deal of variation from place to place; the situation in one place would have affected what went on in another. The loss of wood pasture is a tale within the greater story of the decline of the Swaledale commons as a whole. Just as important as the history of wood pasture is the history of coppicing in Swaledale – the domestic and commercial exploitation of *springs* and small *haggs* – and how this served the lead-smelting industry. There are more charcoal-burners' platforms in Swaledale than most people realise. This story is more about enterprise than about the exercise and loss of traditional rights. But it is also a subject which awaits further investigation.

Notes

1. Rackham 1976.
2. Ibid.; Rackham 1980.
3. Hill 1984, 60.
4. Rackham 1986, 247.
5. Denyer 1991, 81–4.
6. Winchester 1987, 103.
7. Cowley 1993, 22.
8. North Yorkshire County Record Office (NYCRO) – ZQX 5/4.
9. Whitaker 1823, 345–6.
10. Harrison 1879, 134; Whitehead nd. (in NYCRO).
11. NYCRO CRONT 2/GRINTON; Ashcroft 1984, 58, 99.
12. Fieldhouse and Jennings 1978, 134.
13. NYCRO MIC 144.
14. NYCRO MIC 144.
15. NYCRO MIC 144.
16. NYCRO ZBO (M) 5/5.
17. VCH 1914, vol. I, 238.
18. NYCRO ZRT 2/3.
19. NYCRO ZIP, ZQH 2 10/63.
20. Armstrong *et al.* 1950, 467.
21. Winchester 1987, 103.
22. Mitchell 1966; Rackham 1980, 27.
23. Speight 1897, 377, 393; Pontefract 1934, 125.
24. See Fleming 1997, Appendix B.
25. Raine 1881.
26. Ashcroft and Hill 1950, 54–71.
27. Harrison 1879, 228.
28. Ibid., 217–18.
29. 1592 map of Marrick in the Brotherton Collection, University of Leeds Library.
30. NYCRO ZHP.
31. NYCRO ZBO (M) 1/5 and 5/5.
32. Raistrick 1965, 55.
33. Toulmin Smith 1906–10, 32.
34. Cronon 1983.
35. Bogg 1908, 623–5.
36. Hartley and Ingilby 1984, 100.
37. VCH 1914, 239.
38. Fieldhouse and Jennings 1978, 48; Smith 1967, vol. II, 265; NYCRO ZIP 359; Grinton Tithe Map (1841); Fleming 1999.

CHAPTER SEVEN

People, Places
and Pathways

At the heart of the Swaledale communities lay people's homes, the neighbour-hoods where their children began to know the world, and the roads which led not only to fields and pastures but also to friends and relatives elsewhere, to markets and towns and sometimes to work far away from home. Looking through the printed volume of Grinton parish register entries, I was startled to find that there was a Richard Sunter living in Healaugh in the middle of the seventeenth century, just as there is today. But just because some of the old Swaledale surnames persist, we should not assume that the same families lived side by side for centuries. In those same parish registers, new surnames appear and old ones disappear. Immigrants came into the dale to work in the lead mines, and many of them lived in Swaledale as lodgers. Equally, many left the dale, not least in the late nineteenth century when the lead industry was collapsing, and Swaledale speech was heard in Spain and in Iowa.[1] Many of the houses in Swaledale's hamlets and villages date from the nineteenth century, when there were many jobs in the mines and smelting-mills of the lead industry. These settlements are the most concentrated archaeological expression of what Swaledale's past communities were about. In principle, the ground plan of each settlement gives us the opportunity to work out the processes which shaped its origins and growth, because the outline of its present character will have been determined long ago. We can study the relationships between houses and routeways, public space and private space. Brian Roberts, a scholar who has made intensive studies of the morphology of settlements, believes that the plans of villages can be classified into types such as 'homeomorphic cohesive composite' or 'mature agglomerated'.[2] The question then becomes: how do we explain the origins and present distribution of the different types? For archaeologists there are different priorities. Settlements have complex histories which await investigation. One of our foremost landscape archaeologists, Chris Taylor, has described how he tried to work out the historical development of the Cambridgeshire village where he lived over a period of twenty years or so;[3] he was frequently forced to change his mind, as a result of new archaeological discoveries, or because his own perspective had shifted.

As in the case of the commons, the history of settlements is also the history of increasingly sharply defined property rights. There must have been a rough progression, from open access – freedom to settle anywhere – to more regulation of the space within settlements, and there was usually a distinction between living in a *planned* settlement and accepting a prearranged set of rights and obligations, and living in a settlement which grew more naturally. Eventually, rights held by families by virtue of their membership of a community, and their relationships with other families, became the rights of holders of tenements and parcels of land with fixed boundaries, carrying closely defined rights and duties. In this situation, the ground plans of settlements must have developed within increasingly tight constraints. The community may have managed and kept control of its common arable strips and pastures; but there would always have been tensions between community membership and family membership, between neighbourly approaches to the management of communal land or facilities and the demands of particular families with interests and objectives of their own. In the Middle Ages, I have suggested, such tensions would have increased; arguably they would have been at their most intense within settlements, bound up in the close links between families and property in houses, farm buildings, gardens, garths and land which went with individual tenements. The creation of boundaries and regulations provide the framework within which family histories take their courses; much turns upon the rules and expectations surrounding the inheritance and transfer of property.

Another factor enters the equation where there is a different source of livelihood, such as lead-mining. Thomas Armstrong's hero, Adam Brunskill, wanted to make enough money from mining to give it up and become a farmer.[4] The choice between farming and mining, in various permutations, must once have exercised the minds of many individuals and families – on the occasions when they *had* a choice. In thinking about the growth and development of Swaledale's settlements and housing, we have to take account of the impact of incomers attracted here by the lead-mining industry, and their relationships with the older families of the dale. The links between places, people and property fluctuate and change, finding incomplete expression in the landscape. I can do little more than touch on a few themes in this chapter, which is about settlements, and the routeways which link them, ultimately involving the people of Swaledale in the opportunities and problems presented by the wider world.

As the 1:25000 map shows, there is a complex network of routes in Swaledale and on the surrounding moorlands – roads, lanes, tracks, bridle ways and footpaths, their users ranging from the lone hill-walker to the thirty-ton truck. Their present functions vary; they are not all rights of way. But each has a history, which is there to be worked out on the ground. In most of Swaledale's past, traffic consisted almost entirely of pedestrians, riders and pack animals. Although carts must sometimes have been seen on the roads in the past few centuries, loads on farms were often transported on sledges, often horse-drawn, one or two of which can still be seen today. I once came across part of a small one, blocking a stile (Fig. 7.1). Traffic could still be heavy enough to make an impact, however. Reels Head, high on the daleside between Fremington and Marrick, used to be 'threllesgata', meaning 'the road through the gap'.[5] We know from a document of 1304 that this was the old road 'into Swaledale'– historic Swaledale, that is.[6] The 'threllesgata' is documented in the middle of the twelfth century.[7] Above Reels Head, the 'gap' is clear; it has numerous hollow-ways running through it, side by side or criss-crossing each other (Fig. 7.2). Most of them were probably created more recently

FIGURE 7.1. A stile blocked by part of an old sledge near Kisdon.

FIGURE 7.2. Hollow-ways at Reels Head, the medieval 'threllesgata'.

than the twelfth century. A late sixteenth-century map marks a gate across the road here, with the legend 'threllesgate'; by this time the old meaning of the word *gata* was in the process of being lost. Another interesting medieval name is Holgate ('hollow-way'); the route which crosses Marske Beck at Holgate, one of several tracks heading north-east towards the Tees, must be a very old one.

The road from Richmond to Reeth across the moors leaves Richmond by Hurgill Lane, a name which usually indicates the presence of a very old road.[8] There is another mark of this road's antiquity at Marske, where beneath the bridge over Marske Beck it is possible to see the stone ribs of an early, narrower predecessor, said to date from the fifteenth century. In the Middle Ages, many of the becks which flow into the Swale must have been crossed by simple, easily maintained wooden bridges; 'Stop Bridge Lane' in Downholme was originally 'Stock Bridge' referring to a log bridge over Gill Beck. In 1279, there was a complaint about the breaking down of a bridge crossing 'the water of Eske, which is the division between the township of Feldom and the township of Skelton, by which the cattle and men of Skelton passed between the said villages ...'[10] Probably this was Orgate Bridge. Evidently Marske Beck once bore a British name, the Esk. The Swale itself, the turbulent one, was a different matter. What individual or community was prepared to invest in a bridge, and, more importantly, how was it to be maintained down the years? In the middle part of Swaledale there were numerous *waths* (fords), such as Scabba Wath at Low Whita, one between Harkerside and Healaugh, another between Harkerside and Reeth, one beside Marrick Priory, still marked as a ford on the map; and Ellerholme Wath, on the old route from Marrick village to Ulshaw Bridge in Wensleydale. If the fords were not marked on old maps, we could work out the locations of many of them by noting the behaviour of footpaths. The Swale flows through sedimentary rocks, hence down a series of steps, the front edges of which may provide good *waths* when the river is not too high; but one wonders how many of the drownings recorded in the Grinton parish registers resulted from accidents at river-crossings. Grinton Bridge was probably the only continuously maintained medieval bridge over the Swale above Richmond; Leland mentions a 'fair bridge' there in the early sixteenth century,[11] and, as we will see, there are good reasons for believing that this has long been an important river-crossing. Downholme Bridge was not built until the late seventeenth century (though the present one looks later).[12] The seventeenth-century Quarter Sessions records are full of references to bridge repairs and the need for them. For instance, in April 1629, Healaugh Bridge 'in Swawdale-super-Barney becke' was found to be in decay.[13] This was probably the uppermost of the two bridges over Barney Beck today.

Until the Normans took over a place called Hindrelagh and assertively renamed it Richmond, after a place in northern France, there was probably no great need to travel down the dale from Old Swaledale. But the new town was an important political and administrative centre, from which offensive and defensive actions against the kingdom of the Scots were to be co-ordinated; its lord was supposed to command the allegiance of the lesser barons of the area. Richmond developed as a market centre, linked to Grinton and the Upper Dale by a road which went via Hudswell, Downholme and Ellerton. This road briefly joined an even earlier route, the old Roman road from Ulshaw Bridge to Marrick, before taking a course roughly on the line of the present main road. Then it linked up with the road which ran west from the gate of the nunnery at Ellerton (to the west of the church), and along the main street of Ellerton village (now deserted), and on to Swale Farm, the sole survivor of the old Ellerton. From here, the route went south of Hags Gill Farm to Stollerstone Stile, on the Grinton parish boundary, which was traditionally regarded as the gateway to Upper Swaledale. This was Stallerstone yate in the sixteenth century.[14] Then the route went through Cogden, and joined the Grinton village street at right angles, well to the south of the Bridge Inn where the present (nineteenth-century) road meets it. The route is commemorated by a short public footpath leading east from the village street to a sharp bend not far from the cemetery. Right-angled bends in roads and odd lengths of footpath can often be explained in terms of changing patterns of movement.

Grinton means 'the settlement with the green'; the green in question must date from before the Norman Conquest, since Grinton is mentioned in Domesday Book (1086). It seems that in the pre-Conquest period the presence of a green made the place distinctive, which is interesting. The green no longer exists; it must have been small and narrow, on an east-west axis, at right angles to an important road which crossed the Swale here. The church, constructed around 1100 or just possibly earlier, and the churchyard occupy what was probably the western part of the green. It is hard to tell from the earliest map (1786) when and how the eastern end of the green was taken up by houses and garths.[15] The narrow rectangular greens of Swaledale did tend to become 'infilled' by houses, and Grinton is now much more of a 'street village', stretched along the important road from Middleham to Reeth and beyond, which crossed the Swale here. The construction of Grinton Bridge would have made it easier for the people of Reeth to reach their parish church; but it is hard to believe that local traffic was the main reason for the investment involved.

What if the road from Middleham led not primarily to Reeth, but up through Fremington, and over the moor to Hurst, the old lead-mining centre? This route is easy to follow, on the map and on the ground, as it breasts the slope below Fremington Edge (Fig. 3.3). A late sixteenth-century map marks the moorland part of the road as 'the badger waie'.[16] A badger was an itinerant dealer or middleman. This was not a through route; there is no sign on the ground that it continued north, beyond Hurst. Could it have been the route taken by lead merchants from further south, who had the lead transported along this road to Middleham, or to a wharf on the Ure at Ulshaw Bridge?

At first sight this route has no obvious advantage over the old Roman road already mentioned, from Marrick to Ulshaw Bridge. But what if the construction of a bridge at Grinton made all the difference? And what if its costs were met from the same source as the funding for the building of the parish church of Swaldal here? There is, after all, a puzzle to be explained. Grinton is the only developed settlement on the north-facing side of Swaledale; to find the parish church here, rather than at Reeth, is unexpected. After all, Reeth had more agricultural land, on south-facing slopes, and better communications with the string of settlements further west, on the north bank of the Swale. It was well placed to develop a role like that of Middleham, in neighbouring Wensleydale. But it did not; why?

I believe that the critical factor determining Grinton's early importance may have been lead-mining. Admittedly the evidence is limited. Unlike the Derbyshire section in Domesday Book, the Swaledale section does not mention lead-mining.[17] But Grinton does have a beck called Grovebeck, named from a mine or 'groove', and it is rare for old place-names to refer to lead-mining. In 1219, lead-miners in Grinton were promised a return to the working conditions which they had enjoyed in Henry II's time – that is, the later twelfth century. According to Raistrick 'the mines in Grinton were very old; much of the twelfth century production of lead came from them'.[18] Lead-mining requires good fortune, the favour of the Almighty; success provides the means to repay Him. Lead-miners had both motive and opportunity to pay for the building of Grinton church. A bridge at Grinton would have attracted tolls for taking lead south from the Marrick Moor mines. Merchants from the south could have used this road to take them to *two* early mining centres, Grinton and Marrick Moor.

At this period, there may have been considerable rivalry between the Grinton and Marrick lead-miners. When the nunnery at Marrick was founded, in 1165, copious supplies of lead for the roofs came from the old-established mines on Marrick Moor, including those at Copperthwaite, Owlands and Greenas. Stone for the buildings also came from the remote north end of the moor, at Skegdale and Roan Mire; perhaps mixing mining with quarrying provided a steadier income?[19] The two mining communities faced each other across an old boundary. The origin of Grinton church cannot be traced beyond bits of Norman architecture. The twelfth-century church was not the spacious structure of today; it apparently consisted simply of a nave and chancel. Parts of this building survive at either end of the present nave – to the west in the form of the window above the tower arch and some of the associated stone work, to the east as the northern jamb of the chancel arch. But we know that there was a Christian site at Marrick Priory before the Norman Conquest. A fragment of a stone cross-shaft was discovered there in the 1970s; an expert suggested a tenth-century date.[20]

Both churches are beside river-crossings which had to be used by anyone taking lead south (Fig. 3.3). The ford at Marrick was approached by a deep, curving hollow-way which was already there when the twelfth-century nunnery was established, since its edge defined the line of the nunnery's precinct wall. South of the ford, the route was taken up by a hollow-way (still a bridle-way) along the ditch of the old Rue Dyke; there was another ford (Cole End Wath) below Marrick Woodhouse,[21] which led directly into the earthwork's ditch at the point where it reached the Swale. The route continued south past the present Hags Gill Farm, and on to the moor to join the Middleham road. No doubt this route was sometimes used for transporting lead from Marrick and Hurst, perhaps to avoid tolls at Grinton Bridge, and as a viable alternative to the old Roman route.

So it looks as if wealth, rivalry and the quest for good fortune in mining and transportation may have been crucial ingredients in deciding where the early Christian shrines were to be – and why Reeth did not become the parish town of old Swaledale. But in those days, Reeth was probably a place with few pretensions. Nowadays, with its great square green, it is a very obvious 'planned' settlement. But what was it like before the green was laid out? Unfortunately there is no surviving map earlier than the tithe map of 1830, but some of the early history of the place can be worked out from that (Fig. 7.3). Obviously, the big green has been 'infilled' on its eastern side by the group of houses which include the present post office. Reeth was redesigned to focus on the green, intended as a large market-place by an ambitious landlord, Philip, Lord Wharton, who in 1695 obtained a charter to hold a market here, and four annual fairs, one of which was the famous 'Bartle' (St Bartholomew's) Fair.[22] As a would-be market town, Reeth never quite succeeded in the longer term (and has problems of the same sort today). Some of the tall, stately houses, especially on the western side of the green, give it the distinctive atmosphere of a place which has come down in the world.

As the map makes clear, the medieval settlement of Reeth stretched along the road which led from the bridge over the Arkle Beck. Instead of turning through 90 degrees at what is now the corner shop, to reach the south-east corner of the present green, the original road went straight on, along what is now Back Lane. It emerged further west, running through arable land represented now by the magnificent 'strip lynchets' below Reeth School, and on towards Healaugh, along the line of the present right of way. At right angles to this road, I believe, there would have been a narrow green running north, incorporating what is now Anvil Square and the broad strip of cobbles and tarmac on the western side of the present green, where cars are parked nowadays. The map shows the boundaries of some of the medieval crofts and tofts which lay behind the houses on the western side of this early, narrow green. At the north end of this green, Reeth Lane, probably flanked by medieval 'ribbon development', led through the gap between steeply rising ground to the north-west and the knoll on which the Burgoyne Hotel now stands; it went through 'Town End' to the big shared meadow called Sleets, and on past the pinfold to Reeth Low Moor. The extent of the arable land and subdivided meadows suggests the presence of a sizeable agricultural settlement here in the Middle Ages. There should have been tofts and crofts along the eastern side of this narrow green, facing the present line of pubs and shops. Most traces of them would have been eradicated when the big square green was laid out, although perhaps some of these tenements were untenanted after the late medieval recession. Eventually, a fairly level surface would have been required for the cobbles, which extended further east than they

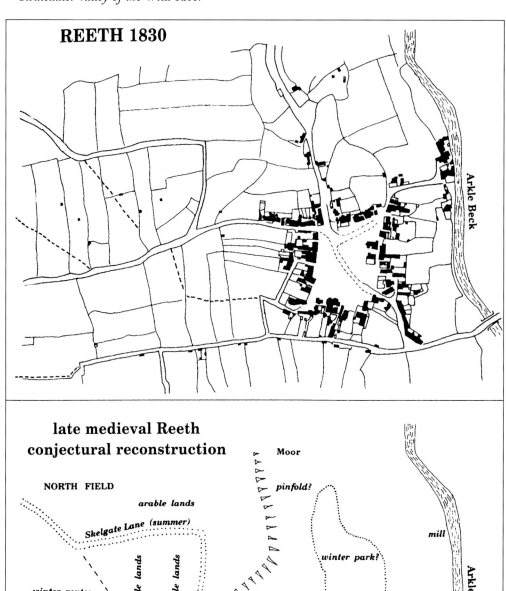

REETH 1830

Arkle Beck

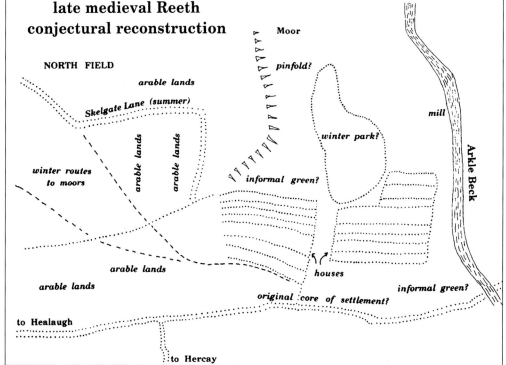

**late medieval Reeth
conjectural reconstruction**

Moor

NORTH FIELD

arable lands

pinfold?

Skelgate Lane (summer)

mill

winter park?

arable lands   *arable lands*

*winter routes
to moors*

informal green?

Arkle Beck

arable lands

houses

arable lands

informal green?

original core of settlement?

to Healaugh

to Hercay

do today, as can be seen when the bonfire lit on November 5th has burnt away the turf. Evidence of the importance of the early nucleus of Reeth, around Anvil Square and along the road from the bridge, can still be seen on the map. There are features on the western side of Reeth which are puzzling at first sight. What is the origin of the elbow-like bend in the road to the west of Anvil Square? An explanation is also needed for the footpath which threads a tortuous path among the modern houses, heads west, swerves north, crosses the Healaugh road, and passes to the east of the school. It then crosses two fields above the school at an angle before leading into Skelgate Lane at the point where the lane starts to run directly up the slope towards Riddings Rigg, having gone round the edges of some rectangular parcels of land.

Taken together, the line of the road with the elbow bend and the rather tortuous footpath indicate the course of the direct route to Reeth Low Moor from the centre of the old village. This path also led to the North Field, the big arable field at the eastern end of Riddings Rigg – though other hollow tracks further north, scarring the bank above the village, would also have led up there. In the Middle Ages, then, Reeth may have been T-shaped, with a long narrow green coming off a through route at right angles. It would be interesting to know what the plan of the eastern side of the settlement was like; perhaps the tofts and crofts of the houses on the eastern side of the narrow green went all the way back to the top of the slope above Arkle Beck.

Walburn, one of the best-preserved deserted medieval villages in Yorkshire, has a similar T-shaped plan (Fig. 7.4). Here, the through route was the old

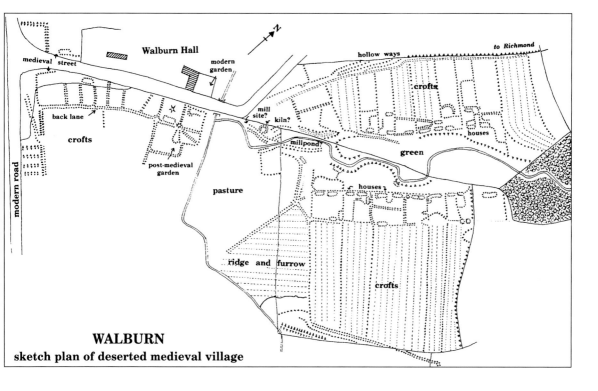

WALBURN
sketch plan of deserted medieval village

Roman road from Marrick to Ulshaw Bridge, and the central axis – I do not know whether to call it a broad street or a narrow green – came off it at right angles, at the place where the A6108 road from Leyburn to Richmond makes a sharp turn, and is joined by the road from Wathgill camp and Stainton. East of this junction, medieval tenements faced each other across the central axis of the village, which led past the present Walburn Hall, over a wooden (?) bridge, and then straight on where the modern main road bends; it ended at the mouth of a gill now swathed in sycamores. From the head of this gill, where the village's main supply of drinking-water must have been located, a beck ran through the green, which had houses, farm buildings, tofts and crofts on each side, still beautifully preserved as earthworks. Not far above the point where this beck meets Gill Beck, by the bridge, there was a corn mill, now virtually destroyed. It probably had a corn-drying kiln nearby, and a little further north a dam and the earthworks of a narrow millpond. All around were Walburn's extensive ploughlands, which show up well in low sunlight or when snow is melting. At some stage in its late medieval life, Walburn must have been a populous place; judging by the depth of the hollow-way leading uphill, behind the crofts on the northern edge of the village, there would have been plenty of traffic on the road from here to Richmond, though this road looks like an afterthought, threading its way along the back lane as it does.

Walburn is a good example of medieval planning. But as we have seen, the medieval settlements at Downholme and Reeth were also planned, at least in part, and although Grinton seems to straggle rather haphazardly up the road towards Leyburn, from the air its plan looks more ordered. There is a good deal of discussion about the date of planned medieval settlements, both in Yorkshire and elsewhere in England. Some apparently pre-date the Norman Conquest by up to a couple of centuries; in Yorkshire many are thought to have been laid out in the late eleventh century, after the notorious 'Harrying of the North' by the Normans in 1069–70 – a campaign whose real effects are still hotly debated by historians.

Settlements like Walburn, or the early Reeth, are expressing an ambivalence which recurs in other Swaledale T-shaped settlements, in which most of the houses lie along an axis which comes off a through route at right angles. Arkle Town, in Arkengarthdale, is another case in point. There is something deeply symbolic here, an expression of the dual nature of the settlement as a community both close-knit and at the same time containing families and individuals involved in many relationships with outsiders. The through route brings opportunities and also trouble. Outsiders may turn off it, and engage with the inhabitants of the place, although its layout gives them little encouragement to do so.

Further west, settlements often look as if they have developed naturally, with a minimum of planning. A characteristic type of settlement was the one which was strung out along the contour – as at Booze, in Arkengarthdale, or above the modern village of Healaugh. Harkerside Place, south-west of Reeth, is the one farm which survives from one of these 'linear' medieval settlements which has gradually lost its population. Its households were distributed along a line which ran just above the most valuable land, with access to water from a nearby spring line. In the Middle Ages this place was called Herthay ('the deer enclosure'); the name was later corrupted to Hercay and Harka. The map shows that Herthay had an extensive moorland common, larger than Grinton's. When the sun is low in the sky, the narrow strip fields low on the slopes below Harkerside Place become very obvious. This was arable land in the Middle Ages; in the closes higher up the slope, the strip boundaries have been ploughed out. Herthay's decline seems to have been gradual; in the seventeenth century, with at least eight growing families, it was not much smaller than Healaugh.

Significantly, a public footpath now follows the axis of Herthay, along the route from Harkerside Place to the modern road just above Swale Hall. Going west from Harkerside Place, this path originally led to what was probably the township's wood pasture zone, represented now by a hillside of junipers. Going east, the path follows the route which once linked Herthay's dispersed farms and gave their occupants access to Grinton; it breaches the westernmost of the Grinton-Fremington earthworks. Along the way, quite a few traces of Old Herthay can be seen. There were three small farms along this route in the nineteenth century; the buildings still stand. Just north-east of the big modern barn at Harkerside Place stands a ruined seventeenth-century house, its stone mullions largely intact; the house faces south, as they all do on this slope. Probably most of the medieval houses and barns were located on the same sites as the much more recent buildings visible today. But scattered along the line from Harkerside Place to a point just east of the earthwork, one can pick out the low, grass-covered walls of several rectangular buildings, most of them quite small, and usually set on levelled platforms. One of them can be seen among a group of trees in front of Plaintree Farm. Envisaging the character of Herthay in the Middle Ages takes quite an effort of the imagination. If there were medieval crofts, gardens and small greens here, their boundaries have not been much respected by the walls of the later closes. The sense of a roadway linking the old farms is probably best conveyed by the positions of the modern gateways which 'line up' along it, to the east of Harkerside Place. A few stiles and narrow 'man-gates', used by riders and pack animals, may also be seen along this line; some have been blocked up. Taken together, the standing and ruined buildings seem to form a 'dispersed' settlement pattern. But the parallel banks which marked out Herthay's *dales* of arable land remind us that this was once a township community.

Just across the dale, Old Healaugh, as I call it (formerly Daggerston, perhaps?) lay above the present village; its houses and outbuildings were also distributed along the contour in a line from Dagger Stones, running across Shaw Gill (which now contains the gated road to the moor), and further east at the level on which a couple of field-barns stand today (Fig. 3.5). One good piece of evidence for Old Healaugh is furnished by the sunken tracks on the moor just above the enclosed land, especially east of Shaw Gill; they are heading down towards various points along the axial line of Old Healaugh, and not into the head of Shaw Gill as they would if they were aiming for the present village. These tracks are transgressed by the enclosure walls, though in places gates were left to allow continued use of the route.

Old Healaugh's 'street', like Herthay's, was really more of an axial line along the contour, linking a scatter of buildings, and overlooked by others further up the slope. There must have been a space where people met and talked. One feature which intrigues me is the large dead elm pollard which stands near the point where the public footpath running east from Thiernswood Hall turns off the 'street' (which is metalled just here) towards the tarmac road to the moor; here one may look through a gateway to the east, along the hollow-way which forms the street's continuation. Nineteenth-century accounts record that village greens in North Yorkshire sometimes carried venerable elms, under which old men used to sit and talk in the open (this is still a characteristic Yorkshire custom, though a draughty bus shelter doesn't have quite the same ambience). There was one of these 'village elms' at Hipswell (just south of Richmond), two in Leyburn (flanking the stocks and the market cross), another just outside the church at Easby; the one in Wensley survived into the mid-twentieth century.[23] The elm pollard at Old Healaugh is near a couple of springs, where people would go to fetch water; was this the informal public space? And was this the late medieval village elm – or the offspring of one which stood here around 1100, when 'High Clearing' gave its name to the new Swaledale manor? As well as casting an unsurpassed shade, as the few survivors demonstrate, these trees must have had a deep symbolic meaning; friends tell me that in Sweden a homestead will often contain a special tree, which is not to be harmed. At Ellerton, there are still traces of a couple of elms which once stood in the field to the west of the modern Ellerton Abbey house, and which can still be seen on a fairly recent air photo; interestingly, they too are located on the street of the deserted medieval village. They may have been descendants of trees which once stood among the houses here. On the north bank of the Swale, west of Reeth and Healaugh, there are quite often *two* lanes or footpaths at different levels on the daleside, serving the upper and lower zones of settlement which I mentioned earlier. Going west from Healaugh, the route splits into two, one branch heading for Feetham, Low Row, Lodge Green and Gunnerside, the other leading to Kearton, Blades and Little Rowleth (above Lodge Green). In some places, these footpaths through the fields are slightly hollow. The lower route is now represented in most areas by the modern road, the descendant of a former highway. (Many highways were put in place in response to decrees and legislation, from the sixteenth century onwards.) But the building of the highway did not force the extinction of the earlier route. There is a classic case at Gunnerside, the historical Gunnersett, to the *west* of the beck (Fig. 4.3). The detailed plan of Gunnerside drawn for the tithe map shows that the houses were built along the north and south sides of a small rectangular green, though the green has been invaded by buildings and gardens. If you stand on the bridge and look a little downstream you can see the remains of an earlier bridge, protruding from the west bank of the beck; notice that it is central to the axis of Gunnerside green. And the route which formerly led to this bridge is perpetuated not by the modern road through Lodge Green, but by a public footpath which leads through the meadows from the east; its original destination was certainly not the public conveniences!

The same thing happens at Satron, where the original route ran between the two rows of buildings; the tithe map shows a footpath (now no longer a right of way) emerging from the west end of Satron and running through the closes beside the highway for over a mile, crossing Oxnop Beck at Mill Bridge (which still exists) and rejoining the highway near Rash. Further east, the footpath to the south of the road between Reeth and Healaugh also has medieval origins; as I pointed out earlier, it is the continuation of the old route through Reeth from the bridge over the Arkle Beck. Why did footpaths like these continue in use, in spite of the provision of highways not far away? A glance at the 1:25,000 map will show the complex local networks which have been preserved in some areas – for example north of Harkerside Place, north of Gunnerside and Lodge Green, and on Whitaside, south of Low Row. The routes taken by some of these paths seem meaningless now. Often, such paths do not look particularly old, and it is the ingeniously constructed stiles which usually focus the attention. Occasionally a path may be slightly hollow, as in the case of the one which leads west from Ivelet. Rights of way have always been the subject of concern. In 1682, 'three persons of Grinton' were charged with 'stopping a footpath'.[24] The Northallerton archives have preserved a letter which is undated, but evidently written in the early eighteenth century by Edward Kearton, concerning a 'complaint of George Chirre and George Robinson relating to a footpath over lands late Walbanks from Whitasyde to Feetham'. Apparently the footpath had fallen into disuse, or was not being maintained; Kearton explained that

> 'the plase whear I live cal'd Fethamholm contain'd 7 or 8 dwellers that is so many famalese and within this 12 years was redeust to one famale and when I had my occation I went on horseback so that this foot road was made little use on. Now the famalese increaseth again and the road may be more usefull'.[25]

Later, footpaths were drawn on maps, such as the tithe maps for Upper Swaledale, which were mostly produced by a local man, Anthony Clarkson, bearer of a local surname. Clarkson lived at Smithy Holme, a mile to the west of Keld. His sudden death in 1847 at the age of fifty-nine came after a morning's surveying;[26] his tombstone, which describes him as 'LAND SURVEYOR', is prominent in the churchyard at Muker. Clarkson made the tithe maps for Reeth (1830) and Grinton and Muker (both 1841). The fact that he was a local man, a small farmer and sometime schoolmaster as well as a mapmaker, must surely have affected his attitude to footpath preservation. And in more recent times, when quite a few small dairy farms on the dalesides were still occupied, and the post was often delivered on horseback, local postmasters and postmistresses insisted that footpaths should be marked on maps.

In terms of Swaledale's social history, such a concern for footpath preservation makes sense. In the past there would have been much more coming and going, with far more people living in the dale than there are today, many walking long distances to work in enterprises on the moors which have now closed down – lead-mines, coal-mines and quarries. Many people had to work on their way to work; some of the beautifully carved knitting-sticks which they used on these long walks, and sometimes carved for their sweethearts, are preserved in local museums at Reeth and Hawes. So there were many people to keep footpaths open – and many homes were not reached by the 'highways'. The idea that a farm holding should form an exclusion zone is a recent one; it is not suited to a world where inheritance is partible, holdings of land are intermingled, many people have common rights and there are few strangers. Making enclosures on the daleside cow pastures did not give one the right to close public footpaths. Even deer parks such as the ones at Healaugh and Marrick had rights of way running through them.

There does seem to be a difference between the density of footpaths on land which was enclosed piecemeal and on land which was enclosed by Act of Parliament, in the early decades of the nineteenth century. A 1774 map of the area between Isles Bridge and Feetham Holme, opposite Low Row, shows a complex pattern of daleside closes, some of them clearly won from an area of former wood pasture, as the character of the boundaries and some of the field-names make clear (Fig. 6.8).[27] The map marks numerous footpaths, most of which survive to the present day. On the other hand, in areas where ruler-straight boundary-walls indicate cow pastures enclosed by Act of Parliament, there are few footpaths. But some through routes *were* maintained across such 'improved' areas – for example the path from Angram to Hoggarths, and the path from High Whitaside to the lead-mining zone on Harkerside Moor. Nevertheless it does look as if the ethic of community had declined considerably by the early nineteenth century.

Some of the maps of the seventeenth and eighteenth centuries remind us that roads which passed through enclosed land were often broader than they are today; they were often used as droveways, and also there had to be space for traffic to move to one side to avoid the worst of the ruts on the existing track. At Stainton, in the late seventeenth century, two broad droveways led from the village to the high road, which by then was confined to a narrow corridor (Fig. 5.3). From Reeth, a broad lane led north on to the moor. At Downholme, in the eighteenth century, the walls flanking the central axis of the village flared outwards, to make a funnel entrance for stock being driven in from the moor (Fig. 7.5).

Within the settlements, the provision of public space varied considerably. At some of the old-established settlements in the upper dale, the houses form two roughly parallel rows, so that the space between them might be described as a small rectangular green – sometimes 'infilled' by other houses. This sort of arrangement occurs at Gunnerside, Thwaite, Satron and Ivelet. The houses face south, and thus do not usually face each other. (It is characteristic of Swaledale

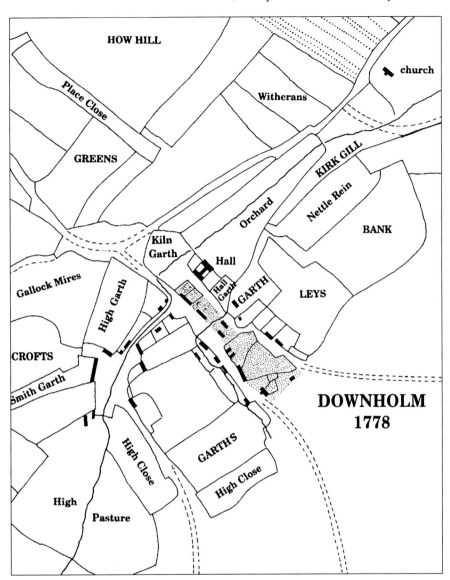

FIGURE 7.5. Downholme, redrawn from a plan of 1778. The stippled area indicated the 'infilled' green.

that, from the road, many houses can be seen only from the back; one of the pleasures of visiting someone here is going round to the front, and seeing their beautiful, secluded garden for the first time). In other places, greens are much less regular in plan, as in the case of the long, straggling green at Feetham and Low Row, the large one at Blades, or the little one behind the houses at Kearton.

Greens were essential to social and economic well-being; they were public spaces, where poultry could graze, children could play, people could work outdoors and gossip, meetings of all sorts could be held, and travellers and local people could meet and deal on neutral territory. Either they were designed – as in the case of the planned north country medieval village – or they happened anyway. In England in general a place with the name 'Green' often turns out to have originated from a cluster of cottages around an area claimed as public space – and it is often a late-developing, peripheral community perhaps formed by migrant workers. Lodge Green probably originated like this, responding to the needs of the lead-mining industry in Gunnerside Gill. It seems to have developed in the sixteenth century, though the 'lodge' element in the name must be older than that.[28] Places like Lodge Green were peripheral, overspill communities, containing incomers as well as those whose fortunes had declined, tradespeople and part-time farmers as well as miners. Presumably some of these households had gates on the commons, inherited or rented or obtained by marriage; and in Swaledale strong bonds must often have formed between groups of miners who were related to one another or worked together in mining partnerships. When the occupants of one of these settlements acted as a group, or when one of the larger families asserted itself, they must have had a good deal of muscle.

The layout at Downholme perhaps provides a good illustration of the relationship between the expanded old-established community and the 'secondary' community on the local green. Whether or not the earlier Downholme was near the church, as I suggested earlier, the Downholme which we see today was carefully planned to face on to the Richmond-Swaledale road. The plan of 1778 shows quite a few surviving boundaries between the crofts, and the fronts of the properties flanking a broad, slightly funnel-shaped green (Fig. 7.5). As at Gunnerside, the original green has been 'infilled' with houses; the familiar 'T-shape' has developed informally, as an extension to the original planned settlement, beside a beck which flows across the main street. But what is striking on the plan is the irregular open space a little further west, where the road to Swaledale is crossed by the north-south road leading towards Walburn. This space looks quite decorous now, with a triangle of grass and a substantial nineteenth-century house covering part of it. But it is marked on all the eighteenth-century maps; and the earliest map which we have (Fig. 5.2) shows two areas called 'Greens' just to the west of this open space. Cursory fieldwork among 'humps and bumps' in a nearby field shows the remains of at least two turfed-over rectangular buildings.

The growth of mining and associated trades must have seriously affected old-established communities. Reeth may illustrate this rather well. There were extensive open arable fields here in the Middle Ages, and the subsequent enclosure of land was almost entirely piecemeal and by local agreement, rather than by measured survey and Act of Parliament. In these circumstances, one would expect a number of farms to remain in the village, as at Healaugh for example. But Reeth itself has only one 'old' farm. Perhaps farms were relocated when Reeth Green was laid out. But the place still illustrates the importance of the non-agricultural sector. As Fieldhouse and Jennings have pointed out, in places like Reeth and Grinton many houses were subdivided to make room for lodgers.[29]

According to John McDonnell, the name 'green' seems to be rarely documented before the sixteenth century (though this is not true for Yorkshire as a whole).[30] The Swaledale tithe maps show that settlements and areas carrying this name vary quite a lot. Thorns Green, just north of Angram, is an area with quite a cluster of 'green' names, most of them between Angram and Keld. But there are other 'green' field-names which relate to small fields or slings of ground beside the road, and a couple of other cases which relate to two or three rather remote fields, such as Sleddale Greens, across the beck to the south-west of Muker, and north of Greenseat. Then there is Cullen Green ('Cow Lane Green?') on the other side of the river from Low Row. Do these names indicate places where incoming settlers, squatters and travellers (including 'gypsies') lived and camped, in varying states of permanence, claiming a little 'public space' to graze a horse or a few geese? Such a place might well have looked like a 'gypsy' encampment, with structures such as 'turf haggs', made of perishable materials. If 'greens' did go with small or vulnerable settlements or encampments of doubtful legality, we should not be surprised that the 'green' names which survived into the nineteenth century are rare, and form no very coherent pattern.

The word 'green' here has not much to do with colour (for obvious reasons, greens may well have looked less green than the surrounding closes!). I think it has much more to do with the idea of common land – like 'greenwood' (which must contain the idea of common wood pasture) and 'green lanes', which were traditional thoroughfares (as opposed to 'the king's highway'). In the late twelfth century the section of the old Ulshaw-Swaledale road which runs not far from Bellerby was recorded as a 'green lane', the clerk smoothly translating the English directly into Latin, *viridis via.*[31] There is another 'Green Lane' which runs across Marrick Moor. No doubt 'green lanes' were also used by travellers, camping overnight; even today, walking along old unmetalled tracks, one may come across the signs of such brief stopovers. Greens, then, seem to have had a complicated history, starting as essential public spaces in villages and hamlets, designed within planned settlements. But even as they were infilled, other greens were being reinvented as secondary 'public spaces' for peripheral communities, families and even individuals asserting a right to subsist in a landscape now much claimed and occupied, with the old communal ethos in gradual retreat. Looked at historically, these late 'greens' for the half-excluded seem like ironic parodies of the more integral greens of earlier times.

Notes

1. Morris 1989.
2. Roberts 1987.
3. Taylor 1989, 207–27
4. Armstrong 1952.
5. Smith 1956, part 2, 222.
6. Harrison 1879, 211.
7. Farrer 1942, vol. V, 76.
8. Hindle 1984, 15.
9. Jervoise 1931, 86.
10. Harrison 1879, 204.

11. Toulmin Smith 1906–10, vol. V, 139.
12. Jervoise 1931, 86.
13. Atkinson 1984, vol. IV, 7.
14. North Yorkshire County Record Office (NYCRO) NCRONT 1/Peacock.
15. University of Leeds Library M 51.
16. In the Brotherton Collection, Leeds University Library, and partially reproduced in Tyson 1989, 12.
17. Raistrick and Jennings 1965, 21–2.
18. Raistrick 1982, 10.
19. Tyson 1989, 13.
20. Tweddle 1990.
21. NYCRO ZHP.
22. VCH 1914, vol. I, 238.
23. Speight 1897, 377, 393; Clarkson 1821, 374.
24. Atkinson 1894, vol. VII, 58.
25. NYCRO ZQH 7. 57/10.
26. Cooper 1960, 52.
27. NYCRO ZRT 2/3.
28. McDonnell 1990, 35.
29. Fieldhouse and Jennings 1978, 257.
30. McDonnell 1990.
31. Farrer 1942, vol. V, 105.

CHAPTER EIGHT

From Microliths to Maiden Castle

As I have explained, today's landscape was largely created in the past four centuries or so, emerging from a late medieval framework which has left its mark on place-names, boundaries, settlements and even the courses taken by footpaths. Every time low sunlight picks out plough-ridges and strip lynchets we are reminded of the back-breaking work of several centuries ago. For the earlier medieval period we have the cross-valley earthworks, and, to some extent, place-names. But before that, we have to rely on archaeological evidence. And since little excavation has been done in Swaledale, this means trying to tell a story based on piecemeal archaeological discoveries and surface observations.

What can be seen on the surface amounts to quite a lot. It is true that in Swaledale there are not many freshly ploughed fields to be searched for flints or pottery. The high watersheds are covered in deep blanket peat. We may scan the sides of erosion gulleys and stream channels, but there are not many of them, so we do not know how many buried walls or cairns might be there, or very much about scatters of flint implements on the buried land surface. Low down in these profiles, there are sometimes traces of wood. Edmund Bogg tells us that the peat on Round Hill, above Ravenseat, was found to contain the remains of 'birch and pine and nut tree'; peat-cutters on the moorland plateaus (location unspecified) apparently came across dark-coloured boles of oak and bird-cherry.[1] Like most of the uplands, these hills were colonised by trees after the end of the Ice Age – willow, birch, hazel and pine giving way to trees like oak, ash, alder and elm, around 6000 BC. Shortly afterwards, blanket peat began to spread on the higher, flatter uplands, starting in the badly drained areas. Flint implements and the waste from making them have been found in sufficient quantity to suggest that this was good hunting country for the Mesolithic people during the four thousand years or so before the development of farming;[2] Tim Laurie has found a magnificent Mesolithic flint axe-head on the hills above Gunnerside. Probably these people would have cleared away scrub and undergrowth, partly in their quest for firewood, and partly because they had noticed that more open areas attracted deer and cattle. They may have enclosed these clearings, impeding the escape of game by making rough barriers of felled trees, which would have developed into rough, semi-natural 'hedges', perhaps a bit like the *gehaeg* enclosures of the Middle Ages which have resulted in most of the place-names which end in 'ey' or 'ay'.[3]

To archaeologists, who use stone implements and pottery to divide prehistory into different phases, the next phase which ought to be visible is the Neolithic (starting around 4000 BC), when pottery-making, cereal farming and livestock herding came in – though there are lively arguments about the pace of change, whether substantial numbers of new colonists came in from continental Europe, and whether late Mesolithic people had already 'domesticated' cattle or pigs. We know that they had domesticated the dog; some of the earliest evidence comes from Star Carr in East Yorkshire.[4] Some archaeologists believe that they combined the growing of cereals with a pattern of seasonal movement, probably using distant pastures and hunting ranges on an annual cycle, as their Mesolithic ancestors had done.

A few stone axe-heads and Neolithic arrowheads have been discovered in Swaledale. The local historian Edmund Cooper, for instance, noted finds of stone axe-heads at Healaugh, and the finding near Muker of a fragment of another, which had probably come from the well-known quarries at Great Langdale in the Lake District; another stone axe-head was found at Thwaite, and leaf-shaped arrowheads came from Calver Hill near Reeth.[5] These finds turn up from time to time; they do not yet tell much of a story. The early Neolithic peoples of East Yorkshire and further south in the Pennines buried their dead in long earthen mounds or long cairns which sometimes contained chambers made of large stone slabs, but we have yet to locate one of these in Swaledale. Later in the Neolithic, from about 3000 BC until roughly 2500 BC, still in the period before copper- and bronze-working were introduced, there were ceremonial centres, with earthworks which defined circular areas (henge monuments), or long narrow 'processional ways' with closed-off ends *(cursuses)*. Such ceremonial centres were created in lowland areas not far from Swaledale, with henge monuments and a cursus at Thornborough, near Ripon, a cursus at Scorton (just east of Richmond), and henge monuments near Penrith; there are also henges in the Pennines, notably at Castle Dykes, near Aysgarth in Wensleydale. Stone circles were also built at this time, some of them perpetuating an earlier tradition of circles of timber uprights. There is at least one stone circle on the north side of Wensleydale, and another at Mudbeck, at the head of Arkengarthdale, in the area known on the map as 'Adjustment Ground', which is really 'agistment ground' – that is, pasture ground, its Norman-French name sometimes being corrupted to 'Jest Room'.[6] The stones at Mudbeck are not exactly monumental; if there are other stone circles like this in the area, they will take some finding.

Also late Neolithic, apparently, are the rock carvings of the Pennines, the 'cup and ring' stones which are particularly abundant on and around Ilkley Moor in West Yorkshire. Recently, Richard Bradley has argued that, whatever the carvings 'mean' (and there were 104 different explanations at the last count!), they were not positioned at random.[7] They were located at places which people had to pass on their way into the hills, when they moved up with their livestock in the spring, and in the natural corridors which led from one upland grazing ground to another. Some of the most complex carvings are located in places which have superb views, as if their creators were simultaneously communing with the powers of the sky and asserting their command over the pastures below.

On the moors flanking the upper valley of the Swale, hardly any of these carvings have been discovered, though there are some on Skelton Moor. One which accords beautifully with Richard Bradley's ideas is located far to the north at Osmaril Gill, prominently displayed in a defile leading from Barningham Moor to the moors of the New Forest. We discovered one ourselves during survey work – a small boulder with seven cups in an arc (Fig. 8.1). This too is in a place with a very commanding view, on the nose of the promontory between the Swale and the Arkle Beck, above Reeth. And on the moors to the south of Ellerton Priory, Tim Laurie has discovered cup-marks on a prominent stone which forms a natural 'signpost' on the route along the northern edge of the plateau, on the way to Stainton Moor. Richard Bradley has portrayed the growth of late prehistoric spirituality as a kind of sequence.[8] First, prehistoric people invested various striking natural features with supernatural significance. Then they started to embellish them in various ways, so that they became what we might call shrines. The next stage was the designing of purpose-built sacred places which may truly be called ceremonial monuments. The spiritual power which was rooted in the wild had been partly 'domesticated', aligned more closely with human dreams and perceptions.

In some parts of northern Britain, late Neolithic carved rocks were incorporated into the large burial cairns of the early Bronze Age – as they were at Addlebrough, in Wensleydale. It is these large burial cairns which come next in the sequence of monuments. On the North York Moors, these old 'howes' stand out where earth meets sky. They have evocative names – Shunner Howe, Lilla Howe, Swart Howe; Old Norse *haugr* means a burial mound. In the Middle Ages, howes made good boundary-marks – and they may have played this role in the Bronze Age too. On the Pennines, the density of Bronze Age cairns is quite variable. Around Swaledale, there is a scatter of prominent burial

FIGURE 8.1. Stone with pattern of cup-marks from the late Neolithic period, Riddings Rigg.

mounds in the area where most of the rock carvings have been found – on the extensive moorland plateau between the Swale, Marske Beck and Arkle Beck, from the Marrick area through Hurst and the New Forest.

The most prominent and best-known of these are How Tallon and Holgate How. On the hills above Marske and Marrick, others crop up on old maps or in descriptions of medieval boundaries; they include Breckon How, Croft How, Hazel How, Cock How, Bradhow and Gaveloak How.[9] And there were evidently howes further east, on the same block of moorland; Henry McLauchlan, who was a good mid-nineteenth-century field archaeologist, mapped two 'tumuli' to the north of Feldom Rigg and another further to the south-east, on the plateau between Marske and Ravensworth.[10]

It is not clear how many of these monuments can still be seen today (though I think I have identified Croft How). This area would have been moorland in the Middle Ages, but much of it has been 'improved' and enclosed in the period around 1800, and cairns could easily have been demolished to provide material for walls or roads. One of the late thirteenth-century references mentions 'Rukke upon Cockhow', an early use of the word 'hurrock'.[11] A 'hurrock' or 'currack' usually means a pillar of piled stones forming a boundary-mark (Fig. 10.3). In the late sixteenth century, there was 'a great horroke of stanis' at Sharrow Hill, on the eastern boundary of Grinton parish.[12]

This rolling but deeply dissected plateau stretches from the eastern edge of Arkengarthdale to the moors above Barningham, Gayles, Ravensworth and Richmond, and from the Stang in the north to the Swale in the south. Despite forming a well-defined and rather mysterious stretch of country, these hills have no name; neither their prehistory nor their history has caught the scholarly imagination. Improved land, recent forestry plantations and military ranges have not made it a particularly attractive area for fieldwork. Thinly populated in recent centuries, it was reached from the north by trackways used by graziers from the villages below, but also traversed by long-distance travellers including merchants transporting lead to the Tees and salt from further north-east. Arthur Raistrick has written about some of these old tracks.[13] Their names are evocative – Hergill Lane, Green Lane, Badger (merchants') Way, Jagger (packhorse) Lane, Stone Man Lane; and there is an older generation of *gata* names – Holgate, Waitgate, Rakegate and Threllesgate. In the Neolithic and Bronze Age, this area would have been an attractive summer grazing zone for people from the lowlands to the north and east. Most of it is well under 1,300 feet (400m) above sea level, distinctly lower than much of the upland further west; peaty, wet areas would have been shallower and relatively restricted in area. Probably these hills, overlooked by the graves of the ancestors, were used as summer grazing grounds for hundreds of years.

There are not many obvious Bronze Age burial mounds on the moors to the west and south of this area, though one cairn which does come to mind is at Jack Standards, on the way from Hollow Mill Cross to the Nine Standards (Fig. 8.2). In the central Swaledale area, Bronze Age death rituals are commemorated by lesser-known monuments called ring cairns. A ring cairn is a circular area,

10–20 yards (c.10–20m) across in most cases, enclosed by a low stone bank or wall. It may have a circle of upright stones protruding from the bank, or lining its inner face. When excavated, a ring cairn often turns out to have had a few cremation burials at the centre, in a pit and perhaps inside a large pottery vessel. Ring cairns and related monuments are found in upland areas in Britain, in south-west England and in Wales as well as in northern England and Scotland; there are quite a number of them on the North York Moors.

The best ring cairn in Swaledale is on Harkerside, though it is marked as a 'hut circle' on the 1:25000 map. Tim Laurie has established that there are quite a few more ring cairns on the moors of central Swaledale, and also further south, on the northern side of Wensleydale, where Tim has been working with Robin Minnitt. Most of the ring cairns occur singly, but they are sometimes found in pairs, separated by up to a couple of hundred yards, as in other parts of the country.

Ring cairns are scattered fairly regularly on the moors to the south of the Swale, from Whitaside in the west to Stainton Moor in the east; north of the river, the pattern is less regular. The Swaledale ring cairns tend to occur at about 1,000 feet (300m) above sea level; as in other parts of Britain, they are not often found on the highest moors. And, as on the southern Pennines, the North York Moors and the hills of south-west Scotland, some of the Swaledale ring cairns occur in association with what archaeologists have come to call cairnfields – scatters of small cairns and stretches of walling, some of which form 'fields', in varying degrees of completeness.[14] There are also 'enclosures', some apparently incomplete, but others roughly kidney-shaped or virtually circular. These antiquities were noticed long ago. A document of the late twelfth century mentions 'Stain-burghanes' (or stone *borrans* – Middle English, meaning cairns) somewhere on Harkerside, and there was a High Borwins Ing near Lodge Green in the early eighteenth century.[15]

Not far away, just west of Bleak House, are the ruins of Ring House, which must have taken its name from the roughly circular ancient enclosure whose southern half can still be seen beside the road from Grinton to Low Whita. On Calverside there are three well-preserved, almost circular enclosures. One is marked on the 1:25000 map, halfway between Calver Hill and Fore Gill Gate. It has given its name to Cringley Hill (from the Old Norse *kringla,* meaning a circle). There is another just to the east of the intakes at Cleasby, and a third on Riddings Rigg; it has been cut through by a later prehistoric wall. Within these moorland enclosures, there are very few structures which could be interpreted as ruined dwellings, though sometimes a wall swerves as if to respect or leave room for a building, which might have been made of wood or turf, and has naturally left no trace on the surface.

The association of cairnfields with ring cairns has long suggested that they represent some kind of Bronze Age occupation of the uplands, though work done in the central and southern Pennines is beginning to discredit the idea that this was just a short episode in the middle of the Bronze Age.[16] These

moorlands were settled from at least the late Neolithic, though probably only in the growing season, roughly the period from Beltane to Samhain in the pre-Christian calendar – early May to early November. Conditions have degenerated since the Bronze Age, when the soil would have been less acid, the peat shallower and less extensive, and the pasture better than it is now. Probably, as the topsoil thinned and surface stone became more of a problem for cultivators, small stone cairns were built, first within the 'fields' or garden areas, and then at their edges. As time went on, stones were cleared more generally on to field boundaries. By the time these upland 'fields' were eventually abandoned, cleared stones had accumulated along their boundaries, sometimes as fairly continuous lines of walling, sometimes as rows of cairns. The parcels of cleared land are frequently irregular in plan, and look as if they represent small-scale garden plots, tilled with hoes or digging-sticks, for occasional crops taken by people who were mainly concerned with livestock.

These areas are not the easiest places for fieldwork. Although the peat is relatively shallow, and the remains of stone walls and cairns are visible on the surface, tall heather obscures much of the archaeology. However, the moors are systematically burnt on a cycle of about fifteen years – so a fair sample of upstanding archaeological features is always on display. When a low wall disappears into a zone of tall heather, it is often still visible to the experienced eye, or can be felt through the soles of one's boots. The best-preserved of these rather fragmentary 'prehistoric landscapes' are found on the moors above Grinton and Harkerside, and across the river, on the flanks of Calver Hill. At the western fringes of both of these areas, there are groupings of larger, more circular cairns; it is tempting to suggest that these were for burials, and not

FIGURE 8.2. A probable Bronze Age cairn at Jack Standards at the west end of Swaledale.

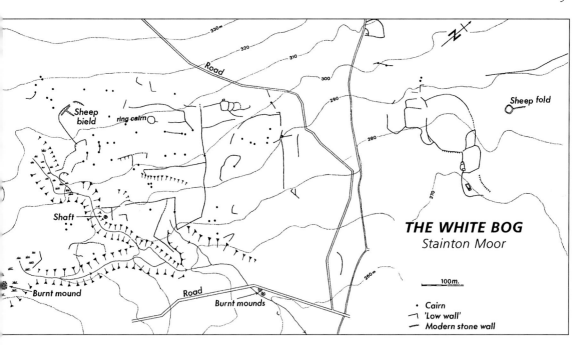

FIGURE 8.3. Plan of prehistoric field system and related features on Stainton Moor. Note ring cairn at northern edge of area.

simply field clearance. On Harkerside and Calverside, and also on Marrick Moor, above Fremington Edge, the 'cairnfield' features occur within a much more organised land division system, laid out later, with long, roughly parallel walls running uphill above the present-day head dykes. This makes for a confusing, archaeologically 'busy' landscape. But there is one area without this later overprint – another of Tim Laurie's discoveries, at The White Bog, on Stainton Moor, a south-facing piece of moorland tucked away on an army range, to the west of Downholme.

Our plan (Fig. 8.3) shows ruined walls or clearance-banks and numerous small cairns on sloping ground above the beck on the western part of the site, dying out well below the top of the hill to the north. A ring cairn, 16 yards (c.16m) in diameter, is located centrally in the upper part of this area. There are fewer small cairns to the east, where there is apparently a separate complex of enclosure walls. On the main, western part of the site, some walls seem to delineate 'unfinished' fields or enclosures. But these features may once have been complete, originally defined by fences or hedges, before parts of their boundaries were 'turned to stone' by clearance or rudimentary wall-building. A few cairns are apparently in lines; it is tempting to 'join the dots' and create one or two more boundaries.

There has also been an element of planning. A central, spinal wall running north-south down the slope is met by two or three walls coming off at right angles, subdividing the land to the west and perhaps to the east as well. In general these walls run through cairnfree zones; they may be relatively late walls whose builders have dismantled older cairns nearby. East of the northern end of the spinal wall, there is a group of three or four very small enclosures joined together, with a wall running off to the west which may have been cut through by the spinal wall. But some of the relationships really defy surface interpretation. For example, how exactly did the mix of straight and curvilinear walls to the east and south-east of these little enclosures come into being, and why do they stop suddenly in places? We may have to read hedges and fences into this landscape, but in areas like this we should probably also think in terms of episodes of clearance, separated by times when grazing livestock was the main activity – and by phases of desertion.

On the southern side of the site are the remains of three 'burnt mounds', the first of three dozen or so which Tim Laurie has discovered in and around Swaledale. These are mounds of stones split and cracked by heat, and now mostly turf-covered. Burnt mounds have been picked up in many parts of Britain and Ireland. In some areas they are quite densely distributed; most of them have been found to date from the Bronze Age.[17] They are usually close to water-courses, and mark places where stones have been heated and dropped into water, perhaps on numerous occasions. All sorts of interpretations have been proposed for burnt mounds. They may have been the sites of large communal feasts, places where brewing, metal-working or cheese-making went on, or possibly saunas or 'sweat-houses', used for healing purposes or by shamans seeking visions of the world of the supernatural. But in some areas these heaps of fire-cracked stones may simply represent the most obvious traces of prehistoric settlement-sites, which is how they are interpreted in Scandinavia, and on Fair Isle.

But what was happening lower down on the dalesides, in the zone which is now farmland? This is the most challenging area to work in. But Swaledale is quite a narrow valley, and if I turn up when conditions are right I can use my zoom lens to capture many archaeological features. As with archaeological air photography, persistence and repeat visits are essential; archaeological sites need particular conditions to look their best, or even to show up at all. The right conditions include low sunlight – morning or evening – and melting snow. Swaledale runs east-west, and the snow doesn't necessarily melt at the same speed on both sides of the river. Often the south-facing side will tend to show white stripes against a green background, while the north-facing side is still displaying long blue shadows on a white blanket. One year I was stupefied to find that the south-facing side of the dale was melting more slowly than the north-facing side! It turned out that more snow had fallen on the south-facing side of the dale – and then thawing had taken place evenly, under an overcast sky. Some of the best observations may be made in the low sunlight of a winter morning, as the hoar-frost on the humps and bumps of an archaeological site thaws differentially, according to which bits are first exposed to the sun. Winter light is best; the trees are leafless and the bracken is down. It is much more difficult to get good results in the hazy sunshine of high summer, though sometimes there are interesting effects just after the fields have been mown. The most ancient field-banks contain stone walls and tumble which retain little moisture; at the end of a dry summer they turn brown or yellow more readily than the surrounding areas.

Different parts of the daleside provide insights into different phases of past

FIGURE 8.4. Burial mound at Swale Hall.

landscape history. In Lower Swaledale, and around Reeth, for instance, medieval strip-fields must have destroyed quite a few earlier archaeological features. It is noticeable that in the zone between Reeth and Healaugh, the best-preserved bits of 'ancient landscape' – house-platforms, settlement-platforms and boundary banks – are in the gap between the arable strips of Reeth and those of Healaugh. In some closes, reseeding for meadows and pastures has created smooth ground surfaces where it is hard to see much, except perhaps when the sun is really low in the sky. So one field may hold a well-preserved Romano-British settlement site, or some ancient field-banks; its neighbour may contain a set of banks delineating medieval strip-fields, or show very little. So there are windows, usually quite small ones, into different aspects of the ancient landscape. The greatest damage has been done on the best land – and also sometimes on the worst, the moor-edge intakes 'improved' in the eighteenth and nineteenth centuries. The best-preserved sites are usually in areas which fall between these categories, on land fairly high on the daleside and within post-medieval closes.

There are some grass-covered mounds in farmland on the daleside; quite a few of them were first noticed by Tim Laurie (Fig. 8.4). Only one, near Swale Hall, is marked as an antiquity on the map. These mounds hardly ever have 'folk names' like the big cairns on the North York Moors. Most of them are too steep-sided and circular to represent heaps of gravel left behind by an ice-sheet, and they are not difficult to distinguish from grassed-over 'flushes' left behind by hillside springs which have since dried up. One or two of them might result from field clearance, perhaps in relatively recent times.

If these are ancient burial mounds, surely they should already have been recognised by early settlers if not by archaeologists? But it has to be remembered that we are the first archaeologists to work here. And it is easy to understand why these mounds were not usually given names. On moorland, with the wider landscape often obscured by cloud or mist, landmarks are the main means of defining paths and boundaries; it is not surprising that moorland cairns have been named. In the well-wooded early medieval daleside landscape, however, the earliest paths would often have been those created by animals – like the 'deer path' *(heort stig)* which gave its name to Hard Stiles, the hillside immediately south-west of Marske. Most boundaries would be those of community land, in distant zones of woodland. Old, dimly known mounds among the trees would not stand out; they would be encountered casually, as land was cleared.

There are, in fact, one or two folk-names for burial mounds in the daleside areas. Sorrel Sykes, in Fremington, was once called 'Sorrow Sykes'.[18] In theory, this might have been a place given one of those despairing names which reflect the difficulty of making a living from its soil. But there is actually a large mound just behind the farmhouse. Here, in medieval Fremington's zone of arable land, it is understandable that a tall, highly visible mound would be recognised as an ancient burial mound, and named something like 'Soar How'. And there was a Borrow Ing somewhere near Lodge Green in the early eighteenth century.[19] The tithe maps for the upper dale also give us Brown How, Black How, Forster How, Dow How and Hutt How, but it is fairly clear that some of these relate to *hōh* (sharp-profiled hill) rather than to *haugr*.

Many of the surviving mounds stand on the edge of natural terraces, immediately above the flood plain of the Swale. There are fewer of them on the more heavily settled north bank than on the south bank, where our provisional map shows that there is a fairly regular distribution of mounds between Grinton and Gunnerside Bridge – and one or two further west. Unfortunately there is nothing to indicate their date. They are not necessarily Bronze Age; some or all of them might be Iron Age, or Romano-British, or even early medieval.

Swaledale has quite a number of 'defended' sites which are probably late prehistoric, though we can only compare them with similar sites elsewhere, since not a single one has been excavated (Fig. 8.5). This should put them in the later Bronze Age or Iron Age, that is, any time between about 1000 BC and the coming of the Romans. Maiden Castle, on Harkerside, is the only one which is well known. But the biggest one is the very damaged hill-fort on How Hill, Downholme. Its rampart and ditch only survive on the west and north sides of the hill; the rest of the circuit was largely obliterated in the Middle Ages. As we have seen, How Hill commands the gateway to Swaledale, and is surrounded by extensive medieval ploughlands. This would fit the conventional interpretation of the larger hill-forts in the south of England, which are portrayed as 'central places', major fortified villages dominated by chieftains who controlled the production and distribution of highly valued trade goods, and perhaps stocks of food; but this view has recently come under fire.[20]

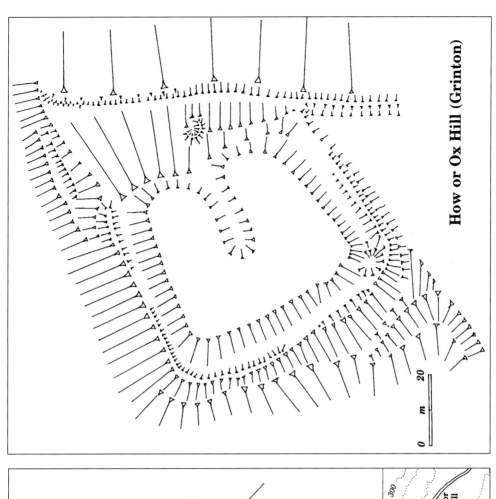

How or Ox Hill (Grinton)

How Hill (Low Whita)

rectangular building

hollow way

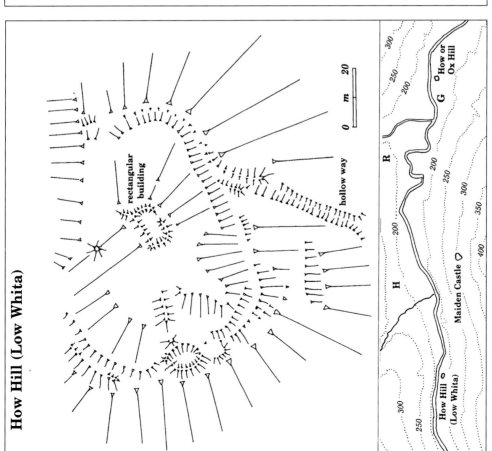

FIGURE 8.5. 'Defended' sites in Swaledale at How or Ox Hill, Grinton and How Hill, Low Whita, with location map (G = Grinton, H = Healaugh, R = Reeth). See also Figures 8.6 and 8.7.

FIGURE 8.6. Defended
knoll at How Hill,
Grinton. For plan, see
Figure 8.5.

As we advance up the dale, it seems that every defensible knoll has been embellished with a bank and ditch. There is How Hill (alternatively, Ox Hill) which dominates the river plain just to the east of Grinton (Fig. 8.6). The enclosure here was roughly square, with an entrance in the centre of the east side. Most of its rampart has been levelled, perhaps by the makers of the early twentieth-century golf course, but the ditch shows up very well in low sunlight. And low sunlight will be necessary if you are to get a good impression of the next defended How Hill, midway between Harkerside Place and Reeth. The top of this small knoll is enclosed by a ditch, roughly square in plan, which shows up well in certain conditions; but the most intriguing site lies just to the south. Across this field run the banks of Herthay's medieval strip-fields, themselves quite heavily abraded by later ploughing. Where they run across an area of slightly higher land, roughly oval in shape, they are slightly better preserved. I have been keeping an eye on this site from the moorland road to the south, taking advantage of various conditions of light and weather, and building up an archive of photographs, each one showing something slightly different. And when the snow thaws or the sun is low in the sky, it is possible to see that this oval area has had a bank (visible mostly on the northern side), a ditch (observable on the southern side) and a hollow-way approaching what must have been an entrance-gap at the east. This site, which has a footpath running past it, is not very like the typical defended enclosures of the Late Bronze and Iron Ages; perhaps it is earlier in date?

FIGURE 8.7. Defended knoll at How Hill, Low Whita. Note how the defences have been slighted by a (Romano-British?) field-bank, and are more degraded on one side of this boundary than on the other. The hollow-way which approaches the ditch on the right does not indicate the position of the original entrance. For plan, see Figure 8.5.

Near Low Whita, there is another How Hill, a sharp bluff just above the river (Fig. 8.7). This would have been a classic heel-shaped *hōh* to Old English speakers; but in Old Norse it was a *hváll*, 'an isolated rounded hill', which is perpetuated in that of the field nearby, which was Whealsey Close in the early eighteenth century, and Whalsay a century later.[21] This hill is also girdled by a bank and ditch, which often shows up well from a distance. There is a hollow-way leading up from the south, but this is a late trackway leading into the ditch and round to the eastern side of the hill, perhaps an approach to the rectangular building which once crowned the hill. Within the enclosed area there are no signs of the house-platforms which one might expect on a site like this. The original entrance was on the western side, though on the ground it is hard to distinguish original features from later disturbances.

Just east of Thwaite is another, smaller rounded knoll, which looks very much like another *hváll*; Fieldhouse and Jennings, trying to identify a dairying settlement listed as 'Waylle' in 1301, decided that it must be Thwaite,[22] and the presence of this hill suggests that they were right to do so. The *hváll* at Thwaite was once surrounded by a bank and ditch, which show up from the air in dry conditions.

The idea that every well-defined knoll in Swaledale was 'fortified' in later prehistoric times, or at any rate occupied by a high-status residence, might make sense of the very odd position of Maiden Castle, which is a fairly typical 'hill-fort', albeit with an extraordinarily long walled entrance corridor – an out-turned entrance, as archaeologists call it. But its position, on a hill shoulder on Harkerside, is very unusual; most hill-forts are on well-defined hills. Perhaps all other potential hill-fort locations were already spoken for when Maiden Castle was planned. But it is more likely, I think, that there was a well-established social and political hierarchy in Swaledale by the first millennium BC, as there was in other parts of Britain. Maiden Castle is larger than the other defended sites in Upper Swaledale; perhaps in the Iron Age mindset the place of highest prestige ought to occupy the highest site, frowning down upon all other residences. There are several other high-altitude hill-forts in northern England alone – Mam Tor in Derbyshire, Ingleborough in the Pennines and Yeavering Bell in Northumberland – which might make sense in these terms.

The name of Yeavering Bell refers to *Gefrin,* the old capital of the Anglian kingdom of Northumbria – which is now a rather uninteresting pasture, far below the hill-fort. Thinking about Swaledale in these terms, should we not ask ourselves whether Upper and Lower Swaledale were already politically differentiated in the Iron Age, so that the relationship between How Hill (Downholme) and Lower Swaledale was equivalent to that between Maiden Castle and Upper Swaledale? If that was the case, the origins of the kingdom of the Swale may lie in the pre-Roman Iron Age, or further back, in the later Bronze Age. But I must now try to bridge the gap between Maiden Castle and the kingdom of the Swale, and turn to the 'ancient landscape' which represents these times.

Notes

1.   Bogg, 1908, 389–90, 422.
2.   Coggins *et al.* 1990; Jacobi 1978.
3.   Simmons 1996.
4.   Degerbøl 1961.
5.   Cooper 1973, 10; Bogg 1908, 208, 403.
6.   North Yorkshire County Record Office (NYCRO) ZWX (M) (MIC 2234/194).
7.   Bradley 1994; Bradley 1997.
8.   Bradley 1993.
9.   Spratt 1993, 92–106.
10.   McLauchlan 1849.
11.   Harrison 1879, 191.
12.   NYCRO CRONT I/Peacock.
13.   Raistrick 1962.
14.   Barnatt 1987; Spratt 1993, 109–18; Barnatt and Smith 1997, chapter 2.
15.   Clay 1935, vol. IV, 346; NYCRO MIC 144.
16.   Barnatt and Smith 1997, chapter 2.
17.   Buckley 1991; Barfield and Hodder 1987; Hodder and Barfield 1991.
18.   NYCRO Reeth Tithe Map (1830).
19.   NYCRO MIC 144.
20.   Hill 1995.
21.   NYCRO ZIF 359; Smith 1967, vol. II, 265; Fleming 1999.
22.   Fieldhouse and Jennings 1978, 48.

CHAPTER NINE

Romans
and Countrymen

On Stainton Moor, as we have seen, land was subdivided as well as enclosed, with three north-south walls running roughly parallel to one another – a very simple 'coaxial' layout, as archaeologists have come to call it.[1] Similar small 'field systems', with roughly parallel walls, were recorded on the North York Moors by the late Don Spratt – for instance at Wheat Beck (Snilesworth), and on Near Moor, above Swainby.[2] Coaxial these systems may be, but they are tiny in comparison with the massive coaxial land division systems of central Swaledale (for which they may well be the prototypes). Only from the air can one gain a true impression of the size of these large coaxial systems, and their persistence in following their chosen axis, as they make their way across terrain broken by streams and glacial overflow channels and up the natural steps formed by Swaledale's sedimentary rocks. On the ground, these boundaries are represented by low, ruined walls, but one needs to get one's eye in to see them outside the zones where heather has been recently burnt off. In some places it is possible to see that these are not just lines of piled stones; they were broad, low walls, with clearly visible facing-stones fronting a core made up of smaller stones (Fig. 9.1). There are three great areas of coaxial land division in the Reeth area. North-east of Reeth is the Marrick Moor system, which runs northwards from Fremington Edge, probably as far as Marske Beck. To the south of Reeth is the Harkerside system, whose coaxial boundaries extend from about 400 yards (c.400m) east of Maiden Castle as far east as Cogden Beck, although there are further coaxial boundaries running across the contour as far east as the Black Hill/Bleaberry Hill area. This land division system is 2.5 miles (4km) wide. The third area of coaxial walls is on Calverside – south and east of Calver Hill, to the west of Reeth. On Riddings Rigg (the eastern shoulder of Calver Hill), there are *two* systems, with different axes of orientation (Fig. 1.5). The relatively small Reeth system, which runs roughly south-east/north-west, is partly overlapped by the bigger Healaugh system, whose boundaries run north-south across the contour and extend almost as far west as Foregill Gate. These three systems are the biggest and best preserved. But there are traces of similar coaxial walled land divisions further west, mostly on the north side of the river. A few high-level coaxial walls run north-south on the exposed limestone to the west of Blades. North of Dyke Heads, to the west of Gunnerside, coaxial boundaries run across the contour, in contrast to the long medieval strip-fields which run *along* the hillside here.

How far out onto the moors did these systems extend? The Reeth system had a clearly defined 'terminal' boundary, or 'top wall', and it also used watercourses

as boundaries. The top wall of the Healaugh system is intermittent. In some places it tends to follow the bottom edge of a sharply rising slope. Sometimes it is not clear how far it represents clearance of stones to the base of the slope, or to what extent stones fallen from above have also made their contribution. By contrast, at the upper end of the Harkerside system some of the coaxial walls *climb* the extra steep slopes below High Harker Hill, before fading away. Further east, they extend as far south as Grovebeck Gill. To the east of How Hill one or two of them run out all the way to Ridley Hush, demonstrating that at least part of the Harkerside system extends two-thirds of the way from the Swale to the Swaledale-Wensleydale watershed.

What happens when these old boundaries approach the top walls of present-day farmland? This is where we run into problems. The moorland intakes of the 'improvement' period, around 1800, were very destructive, and ancient walls have often been completely robbed out, within the intakes as well as immediately above the top walls. But in earlier times, the makers of daleside riddings were less gung-ho; quite a number of ancient field boundaries were preserved and are now visible as green banks beneath or beside walls which

FIGURE 9.1. *Left*: ancient wall on Calverside. Note the carefully built faces. *Right*: excavated wall in farmland, near Healaugh.

FIGURE 9.2. Excavated wall junction, Riddings Rigg, Calverside. The two prominent stones are facing stones of a wall of the Healaugh system, riding over the face of a wall belonging to the Reeth system.

stand today. Many of them run across the contour, just like the old walls on the moors above. On the modern map, it is striking how many field-walls run up and down slope in the area around Reeth, Healaugh and Harkerside. It is no coincidence that this zone lies just below the moors where ancient walls are best preserved. The obvious question is – did the early boundaries extend all the way down to the edge of the Swale flood plain? In this zone, which not surprisingly became our main research area, Tim Laurie and I spent quite a lot of time trying to find clear-cut cases where ruined walls on the moors can be shown to continue as old field-banks into present-day farmland.

The task is not an easy one; we have had quite a few arguments, the more confident one being characterised as too credulous, and the more cautious one being reproved for his timidity! There are ways of sorting the problem out, however. For instance, between different intakes there are gaps containing unimproved land. One of these zones, on the steep hillside above Healaugh, has three coaxial walls running through it. One of them lines up directly with a very pronounced field-bank which runs right down to the level of Healaugh village. Further east, just to the west of Riddings Farm, is a rare place where it is possible to see a couple of old boundaries coming straight off the moor into farmland; one of these is quite a long, continuous feature, running through the modern fields. There is just enough evidence, on Calverside and Harkerside, to link the coaxial boundaries of the moors with those of the dalesides, though understandably enough the boundaries of the Marrick system did not cross Fremington Edge, except on the gentler gradient of the Reels Head area, where they seem to have run down to a 'bottom wall' running along the contour, and quite high up the slope.

On farmland, where an old field-bank is exposed in section – cut by a modern track, for instance – it is sometimes possible to see that it contains a wall just like the ones on the moors. Near our main excavation site we cut a trench through a very broad, gently swelling bank in farmland just east of Healaugh, and discovered that it covered a carefully built ancient wall, faced on both sides with a core of small stones, just like the old walls on the moors. So the *style* of the walls makes another link between moor and daleside (Fig. 9.1).

On the moors, the large coaxial systems do not seem to contain many obvious contemporary settlement sites, though we have to remember that structures of wood or turf would not normally leave surface traces, unless they were built on levelled platforms. But the moorland zones have escaped the destructive effects of medieval fields and later closes – so they are quite good places to work in. As I have explained, on Riddings Rigg to the west of Reeth, the Healaugh and Reeth systems conform to different axes of orientation. Here we were able to establish a *sequence* of boundary systems. We have excavated one of the points where walls from the two different systems intersect, and have been able to show that facing stones of one of the Healaugh system walls overlay a wall of the Reeth system (Fig. 9.2). So the Healaugh system was the later of the two. Not far away, a circular walled enclosure can be shown to be earlier than a wall of the Healaugh system which cuts right through it.

A plan of the ancient walls on this eastern shoulder of Calver Hill shows quite a lot of what archaeologists call 'chronological depth'; it is obvious that not all of the features on the plan were contemporary. There must be a sequence of some kind. In this area quite a few of the old walls have been robbed out or disappear into heather or bog, and often it is only the logic of the layout which encourages the field archaeologist to keep going. To some extent we can use commonsense principles to put complex sets of walls into a sequence (Fig. 9.3). Having confirmed by excavation that the Healaugh system is later than the Reeth system, we may be pleased to note that two of the Healaugh system walls appear to stop at walls which must have been there already; one was part of the Reeth system, and the other linked two Reeth system walls, implying that the Reeth system was already there when the Healaugh system was laid out.

If we call the Healaugh system phase III, phase II was the Reeth system, its coaxial walls ending on a long, wandering "terminal" three-quarters of a mile (over one kilometre) long, which ran right over the ridge and down the hillside, presumably as far as Arkle Beck. Further walls on the same axis strike out to the north-west, on the other side of the terminal. Perhaps we should envisage wooden fences, hedges or boundary markers carrying on into the distance. In the same zone there is a shorter boundary, some 700 yards (c.700m) long; for various reasons, we can work out that it must have been earlier than the terminal of the main Reeth system. That gives us a phase I, a catch-all phase into which I have put everything demonstrably or probably 'early'. The 700-yard (c.700m) wall looks like the outer boundary of a fairly large parcel of land to the south, but it is not clear that it went with a coaxial system; it may simply represent the outer edge of an intake. There is little 'detail' in these land division systems – very few 'fields' or enclosures or plausible house foundations, and only a small number of clearance cairns. Probably these walls formed subdivisions of upland pasture.

The coaxial layouts on Harkerside and Marrick Moor are simpler than

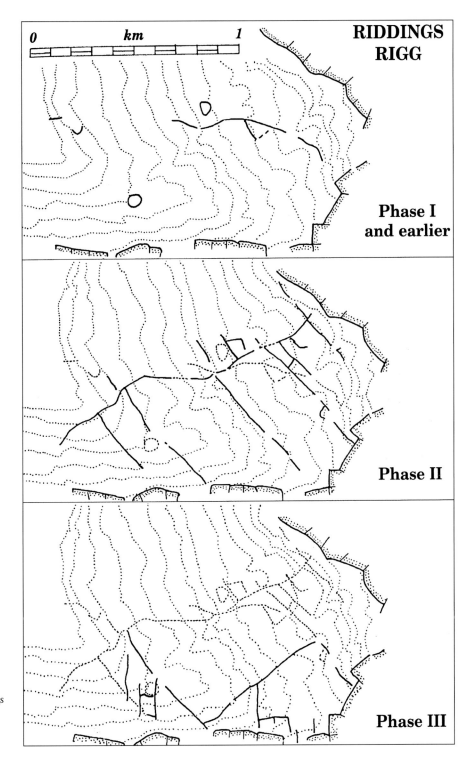

RIDDINGS
RIGG

0   *km*   1

**Phase I
and earlier**

Phase II

Phase III

ᴳURE 9.3. Phase
ɪagram for the coaxial
ld systems on Riddings
gg (Calverside). For
ᴙther explanation, see
ᴋt.

those on Riddings Rigg, with fewer indications of chronological depth. Their terminal walls come and go, and indeed the Healaugh system probably never had a continuous top wall following a well-defined course. Further west on Calverside, there are places where the terminal is well built, But in other areas the coaxials just fade away, as if unfinished (which they may be). There are indications that the Healaugh system also had a lower top wall, which ran along the contour only just above the modern enclosed land. Perhaps this lower top wall formed an early upper limit of the Healaugh system, which was later surpassed, like the terminal of the Reeth system. We cut five sections through this lower top wall. Nowhere was it built on peat, and in places it was possible to observe that it had been constructed on a stone-free soil, implying a good deal of worm-sorting, with less acidic conditions than are present today, and probably better-quality pasture land.

On the moors, there are 'droveways' or 'lanes' in some places, integrated into the coaxial systems (Fig. 9.4). At the western end of the Harkerside system

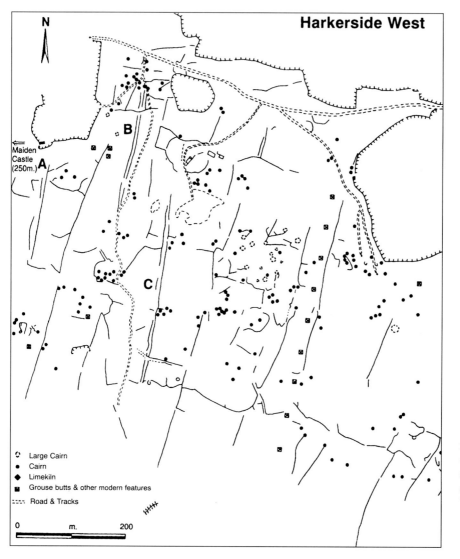

FIGURE 9.4. Part of the Harkerside system above Harkerside Place, showing walls, cairns and 'droveways' (A, B and C).

there are three of these, A, B and C, approximately side by side and following the axis of the system, as well as a short stretch of 'lane' apparently crossing droveway C, and an even shorter one further east, which does not follow the axis but seems nevertheless part of the boundary system. These features are puzzling. They ascend to different levels on the hillside. Droveway A does not seem to be necessary, since it is just beyond the western edge of the system. Droveway C is apparently blocked off near its southern end, like one of the droveways on Calverside. Perhaps originally there were narrow gateways here, which were blocked with stones so that we cannot see where they were. In general, droveways are rare; is this because most of them had one side defined by wooden fencing? The important point about the Harkerside droveways is that they suggest the movement of livestock between the daleside and the moors beyond the enclosed land.

On Calverside we dug a trench across one of the coaxial boundaries of the Healaugh system. Fortunately, there was quite a lot of charcoal, both beneath the 'wall' and on its western side, where it formed a well-defined horizon in soil which had built up against the wall. We managed to obtain three radiocarbon dates for the charcoal, from the Godwin Laboratory in the University of Cambridge. They turned out to date from approximately 300 BC, although the strongly fluctuating proportions of carbon 14 in the atmosphere at this time make it extra difficult to use radiocarbon dates with precision. But taken at face value, the dates should indicate that this wall was in position by about 300 BC, in the middle of the Iron Age, and that it is unlikely to be much older, unless we choose to set aside the date *beneath* the wall.

This would fit in with the evidence of pollen analysis. One of the most useful approaches to landscape history is to persuade a palaeobotanist to take a long column of peat from a suitable location and count the pollen grains of trees and plants preserved in a series of samples, from the earliest at the bottom to the latest at the top. The changing pollen percentages may then be interpreted in terms of changing vegetation. We sampled about 6 feet (c.2m) of peat in a glacial overflow channel on Ellerton Moor, beside the Grinton-Leyburn road, and Elizabeth Livett analysed it. The site is not very far from the Harkerside land division system, and there are coaxial boundaries on Ellerton Moor itself, north of the sampling area.

At the bottom of the diagram, the pollen rain is dominated first by hazel and birch, then mostly by birch. Then comes a dramatic fall in tree pollen, with a sharp decrease in the pollen of birch, and smaller falls recorded for hazel, oak and alder; at the same horizon there is a massive increase in the pollen of grasses, and plantain increases sharply. This represents a major clearance of trees, whether by fire, axe or browsing animals. This episode took place sometime between two radiocarbon dates – the earlier one with a bracket of 510–380 BC, the later with a bracket of 1 BC to AD 80. In other words, there was a major clearance in the middle of the Iron Age, broadly the same time as the dates for the charcoal associated with a coaxial wall of the Healaugh boundary system. After this, our pollen diagram shows a short-lived recovery of trees, not only of birch – which may have been the dominant tree locally, on the moor itself – but also of hazel, oak and alder. This seems to relate to the period around the Roman conquest, in the first century AD. Then there is a major rise in evidence for clearance and open country, which apparently covers the second and third centuries and perhaps much of the fourth as well. Heather, a significant component of the Iron Age pollen rain, now becomes even more important; from now on, heathland evidently became firmly established, probably spreading as a consequence of more intensive human use of this relatively fragile environment.

We have to be careful about extrapolating the results from a single pollen diagram to a whole region. Some pollen cores maybe picking up pollen mainly from the immediate locality. Phases when the landscape was open will give us a more regional picture than times when the bog from which we have drawn our sample was surrounded by woodland. But as it happens the idea of a major opening up of the landscape in mid-Iron Age times is not altogether unexpected, because pollen diagrams from other parts of northern England have produced much the same findings. Valley Bog in County Durham; Whirley Gill in Wensleydale (only 6 miles (10km) from Ellerton Moor, and just south of the Swale-Ure watershed, not far from the road between Whitaside and Askrigg); Fen Bogs, Harwood Dale Bog and Hambleton Dike on the North York Moors; Green Gates and Lanshaw 2 on Rombald's Moor near Ilkley in West Yorkshire; and Leash Fen and Featherbed Moss in the south Pennines, have all produced evidence for major clearance associated with radiocarbon dates in the mid-Iron Age. Clearances which may be slightly earlier in the Iron Age, and also dated by radiocarbon, occur at Simy Folds (Upper Teesdale), Stainmore in the north Pennines, Penhill in Wensleydale, Hebers Gill (Rombald's Moor, West Yorkshire) and Rishworth Moor in the southern Pennines.[3] In some places, sites not far distant from one another have picked up extensive local 'horizons' of clearance, as in Nidderdale and around Rombald's Moor near Ilkley. Areas perhaps 2 or 3 miles (3–5km) across were implicated, and there seems to have been an even larger area of open land on the moors to the west of Sheffield.

One might call this clearance horizon the Great Brigantian *landnam*. It covers the area occupied in the later Iron Age by the Brigantes, whose name translates as 'the highlanders'. *Landnam* is a Danish word, borrowed by palaeobotanists; it means 'land taking'. The 'causes' of the Great Brigantian *landnam* are debatable; it is a horizon which has hardly been noticed yet by prehistorians. We might argue that it reflects the first serious impact on the landscape of iron axes and/ or iron ploughshares. There is not very much direct evidence to support this idea. But there *is* a suspicion that this was roughly the time when the rotary quern was introduced to Yorkshire; at any rate it was widely used around here in the later Iron Age. These 'beehive querns' (so-called because of their shape) were much more efficient hand-mills than the 'saddle querns' of earlier times. In the Yorkshire Iron Age, querns of good-quality stone were evidently worth transporting considerable distances. Querns made of Millstone Grit from the Pennines were reaching north-east Yorkshire; conversely, querns found at Hutton Rudby and Crathorne, just off the north-west corner of the North York Moors, were made of Yoredale Series sandstone from the Pennines. It is likely that they came from a quarry somewhere in the Swaledale or Wensleydale area. New quarries were evidently being opened up.[4] Perhaps cereal production in northern England was reaching new levels in the mid- to late Iron Age.

Accounting for such changes is not easy for prehistorians, who work without written records. We are reluctant to explain them simply in terms of technological change; there was more to the Industrial Revolution than a few mechanical inventions. New agricultural technology is usually developed or applied in order to expand production, as the population increases, or in response to social and political change. But demographic explanations are also tricky; we cannot convincingly use a hypothesis about increasing population to explain the development of more open landscapes in the Yorkshire Pennines if the main evidence for that population increase is the evidence for more open landscapes; clearly this would be a circular argument. But nevertheless the link may have existed.

An expansion in production might have been triggered by increasing social competition – groups of people trying to outdo one another by spending more and more on elaborate gifts, marriage payments, funeral feasts, sacrifices to supernatural beings and so on. The effects might be felt especially in the field of livestock production (cattle have often been used rather like money, as a medium of exchange); demand for large extra areas of upland pasture might have grown considerably. Increased claims on resources might have been made by kings, chiefs, or clan leaders, as they competed to outdo or gain power over one another, setting off a chain reaction which affected the landscape at a regional scale – hence the widespread occurrence of the Great Brigantian *landnam*. Those who controlled the hill-forts and occupied the defended hilltops of Swaledale may have had the power, intermittently at any rate, to concentrate and use certain resources – labour, military force, trade goods such as metals, perhaps a livestock surplus – in their own interests or those of their communities.

There are other large coaxial land division systems in the Pennines. They have been picked up in Wensleydale, for instance, and in Upper Wharfedale, near Conistone.[5] On the basis of the evidence so far – and I admit that it could be better – I believe that the large coaxial systems of Swaledale were probably laid out in the middle of the Iron Age; the Reeth system may be somewhat older. Part of the reason for suggesting a late prehistoric date for these land division systems is that, on the dalesides, Romano-British settlements and fields seem to be fitted into them – and on that basis the coaxials should be early Roman at least. It is also significant, I think, that the coaxial field system on Harkerside stops about 400 yards (c.400m) short of the hill-fort of Maiden Castle, as if to respect the space immediately around it; if that interpretation is correct, it would probably imply an Iron Age date for the Harkerside system.

In our research area, the difference between the archaeology of the farmland and the archaeology of the moors is not just a matter of surface appearances. In the farmland, quite a number of settlement sites can still be seen on the ground

- or spotted from distant vantage points such as the road above Harkerside Place, or between Reeth and Healaugh. Cut into the hillsides are groups of 'house-platforms' – circular, ovoid or rectangular – and larger, roughly circular or ovoid 'settlement-platforms', sometimes containing several platforms for buildings. These settlement-platforms were not simply open terraces; in some places there is evidence that walls ran along their front edges. The best-preserved sites are usually found in the areas least favoured for medieval cultivation – so they tend to be on the more steeply sloping land, for example to the north-east of Healaugh, and just across the river, on the steep slopes around Ivy House. A very good example of a large settlement-platform, with some old field-banks attached to it, can be seen by looking south from Scabba Wath Bridge, between Healaugh and Feetham; as I have already argued, this was a wood pasture zone in the Middle Ages, and this must have helped to preserve the site.

FIGURE 9.5. View from Reeth School, showing aspects of the ancient landscape in Harkerside farmland (for more detailed description, see text).

One or two of the ancient settlement sites are square or rectangular in shape, and consist of a number of small enclosures; in some cases, this is because they have been fitted into a pre-existing rectangular field pattern. The ancient fields here are not well preserved over large areas, like the famous ones at Grassington in Upper Wharfedale;[6] it is not surprising to hear that Arthur Raistrick did not believe that there were early field systems in Swaledale. What happens is that we can pick out *fragments* of ancient field systems, like the ones at Scabba Wath, where there are small 'windows' of good preservation in individual closes. These fragments are quite diverse. A few of these old boundaries are curvilinear;

they may date from Bronze Age times, like the ones on the open moors. Some of them form fairly narrow 'strip-fields' running up and down the hill-slopes. They might be confused with the rather similar medieval strip-fields which are after all very common in our research area, especially between Reeth and Healaugh and below Harkerside. But the ancient strip-fields have clearly defined staggered or slightly 'scalloped' lynchets at their lower ends, against which soil accumulated – unlike their medieval successors, which tend to have longer, straighter boundaries at their lower edges. In any case the fact that Romano-British settlement sites are occasionally fitted into the upper ends of strip-fields ties the latter clearly into at least the earlier Roman period.

It is generally believed that the English medieval open-field system developed in the last couple of centuries before the Norman Conquest. It is not at all clear what preceded it; sometimes, as at Wharram Percy in East Yorkshire, it seems that some of the ridge and furrow was fitted into parcels laid out in Roman times.[7] In Swaledale, given that the Roman fields were defined by low walls – perhaps topped by hedges – any later farmers who were not inclined to fit their fields into those already in existence would be letting themselves in for a good deal of extra work. It is likely that some of the medieval strip-fields running up and down slope between Reeth and Healaugh, and below Harkerside, are based on Roman field systems.

A good deal of detailed analysis remains to be carried out on the archaeology of farmland in our research area. There is space here to mention some of the most significant characteristics of the most important elements of this complex, partially surviving 'ancient landscape'. There is a good deal to see on Harkerside, for example, if one surveys the daleside from just outside Reeth School (Fig. 9.5). One can look south-west and pick up the banks of medieval strip-fields in the field behind How Hill. In this field, one of these banks splits into two, showing how the medieval boundary first follows the ancient field-bank and then diverges from it – a fragment of 'chronological depth'. The east wall of the next field has a pronounced swerve in its course, about halfway along; here it has climbed on to part of an old bank surrounding a small, roughly circular enclosure. In good shadow conditions, one can often see what remains of the rest of this enclosure, and some rather ploughed-down curvilinear banks between it and How Hill.

Some 200 yards (c.200m) to the east of the extensive farm buildings of Harkerside Place is the former Plaintree Farm. A couple of fields further east, tucked in just below rising ground, a sort of grid pattern of small embanked enclosures can be seen in reasonable light conditions. We have done a more detailed survey of this area; our plan gives a good impression of the complexity of archaeological features in an area of good preservation (Fig. 9.6). These features are well preserved because they lie along the axis of the old Hercay; Plaintree Farm probably has a medieval ancestor. The pattern of archaeological survival is very different in Hercay's arable zone, which lay downslope and immediately to the north (field D on the plan). Modern fields A and B straddle an ancient settlement site, but there are also medieval features (a and b may well be medieval buildings). Further east, there is an irregular parcel of land which has largely determined the

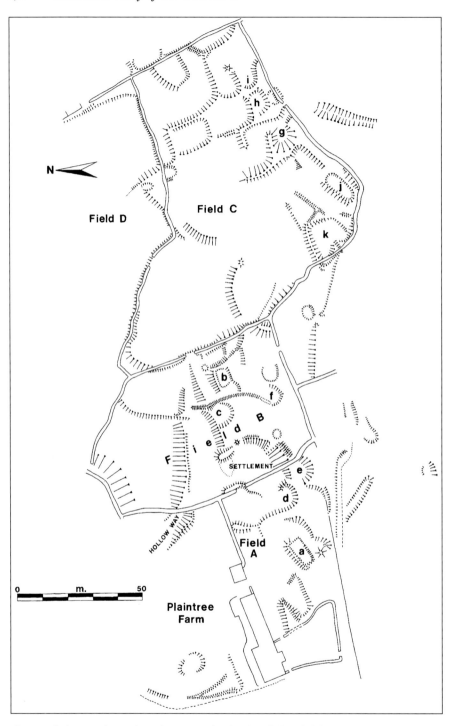

FIGURE 9.6. Plan of earthworks to the east of Plaintree Farm (for more detailed description, see text).

shape of the modern close here. At the back of this field are various building-platforms (i–k), associated with rectangular 'paddocks' which lie at the head of some long fields which evidently continued to the north, in field D, and share some layout principles with them. It seems that this settlement site has actually been set into the upper ends of the fields. This looks like a Romano-British settlement site, though there may be medieval features here too.

Further east, it is possible to pick out the westernmost of the Grinton-Fremington earthworks; just west of it, an old boundary bank can be seen, running uphill and converging on the earthwork. This is another case of chronological depth; the boundary bank must be earlier than the earthwork. The other earthwork, How Dyke as it was called in the Middle Ages,[8] lies 500 yards (c.500m) further east, and has exactly the same relationship with the old field layout. Between the western earthwork and another former farm at Whitbecks, a rather unusual settlement site is often visible from across the river – a series of long platforms set into the lower end of an ancient field. In the area to the west of Swale Hall, which was probably called Meldykes ('between the dykes') in the Middle Ages,[9] there are strip-fields and ridge and furrow. There are also ancient settlement sites here – a near-circular enclosure immediately west of Swale Hall, half-wrecked by fairly recent farm buildings, and a similar one about 200 yards (c. 200m) further west, in a modern field corner. It contains a couple of definite circular house-platforms and two or three further possible sites of buildings. Higher up the slope, and a little further west, is a cluster of small rectangular enclosures which probably represents a Romano-British settlement site, partly 'slighted', as landscape archaeologists say, by the linear earthwork to its west (Fig. 2.1). Quite a lot of the ancient landscape can also be observed from the rather dense network of public footpaths, though it is probably best to get an idea of the most visible sites from across the river first. There are also footpaths on the north bank of the Swale, between Reeth and Healaugh, but a quick initial look at this hillside is best taken from the road running west from Grinton. You need to stop in two places – just west of Bleak House, and then above Ivy House. To the west of Reeth, the flights of magnificent strip lynchets have destroyed much of the ancient landscape. But there are very well-preserved archaeological sites in a zone which starts just below Riddings (not to be confused with the conspicuous Riddings Farm further east) and runs between the next two abandoned farms to the west, continuing at a fairly high level into the fields to the north-east of Healaugh (Fig. 9.7).

Coming downhill from Riddings is a strikingly straight wall which serves as a boundary for four fields (Fig. 9.8). At the top right-hand corner of the 'south-east' field of this quartet are two house-platforms ('a' on Fig. 9.8) – the western one is particularly noticeable – and below them are some small squarish enclosures, fringed to the west by a hollow-way, which seems to have been blocked off near the top. This hollow-way gave access to an ancient settlement site at the bottom of the 'northwest' field, with circular house-platforms – apparently four of them – close together in the eastern half of a platform set on an old landslip ('b' on Fig. 9.8). The hollow-way also goes *past* the settlement, into a funnel-shaped outlet just above the settlement, containing a (later?) house-platform.

The next field going west contains two house-platforms ('c' on Fig. 9.8), each in its own small enclosure – or perhaps placed in a pre-existing enclosure? – and there may be others. They may have been outliers of a group of roughly

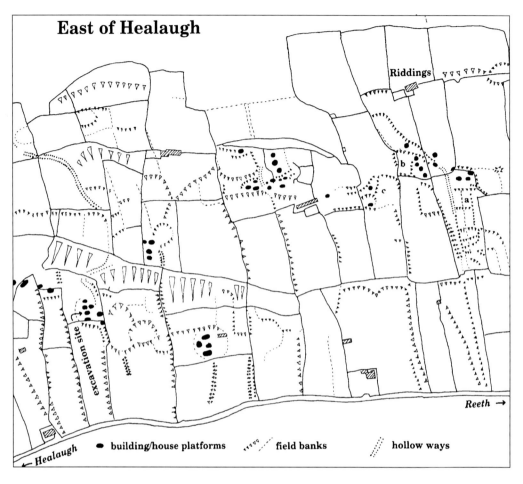

East of Healaugh

Riddings

Reeth →

← Healaugh

● building/house platforms   field banks   hollow ways

FIGURE 9.7. Plan of the daleside between Riddings and Healaugh, showing sites illustrated in text.

FIGURE 9.8. Ancient settlements east of Riddings, on the daleside between Reeth and Healaugh (for plan, see Figure 9.7.). There are two house-platforms just above 'a', and other settlements below 'b' and to the left of 'c'. See text for further comment.

circular platforms most of which are located in the next field but one going west, immediately above the next abandoned farm. (The description which follows can be followed by reference to the plan on Fig. 9.7). There are five or six just above the farm, and three in a squarish enclosure which may have started life as a prehistoric field. One of these is large and circular and almost too good to be true; one wonders if it has been reused in more recent times, for example as a haystack base. Just north-west of the farm's western end, an old track gives access to a well-defined settlement, with perhaps five building-platforms crowded into their own small platform-enclosure, tucked below the massive lynchet of an almost square ancient field. But the narrow track which gave access to this settlement also went past it, into a broad 'droveway' between two fields. Looking over the modern wall at the top of this droveway, into a narrow walled sling which once held a belt of conifers, it is impossible to see anything definite. But immediately beyond the sling, on the moor, there is a short and narrow walled lane, part of the Healaugh coaxial system. It lines up very well with the droveway, and is a good piece of evidence for the integration of the boundaries in present-day farmland with those on the moors. But the area which we have just looked at also shows that not all the daleside fields can simply be regarded as fitting into coaxial systems. Some of them are small and sometimes irregular. They are fragmentary, but it is quite likely that, like their equivalents on the moors, they predate the coaxial boundaries.

Going west, the last abandoned farm is high up, to the north-west of the area which we have just been looking at. Two fields below this farm is another ancient enclosure, which has plough-ridges running right over it and a robber-trench along its southern and eastern sides; just west of it there are at least four house-platforms (Fig. 9.9). At the foot of the steep slope below the

FIGURE 9.9. A group of ancient settlements on the daleside to the east of Healaugh. Note the old field-banks underlying the pattern of modern walls.

ploughed-over enclosure, there are two other enclosures. One of them is the most conspicuous settlement-platform one could imagine; it is quite small, and has the smooth surface of a green on the golf course from hell. It has probably been reused in recent years but there is no reason to doubt that it is ancient; there are traces of a wall along its front edge, and old field-banks run up to it. In the field to the east is a larger enclosure which is not quite so easy to see. It lies in front of quite a large field-barn and contains several house-platforms. Finally, there are two fields to the west of the one which contains the 'golf course' platform. A deep hollow-way runs up to the south-east corner of the upper one of these fields, whose interior is mostly concealed from the south by a large ash tree. The eastern bank of this hollow-way swings back and joins the 'golf course' platform, while the hollow-way's western bank runs down the hillside, just west of a modern field-wall.

These three settlements lie side by side on a steep hillside, just below an even sharper rise in the ground (Fig. 9.9). Two of them are on a natural bench, but the westernmost settlement is a series of ovoid platforms cut into a considerable slope; the roof of one building would have been on the same level as the floor of another. Presumably when this group of settlements was established, the better sites further east were already taken. This seems good evidence that in the late Iron Age and Romano-British periods the daleside was densely settled. The same conclusion might be drawn from the fact that building platforms have also been cut into the correspondingly steep slope just across the river, near Ivy House.

The appearance of the old field-banks close to these settlements owes something to geology and the effects of soil creep and landslip. But there is something coherent, almost familiar, about this fragment of ancient landscape within the modern fields. The settlements have coaxial boundaries running downslope from them. But there are also three coaxial boundaries – two just east and just west of our three settlements, and the third running between the central and the eastern settlements – which run *past* the zone of habitation. The central one ran up the steep bank above the settlements, to meet the settlement on the shoulder above, while the eastern one must also have climbed this bank. So there was a larger coaxial framework, into which the smaller fields just below the settlements have apparently been fitted.

The westernmost settlement is approached by a short length of hollow-way which conforms in part to the coaxial layout. Our excavations have shown that this route continued as a cobbled track running up the eastern side of the settlement, almost certainly between the buildings, and probably climbing the steep bank above by the ramp which is followed by a modern track. It may have continued as a hollow-way leading north-west from the top of the bank here. This makes the Healaugh settlements comparable to those further east, where, as we have seen, there are two clear-cut cases of trackways coming uphill, giving access to settlements, and then carrying on past them up the hillside. The implication is that the pattern of land-use required access to the lower ground – meadows beside the Swale, perhaps? – and to the subdivided pastures

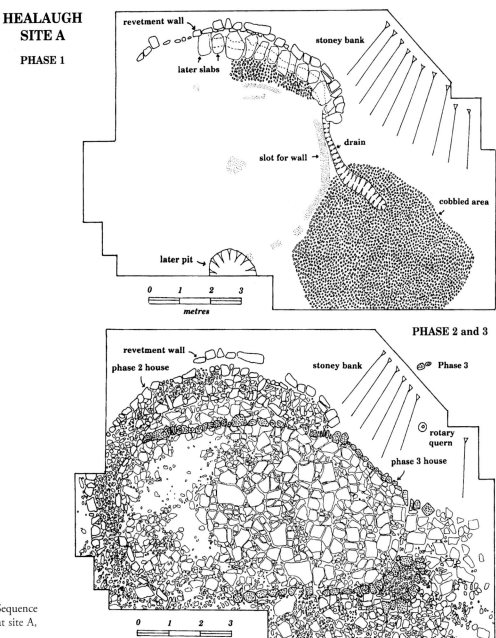

HEALAUGH SITE A

PHASE 1

revetment wall

later slabs

stoney bank

slot for wall →

drain

cobbled area

later pit →

0 1 2 3
metres

PHASE 2 and 3

revetment wall

phase 2 house

stoney bank

Phase 3

rotary quern

phase 3 house

0 1 2 3
metres

FIGURE 9.10. Sequence of settlement at site A, Healaugh.

further upslope. Although no comparable hollow-ways have been identified in the Harkerside farmland, we have already noted that 'droveways' integrated into the coaxial system just east of Maiden Castle provided access to the open pastures beyond the Harkerside coaxial system (Fig. 9.4).

We have excavated one of the house-platforms in the westernmost settlement (Figs 9.10, 9.11). In its present form it is ovoid, like its neighbours, but we

FIGURE 9.11. Healaugh site A: house-platform at an early stage of excavation, with others above it.

FIGURE 9.12. Healaugh site A: the circular house.

discovered that the first house on it was circular and stood on the western half of the platform. It was made of timber, its wall of upright planks set in what archaeologists call a 'ring groove', with an efficient drain running round the back of the house, covered with slabs. To the east there must have been a small working area, with a broad, heavily worn pathway leading to the building. The timber house was succeeded by another circular house, but this time one with a well-built stone wall, and stone paving in the interior, which was 20 feet (6m) in diameter (Fig. 9.12). This house would presumably have had a conical thatched

FIGURE 9.13. Healaugh site A: the ovoid house.

roof, rising from a ring beam on the top of the wall. The worn-down area to the east of the house was carefully metalled with small cobblestones.

Then came a dramatic change. The circular house was converted into an ovoid house, and extended to the east, over the cobbled area which covered the rest of the platform (Fig. 9.13). This area was now covered with paving slabs, and a wall-face was built to revet the rear edge of the platform and form the rear wall of the house. Most of the wall of the circular house was dismantled; a little of it was reused, and at the back a section of it was masked by the new back wall of the ovoid house. This ovoid or elliptical building measured about 30 by 16½ feet (9.3m by 5.1m) internally; its roof would have been supported by timber pillars set on 'pad-stones' (indistinguishable from flooring slabs) and locked together by the wooden roof structure. The doorway was at the east end, with the door swivelling in a shallow rebate in the surface of a paving slab. Probably the change from circular to ovoid house took no longer than the time needed to carry out the conversion. We can see from the pattern of some of the paving slabs that some of them originally floored the circular house and remained in place after the conversion. Also, the walls of both the circular and the ovoid house were built in 'post and panel' style – roughly square slabs set on end alternated with panels of dry walling. There may have been more of a break between the timber house and the circular stone house, however, since the two phases were separated by a pit dug near the front edge of the platform.

The floor of the ovoid house and the wall of the circular house contained fragments of beehive querns, and there was also a more primitive saddle quern on the paved floor (phase uncertain) which was either reused as a paving slab or abandoned when still in use as a quern – it was impossible to tell. The pottery from the site has still to be studied in detail, but an expert tells us that it runs from the very late Iron Age to second-century Roman and perhaps later. So it looks as if the early Roman period in Swaledale saw the conversion of some traditional late prehistoric round-houses, timber or stone-footed, into ovoid houses. Now that we know about this, it may be possible to look more closely at some of the better-preserved ovoid 'house-platforms' and see whether evidence for this conversion can be seen on the surface.

Evidence from our Healaugh site also suggests that during the 'ovoid house' phase, that is from the early Roman period, the inhabitants of the Healaugh settlement may have let the wall of their enclosure fall into disrepair. As I mentioned earlier, a trench through the bank to the west of the house-platform which we excavated revealed a well-built wall, with a core of small stones and carefully constructed faces (Fig. 9.1., right). This wall, together with the rather straight wall to the east of the houses, probably formed an enclosure for the settlement. I prefer this hypothesis to the idea that these walls defined some kind of small (but very sloping!) field, abandoned when the house-platforms were cut into it. The reason for believing that the ovoid houses were 'in the open' is that part of the western enclosure wall has been removed by means of a 'robber trench'. But this does not display the freshness of a robber trench made in the last three or four centuries; this is an *ancient* robber trench, the kind which is hard to see until one gets one's eye in. And what is more, the lowest of the ovoid platforms here seems to have transgressed on to the line of the enclosure wall, as it curved east to form the southern boundary of the settlement. In other words, the settlement was once enclosed by a wall, which was later robbed and built over, probably in phase 3.

There are of course numerous 'unenclosed' house-platforms in our research area which would echo the situation at Healaugh – as well as ovoid platforms apparently *within* walled enclosures. The number of platforms on steep hillsides and the presence of 'overspill' platforms just *outside* settlements make it tempting to suggest that in Roman times population density was relatively high – which accords with a good deal of evidence from other parts of Britannia. Sometimes this Romano-British population peak is explained by the presence of the Roman army, or the growth of a market economy in peaceful conditions, but in Swaledale it looks as if the population was already building up in the latter part of the Iron Age, if not before. It would be nice to think that we could measure this in some way – but it would be premature, on the basis of one excavation, to assume that all circular houses are early – 'survivals' from the Iron Age – and all ovoid ones are early to mid-Roman. Sampling enough sites to make generalisations would be expensive and time-consuming. But somewhere in the Pennines, such work should be attempted.

The methods of landscape archaeology should allow us to do a good deal more work in advance of such excavations – using the areas where preservation is best to work out what is typical, what is the range of variation within these ancient settlements and field systems, what these farmers were trying to achieve in terms of where they lived and the areas they were trying to farm. The landscape archaeologist has to tease out the details, looking at the dalesides in the best light conditions, taking photographs, making sketch-maps and then ground plans and then going back and trying to make sense of it all in terms of sequence and pattern. There is a lot more work to be done here!

Notes

1. Fleming 1987.
2. Spratt 1993, figs 47, 50.
3. Honeyman 1986; Bannister 1985; Spratt 1982; Hicks, 1971; Turner 1979; Bartley 1975.
4. Hayes *et al.* 1980; Heslop 1988; Spratt 1993, 143–6.
5. King 1985.
6. Raistrick 1938.
7. Beresford and Hurst 1990.
8. Fleming 1994, 28.
9. NYCRO Grinton Tithe Map (1841).

CHAPTER TEN

History and the Swaledale Landscape

Archaeologically speaking, Swaledale has been something of a Cinderella. The archaeology of the North York Moors, just across the Vale of Mowbray, is quite well understood, thanks to John Atkinson, Frank Elgee, Don Spratt and Ian Simmons among others.[1] The work of Arthur Raistrick and Alan King has introduced us to the rich archaeology of Upper Wharfedale and Ribblesdale, further south.[2] Dennis Coggins has given us a good account of the archaeology of Upper Teesdale, to the north.[3] But when Tim Laurie and I first started working together in 1983, we were entering territory which was virtually unknown. It is true that there were document-based histories of Swaledale – a short one by Edmund Cooper, and a longer one collated by Fieldhouse and Jennings.[4] But there was not much to read about the history of the landscape, despite the fact that this is one of the best-loved dales in northern England.

Having worked on the landscape history of Swaledale, I feel rather like the film director who made a film about Paris and called it *One or Two Things that I Know about Her*. In this book I have explained how I have got to know 'one or two things' about Swaledale – using a mixture of fieldwork and documentary work, applying approaches and insights often derived from elsewhere. It has been hard work, but it has also been rewarding and enriching. Odd memories return sometimes; I vividly recall lying awake in a tent under the trees, at the dawning of a beautiful early summer's morning, listening to the owl and the cuckoo calling at the same time. Sometimes I got up at dawn, to try to catch the very longest shadows, hoping that a new site would reveal itself or that one known already might appear literally in a new light. To study the past in one locality can easily become an obsession. It is tempting to become deeply involved with some special area, perhaps one as small as a single parish. The methods and approaches required for studies of local history are quite well known by now. Even Ambridge, the mythical west Midland setting of our much-followed radio series *The Archers* ('an everyday story of country folk') has its very own published history.[5] It comes complete with maps and facsimiles of documents. It is all too plausible in its grasp of the fundamentals of 'mainstream' English landscape history, although it has to be said that the radiocarbon dates obtained for the earliest church at Ambridge, which came out after the book was published, caused controversy in archaeological circles!

In a sense, we can now almost research and write local studies in our sleep. Sooner or later, most parishes and regions in Britain will have their chroniclers. These studies will often be very detailed; after all, it is deep local knowledge which gives their authors their authority. But there is a danger that these studies will become neat little packages. They will literally go over much the same kind of ground. It is the *place* which is central to the story, the place that is being celebrated. Writing about a well-loved place becomes like writing a love-letter, in which it is important to insist that the beloved is unique and special. Yet the reality is otherwise.

In local studies, the familiar cast of characters usually put in their appearance. Words like 'tradition' and 'heritage' soon come to seem like meaningless compliments. Should we not try to get away from the local study as love-letter, and try to write about the conflicts, the uncertainties, the paradoxes, the unfinished and the unfolding – in short, to convey some sense of an ongoing relationship between researcher and landscape, between the present and the past? And might not this relationship be stormy, difficult, ambiguous at times?

In the archaeology of landscape, no-one will ever establish the limits of what is observable, of the connections that may be made, of the questions to be asked. Sooner or later some archaeological excavation, perhaps undertaken as a relatively small-scale 'rescue' project, will unearth something which will make us rethink our standard assumptions. At the ruined church of Wharram Percy on the Yorkshire Wolds, the best-known deserted medieval village in England, the five phases which were picked up by architectural historians became thirteen once the archaeologists had completed their excavations there.[6] Before our excavation at Healaugh, we could not have guessed that an ovoid 'house-platform' had once carried a circular building.

To be a landscape archaeologist, then, is like being in an artist's workshop, in which completed projects (perhaps covered in dust) jostle with works still in the midst of the creative struggle, sketches and rough-outs which may or may not come to fruition, and stimulating things brought in from outside. There is no sense of completion; even the finished works can be looked at in new ways – if not by the original artist, then by the critics. But it is precisely this sense of the potential for further creation which makes the enterprise exciting. I believe that it is mainly archaeology, in the landscape and under the ground, which gives local studies their cutting edge. So in the nature of the case, this book cannot be a neat package. In the space which remains to me I will try to discuss 'the state of the art', as far as the history of the Swaledale landscape is concerned.

So what about the unfinished – apart from the details of the 'ancient' landscape'? We still lack a history of the river, the 'turbulent one' itself. Those who like to gaze across the valley from the roadside just west of Reeth will have understood something of the restlessness of the Swale, as it toys with the notion of creating an oxbow lake. There are quite a number of places in Swaledale – between Reeth and Marrick, for instance – where one can observe old river-channels, and places where the Swale has snaked across its flood-plain and scoured the edges. With the help of environmental archaeologists and physical geographers, archaeologists have come to understand how the sediments in river valleys may record the work of humans who have lived upstream – changing run-off patterns by opening up the woods, increasing the sediment load by cultivating the hillsides, sometimes altering the behaviour of the river itself and the conditions of existence for people living further downstream.

In Swaledale, such a study ought to pick up the effects of lead-mining – not least the practice of hushing,[7] the deliberate and dramatic downhill release of water previously accumulated behind a dam, in order to get rid of overburden and expose the potential for mineral extraction visible in the underlying rock. The relationship between sediment depth and the extent of upstream clearance and cultivation is not necessarily a simple one, especially when it is complicated by mining activities; but we ought to be able to get some idea of the intensity of cultivation. It seems particularly important to establish this for the late prehistoric and Romano-British periods. We need to understand how much difference, if any, 'the coming of the Romans' made to the scale and character of local agriculture, and how far major economic changes in the region during the late Roman period affected life in the Pennine dales. We also need to understand more about 'the Great Brigantian *landnam*', the mid-Iron Age 'clearance episode' which seems to be detectable not only in northern England but also elsewhere. Ever since the 1920s, when Arthur Raistrick started to discuss the field systems of the Pennine dales, we have never been quite sure how to apportion the visible field boundaries and settlement sites between and within the late prehistoric and Romano-British periods. Martin Millett has recently explained how the Roman government perpetuated and built upon the local social and political setup whenever it could, and certainly it seems that in Swaledale the basic structure of what was to become the densely occupied Roman landscape was probably already in being when the valley became part of Britannia.

Mention of sediments reminds me that I have hardly discussed lead-mining, which has had a serious impact on the appearance of the landscape, the actions of the rich and powerful, and the working lives of many of the people of Swaledale (Fig. 10.1). Farming and woodland management, for instance, must have been closely linked with the demands of lead production. In the case of woodland management it is hard to understand the balance between coppicing and pollarding for fodder, timber and firewood around the farm, and the commercial production of wood and charcoal for the lead-smelters. There is a good deal of work to do on the archaeological landscapes of the areas where lead was once mined and smelted. Archaeologists are often pessimistic about the chances of picking up traces of 'early' mining, believing that they will have been obliterated by the larger-scale mining of more recent centuries. But that has not been our experience in Wales, where several prehistoric mines have been confidently identified.[8] Locating old mines is often a question of persistence, of knowing what to look for, and exercising a certain amount of lateral thinking.

We also need to understand more about the development of houses and other buildings in Swaledale (Fig. 10.2). Fortunately, these are the subject of a study being carried out by Barry Harrison and a group of local people, so we should soon know more about it. 'Vernacular architecture', as it is called, is an area of rather specialised knowledge, and its practitioners have to persuade householders to let them indoors. Only a thorough internal inspection will allow the specialist to reconstruct a house's history.

In the mid-sixteenth century, John Leland, writing about Richmond and Grinton, said: 'the houses of these two tounes be partly slatid, partly thakkid', so some stone slates were already being quarried then.[9] Two hundred years later, many of the houses and the field-barns in Swaledale would still have been thatched. A few thatched buildings survived into the age of photography; they could be seen in the early twentieth century at Hurst, and a thatched barn at Shaw lasted into the 1960s.[10]

Sometimes evidence for change can be seen from outside. Farmhouses may have had their roofs raised, or new window and door openings put in, but it is often possible to work out what has happened. Sometimes a house which looks nineteenth century may betray signs of a more interesting history, in the form of an old chimney stack rising half or one third of the way along the roof-ridge. Frequently, dressed stone window surrounds, with their carved mouldings, will have been reused. You may observe that mullions have been removed to make the windows more fashionable and let in more light, or that stones with carved mouldings are no longer in their original positions. Raising the roof, or redesigning the hall and stairway, often forced the owners of a house to make further modifications; the result is a display of windows in odd positions, at various different levels, in heterogeneous styles and sizes.

The relationship between house structure and family structure is also worth thinking about. In some places there are long 'rows' of cottages, most notably perhaps at Lodge Green. According to Barry Harrison, there is a little physical evidence which suggests that the concept of the long 'row' may go back to the Middle Ages – although not, of course, the standing structures which we see today. There is a medieval name which supports this idea; one of the settlements mentioned in 1297–8 was called 'Ratonrawe'.[11] This was almost certainly the settlement mentioned as 'next Arclegarth' in 1293; it may have been the place now simply called Raw. The name itself suggests why the place may not have survived, or was given another name; it means 'Rat Row'.[12] At Low Row itself, it is possible that the existence of a long, compartmented 'row' of houses led to the old 'Wra' name (meaning 'the nook') being understood to mean 'row' – so 'Low Row' made sense in those terms. The place-name 'Raw' also gave rise to a distinctive Swaledale surname; there are still Raws in Cwm Ystwyth, in mid-Wales, descendants of a locally famous family of mine-captains whose ancestor left Swaledale in the early 19th century.

In other parts of Yorkshire, we know that the frameworks of medieval buildings were based on two or more pairs of timber 'crucks' rising from low walls or pad-stones. In principle, any number of pairs of crucks could be raised, to form a long house subdivided into several bays, on much the same principle as the long peat stores constructed at Surrender and Old Gang mills. Such a

FIGURE 10.1. A reminder of Swaledale's industrial past in Gunnerside Gill.

multi-bayed structure would have been appropriate for an extended family which practised partible inheritance – or in a place where incoming groups of miners needed to find lodgings. If such structures existed, we would not expect to find them in planned villages like Walburn, but rather in places with more space – less formal settlements, strung along the contour, such as Old Healaugh or Herthay (Harkerside), and settlements clustered around informal greens, such as Low Row, Blades or Lodge Green. If rows were divided into several different tenancies, one might expect to see each 'bay' (that is, each cottage in the row) being repaired and rebuilt piecemeal, so that eventually one would end up, in one or two places, with the nineteenth-century row which we see

FIGURE 10.2. Low
Oxnop: a fine late
seventeenth-century
house.

today. On hillsides, we might expect that the platforms originally taken up by
these rows would now have farms and ancillary buildings standing on them.
It's a plausible theory; proving it would be quite a challenge!

I have not mentioned the numerous old lime-kilns in Swaledale, which are
currently under study. It would be interesting to work on boundary markers
– hurrocks or curracks, standards, stone men and bounders, especially those
which follow the great watersheds to the north and south. As artefacts and as
preservers of names, these boundary markers may be revealing (Fig. 10.3). Their
very names are evocative – Snowden Man, Whitestone in Fellend, Grey Yaud,
Little Punchard Standard, Seavy Man...

These are some areas of landscape study where research might profitably be
undertaken in the future. But where are we now, after the rather patchy history of
the Swaledale landscape which emerges from these pages? Does this sort of research
involve anything more than simply 'reading' the local landscape, reconstructing
a series of stage-sets for actors long departed, and revealing intimate historical
secrets about particular places? The history of every place is special, of course, and

worth finding out about, but no place is an island (least of all islands themselves!). There are all sorts of links to the outside world. This is not just because of the connections made by roads and rivers, and the comings and goings of different people – the possibilities created by geography and history. The most interesting links are created because every place is eloquent in one way or another about historical processes and offers us opportunities of interpreting them in different ways. Local landscape histories should carry wider meanings.

Swaledale's landscape history echoes the experience of England in general. Before the landscape of walled closes and field-barns which dominates Swaledale today, there were apparently two periods when the population peaked and the land was intensively occupied – in Roman times and in the later Middle Ages. Frameworks for systems of planned land division were probably set up in the middle Iron Age, around 300 BC, if not earlier. In the Roman period the landscape must have looked as 'settled' as that of today, if not more so, with broad walls running up and down the dalesides, perhaps topped with elm hedges, and interrupted at frequent intervals by walled enclosures containing groups of ovoid huts, with others close by, each on its own terrace. In the later Middle Ages, the daleside landscape must have been more open, but hedges and walls were probably already beginning to appear among the ranes and *dales* in arable fields and hay meadows, and around the earliest intakes in the cow pastures and on the edges of the moors. Wood pasture was in retreat, but groups of pollards survived in most old wood pasture areas. Townships had formed, some based on planned settlements (especially in Lower Swaledale), others drawing together scattered farmsteads.

FIGURE 10.3. Swaledale stone. *Left*: Kisdon Standard, a typical hurrock; *centre*: a dressed boundary stone; *right*: the stoop for the gate between Low Cow Pasture and Little Rowleth Pasture – note the evidence for several rehangings.

By this time the commons were closely managed and regulated, but the system was under siege from within and without. Moorland commons have survived, and some common cow pastures lasted for a long time; as we have seen, rights of way dating from before the enclosure of the dalesides persisted well, and so did ekes and pounds and other features of more collective organisation. Many place-names evidently survived for hundreds of years, including 'alternative' names which should really have become redundant in the wake of historical change. Oral tradition and 'folk customs' are not just randomly surviving curiosities; folk versions of history are often rooted in political and social pressures and tensions. Some of the more persistent survivals of names and traditions must have been generated by political attitudes – resistance to distant landlords, rivalry between communities and families, maintenance of a collective ethos which some must have followed more loyally or insistently than others. For various reasons, in this book I have usually chosen to write about communities, rather than the property rights and financial relationships of individuals and families. This is not, I hope, because I have an idealistic view of the medieval 'community' or wish to downplay the role of money, markets, enterprise and power politics. It is rather that I am interested in how small-scale communities behave and regulate themselves, particularly in the context of various threats to their livelihoods – demographic and ecological problems as well as social competition and predation. Perhaps because I am a prehistorian and would like to take the long view, for me this is a good part of what landscape history is about.

It is difficult now to think back to a more relaxed commons phase, earlier in the Middle Ages, when interdependence was more important than competition. But if we have to contemplate the Roman period or the later Middle Ages, when land came under pressure, we also have to envisage times when the landscape was much wilder and more wooded, when it was clearances rather than woods which stood out and were identified by name. It is the names of places and features well away from main settlements which evoke these times most vividly In the Swale valley above Muker, we have to envisage the eagle's nest in Arngill, and just below, on the valley floor, the place where deer played – Hartlakes (perhaps there was a mud wallow here, in a flood channel of the river). 'Cocklakes' may have been where capercaillies enacted their remarkable courtship performance. Cranes may once have danced at Trangholme, which is also in the Swale valley above Muker; a little further up, names like Catrake and Cat's Hole remind us that the 'true yellow wild cat' was only exterminated in Yorkshire in the mid-nineteenth century.[13] Glead Gill, above Grinton, must once have been the haunt of the kite. Owlands, in the improved land on Marrick Moor, was once Ulveland – the name refers to wolves, and probably the same applies to Uldale, in the far west of Swaledale. The name 'Gildersty' which crops up occasionally among field-names – it occurs just across the river from Rowleth Wood, for instance – means the snare-path. People named the land after animals and birds which their descendants would later hunt to extinction.

These names are evocative. But there is no escaping the fact that the centuries between Romans and Normans are difficult to work with. The patterns and frameworks provided by names and boundaries are a limited substitute for a landscape rich in archaeology – especially the relationships which can be studied when extensive field systems are involved – or a land copiously documented in written archives. And the fact that we are dealing with named peoples with familiar, distinctive images – 'Celts', Anglo-Saxons' or 'Norse' – may deceive us into taking too much for granted. But nevertheless, these periods of 'wildscape' are worth thinking about, not least because they may provide quite good analogies for those prehistoric periods when farming, herding and hunting took place in a largely wooded landscape.

We might imagine Swaledale's landscape history, then, in terms of a double cycle, from prehistoric wildscape to late Roman fieldscape, then a reversion to Dark Age wildscape followed in turn by the later medieval fieldscape and the pattern of parishes and townships which has formed the framework for today's landscape. But we can only accept such a cycle by setting aside aside our profound ignorance of what happened in the post-Roman period (the 'Dark Ages') in terms of depopulation, plague, woodland regeneration, immigration, emigration, demography and the development of new social and political identities. And in any case, this double cycle is an abstraction. Wildscape and fieldscape will be more interesting as concepts if they help us to think about the true subjects of landscape history – people. Woven into the fabric of the Swaledale landscape are themes of competition and interdependence, power and powerlessness, the ethos of independence and of the collective, the determination to impose and the will to resist. The journey through the long valley of Swaledale, from Richmond to Hollow Mill Cross, may generate a set of two-dimensional photographs. But as I hope this book has demonstrated, landscape's most interesting dimension is its history.

Notes

1. Atkinson 1891; Elgee 1930; Spratt 1993; Simmons and others in Spratt 1993, 15–50.
2. Raistrick and Holmes 1962; King 1970, 1985.
3. Coggins 1986.
4. Cooper 1973; Fieldhouse and Jennings 1978.
5. Aldridge and Tregorran 1981.
6. Beresford and Hurst 1990.
7. Millett 1990.
8. Crew and Crew 1989; Dutton and Fasham 1994.
9. Toulmin Smith 1906–10, vol. IV, 26.
10. Pontefract and Hartley 1939, 203; Fieldhouse and Jennings 1978, plate 6.
11. McDonnell 1990.
12. Smith 1967, vol. I, 118.
13. Bogg 1908, 645.

Bibliography

Addy, S. O. (1913) *Church and Manor*, London.

Alcock, L. (1987) *Economy, Society and Warfare among the Britons and Saxons*, Cardiff.

Aldridge, J. and Tregorran, J. (1981) *Ambridge: An English Village through the Ages*, Borchester.

Armstrong, A. M., Mawer, A., Stenton, R. M. and B. Dickinson, B., (1950) *The Place-Names of Cumberland*, Cambridge.

Armstrong, T. (1952) *Adam Brunskill*, London.

Ashcroft, M. Y. ed. (1984) *Documents Relating to the Swaledale Estates of Lord Wharton in the Sixteenth and Seventeenth Centuries*, Northallerton.

Ashcroft, M. Y. and Hill, M. A. eds (1980) *Bilsdale Surveys 1637–1851*, Northallerton.

Atkinson, J. C. (1891) *Forty Years in a Moorland Parish*, London.

Atkinson, J. C. ed. (1894) *North Riding Records*, London.

Bannister, A. J. (1985) *The Vegetational and Archaeological History of Rombald's Moor, West Yorkshire*. Unpublished Ph.D. thesis, University of Leeds

Barfield, L. and Hodder, M. (1987) 'Burnt mounds as saunas, and the prehistory of bathing', *Antiquity*, **61**, 370–9.

Barnatt, J. (1987) 'Bronze Age settlement on the East Moors of Derbyshire and South Yorkshire', *Proceedings of the Prehistoric Society*, **53**, 393–418.

Barnatt, J. and Smith, K. (1997) *English Heritage Book of the Peak District*, London.

Bartley, D. (1975) 'Pollen analytical evidence for prehistoric forest clearance in the upland area west of Rishworth, West Yorkshire', *New Phytologist*, **74**, 375–81.

Bassett, S. (1989). 'In search of the origins of Anglo-Saxon kingdoms', in S. Bassett ed. *The Origins of Anglo-Saxon Kingdoms*, Leicester.

Beresford, M. and Hurst, J. (1990) *The English Heritage Book of Wharram Percy*, London.

Bogg, E. (1908) *Richmondshire*, London.

Bradley, R. (1993) *Altering the Earth*, Edinburgh.

Bradley, R. (1994) 'Symbols and signposts – understanding the prehistoric petroglyphs of the British Isles', in C. Renfrew and E. Zubrow eds *The Ancient Mind: Elements of Cognitive Archaeology*, Cambridge, 95–106.

Bradley, R. (1997) *Rock Art and the Prehistory of Atlantic Europe*, London.

Britton, E. (1977) *The Community of the Vill*, Toronto.

Brown, W. ed. (1896) *Yorkshire Lay Subsidies*, Leeds.

Buck, S. J. (1989) 'Cultural theory and management of common property resources', *Human Ecology*, **17**, 101–16.

Buckley, V. ed. (1991) *Burnt Offerings: International Contributions to Burnt Mound Archaeology*, Dublin.

Clarkson, C. (1821) *The History and Antiquities of Richmond in the County of York*, Richmond.

Clarkson, T. J. (1993) 'Richmond and Catraeth', *Cambrian Medieval Celtic Studies*, **26**, 15–20.

Clay, C. T. ed. (1935) *Early Yorkshire Charters*, Leeds.

Coggins, D. (1986) *Upper Teesdale: The Archaeology of a North Pennine Valley.* Oxford.

Coggins, D., Laurie, T. and R. Young (1990) 'The Late Upper Palaeolithic and Mesolithic of the North Penine dales in the light of recent fieldwork', in C. Bonsall ed. *The Mesolithic in Europe*, Edinburgh, 164–74.

Cole, J. W. and Wolf, E. R. (1974) *The Hidden Frontier: Ecology and Ethnicity in an Alpine Valley*, New York.

Cooper, E. (1948) *Muker: The Story of a Yorkshire Parish*, Clapham.

Cooper, E. (1960) *Men of Swaledale*, Clapham.

Cooper, E. (1973) *A History of Swaledale*, Clapham.

Cowley, W. (1993) *Old Stones, Old Fields, Old Farms: A History of the Snilesworth Area* (privately printed).

Crew, P. and Crew, S. eds (1989) *Early Mining in the British Isles*, Blaenau Ffestiniog.

Cronon, W. (1983) *Changes in the Land: Indians, Colonists and the Ecology of New England*, New York.

Degerbøl, I. M. (1961) 'On a find of a preboreal domestic dog (*Canis familiaris*) from Star Carr, Yorkshire, with remarks on other domestic dogs', *Proceedings of the Prehistoric Society*, **27**, 35–55.

Denyer, S. (1991) *Traditional Buildings and Life in the Lake District*, London.

Dutton, P. A. and Fasham, P. J. (1994) 'Prehistoric copper mining on the Great Orme, Llandudno, Gwynedd', *Proceedings of the Prehistoric Society*, **60**, 245–86.

Edwards, J. F. and Hindle, B. P. (1991) 'The transportation system of medieval England and Wales', *Journal of Historical Geography*, **17 (2)**, 126.

Ekwall, E. (1960) *The Concise Oxford Dictionary of English Place-*Names, Oxford.

Elgee, F. (1930) *Early Man in North-East Yorkshire*, Gloucester.

Everitt, A. (1986) *Continuity and Colonization: The Evolution of Kentish Settlement*, Leicester.

Farrer, W. ed. (1942) *Early Yorkshire Charters*, Leeds.

Faull, M. (1974) 'Roman and Anglian settlement patterns in Yorkshire', *Northern History*, **9**, 1–25.

Faull, M. L. (1981) 'The Roman period [and] The post-Roman British period', in M. L. Faull and S. A. Moorhouse, eds *West Yorkshire: An Archaeological Survey to A.D. 1500*, Wakefield.

Faull, M. L. and Moorhouse, S. A. eds (1981) *West Yorkshire: An Archaeological Survey to A.D. 1500*, Wakefield.

Faull, M. L. and Stinson, M. eds (1986) *Domesday Book: Yorkshire*, Chichester.

Fieldhouse, R. and Jennings, B. (1978) *A History of Richmond and Swaledale*, Chichester.

Fleming, A. (1987) 'Coaxial field systems: some questions of time and space', *Antiquity*, **61**, 188–202.

Fleming, A. (1994) Swadal, Swar (and Erechwydd?): early medieval polities in Upper Swaledale', *Landscape History*, **16**, 17–30.

Fleming, A. (1996) 'Early roads to the Swaledale lead mines', *Yorkshire Archaeological Journal*, **68**, 89–100.

Fleming, A. (1997) 'Towards a history of wood-pasture in Swaledale (North Yorkshire)', *Landscape History*, **19**, 31–47.

Fleming, A. (1999) 'Swaledale: a lost vaccary and a palimpsest of place-names', *Northern History*, **36**, 159–62.

Fleming, A. (2008) *The Dartmoor Reaves*, Oxford [first published in monochrome in 1988]

Gawne, E. (1970) 'Field patterns in Widecombe parish and the Forest of Dartmoor, *Transactions of the Devonshire Association*, **102**, 49–69.

Gelling, M. (1974) 'The chronology of English place-names', in T. Rowley, ed. *Anglo-Saxon Settlement and Landscape*, Oxford, 91–101.

Gelling, M. (1978) *Signposts to the Past*, London.

Gelling, M. (1984) *Place-Names in the Landscape*, London.

Godwin, F. (1990) *Our Forbidden Land*, London.

Gregson, N. (1985) 'The multiple estate model: some critical questions', *Journal of Historical Geography*, **11 (4)**, 339–51.

Guilbert, G. and Taylor, C. (1992) *Grey Ditch, Bradwell, Derbyshire–Preliminary Report* (typescript MS).

Hardin, G. (1968) 'The tragedy of the commons', *Science*, **162**, 1243–8.

Harland, J. (1873) *A Glossary of Words Used in Swaledale. Yorkshire*, London.

Harrison, G. H. de S. N. (1879) *The History of Yorkshire, vol. I: The Wapentake of Gilling West*, London.

Hartley, M. and Ingilby, J. (1984) *A Dales Heritage*, Clapham.

Hayes, R. H., Hemingway, J. E. and Spratt, D. A. (1980) 'The distribution and lithology of beehive querns in northeast Yorkshire', *Journal of Archaeological Science*, **7**, 297–324.

Heslop, D. H. (1988) 'The study of the beehive quern', *Scottish Archaeological Review*, **5**, 59–64.

Hey, D. (1979) *The Making of South Yorkshire*, Ashbourne.

Hicks, S. P. (1971) 'Pollen-analytical evidence for the effect of prehistoric agriculture on the vegetation of North Yorkshire', *New* Phytologist, **70**, 647–67.

Higham, N. (1986) *The Northern Counties to AD 1000*, London.

Hill, D. (1984) *In Turner's Footsteps*, London.

Hill, J. D. (1995) 'How should we understand Iron Age societies and hillforts? A contextual study from southern Britain', in J. D. Hill and C. Cumberpatch eds *Different Iron Ages: Studies of the Iron Age in Temperate Europe*, Oxford.

Hindle, B. P. (1984) *Roads and Trackways of the Lake District*, Ashbourne.

Hodder, M. and Barfield, L. eds (1991) *Burnt mounds and hot stone technology*, West Bromwich.

Honeyman, A. (1986) *Studies in the Holocene Vegetation History of Wensleydale*. Unpublished Ph.D. thesis, University of Leeds.

Hoskins, W. G. (1952) 'The making of the agrarian landscape', in W. G. Hoskins and H. R. R. Finberg, *Devonshire Studies*, London, 289–333.

Hoskins, W. G. and Stamp, L. D. (1963) *The Common Lands of England and Wales*, London.

Jacobi, R. (1978) 'Northern England in the eighth millennium bc: an essay', in P. Mellars ed. *The Early Post-Glacial Settlement of Northern Europe*, London.

Jervoise, E. (1931) *The Ancient Bridges of the North of England*, London.

Jones, G. (1986) 'Holy wells and the cult of St. Helen', *Landscape History*, **8**, 59–74.

Jones, G. R. J. (1971) 'The multiple estate as a model framework for tracing early stages in the evolution of rural settlement', in F. Dussart ed. *L'Habitat et les paysages ruraux d'Europe*, Liege, 251–67.

Jones, G. R. J. (1985). 'Multiple estates perceived', *Journal of Historical Geography*, **11 (4)**, 352–63.

King, A. (1970) *Early Pennine Settlement*, Clapham.

King, A. (1985) 'Prehistoric settlement and land use in Craven, North Yorkshire', in D. Spratt and C. Burgess eds *Upland Settlement in Britain*, Oxford, 117–34.

Kirkham, N. (1968) *Derbyshire Lead Mining through the Centuries*, Truro.

Lancaster, W. T. ed. (1912) *The Chartulary of the Priory of Bridlington*, Leeds.

Lewis, L. ed. (1975) *Hird's Annals of Bedale*, Northallerton.

McDonnell, J. (1990) 'Upland Pennine hamlets', *Northern History*, **26**, 20–39.

McLauchlan, H. (1849) 'On the Roman roads, camps and other earthworks, between the Tees and the Swale, in the North Riding of the County of York', *Archaeological Journal*, **6**, 219–25 and 336–51.

Millett, M. (1990) *The Romanization of Britain*, Cambridge.

Mitchell, F. (1966) 'Dating the "ancient oaks"', *Quarterly Journal of* Forestry, **60**, 271–6.

Morris, D. (1989) *The Dalesmen of the Mississippi River*, York.

Östrom, E. (1990) *Governing the Commons: The Evolution of Institutions for Collective Action*, Cambridge.

O'Sullivan, D. (1985) 'Cumbria before the Vikings: a review of some "Dark Age" problems in north-west England', in J. R. Baldwin and I. D. Whyte eds *The Scandinavians in Cumbria*, Edinburgh, 17–35.

Pennar, M. trans. (1988) *Taliesin Poems*, Llanerch.

Phillips, S. K. (1984a) 'Identity, Social Organisation and Change', unpublished Oxford D.Phil. thesis.

Phillips, S. K. (1984b) 'Encoded in stone: neighbouring relationships and the organisation of stone walls among Yorkshire Dales farmers', *Journal of the Anthropological Society of Oxford*, **XV (3)**, 235–42.

Pontefract, E. (1934) *Swaledale*, London.

Pontefract, E. and Hartley, M. (1939) *Yorkshire Tour*, London.

Rackham, O. (1976) *Trees and Woodland in the British Landscape*, London.

Rackham, O. (1980) *Ancient Woodland: Its History, Vegetation and Uses in England*, London.

Rackham, O. (1986) *The History of the Countryside*, London.

Rackham, O. (1989) *The Last Forest*, London.

Raine, J. (1881) 'Marske, in Swaledale', *Yorkshire Archaeological Journal*, **6**, 172–286.

Raistrick, A. (1926) 'The glaciation of Wensleydale, Swaledale and adjoining parts of the Pennines', *Proceedings of the Yorkshire Geological Society*, **20**, 366–410.

Raistrick, A. (1938) 'Prehistoric cultivations at Grassington, West Yorkshire', *Yorkshire Archaeological Journal*, **33**, 166–74.

Raistrick, A. (1962) *Green Tracks on the Pennines*, Clapham.

Raistrick, A. (1965) *A History of Lead Mining in the Pennines*, London.

Raistrick, A. (1968) *The Pennine Dales*, London.

Raistrick, A. (1982) *The Wharton Mines in Swaledale in the Seventeenth Century*, Northallerton.

Raistrick, A. and Holmes, P. F. (1962) 'Archaeology of Malham Moor', *Field Studies*, **1**, 73–100.

Raistrick, A. and Jennings, B. (1965) *A History of Lead Mining in the Pennines*, London.

Redmonds, G. (1973) English Surname Series, I: *Yorkshire West Riding*, Chichester.

Rivet, A. L. F. and Smith, C. (1979) *The Place-Names of Roman Britain*, London.

Roberts, D. B. (1987) *The Making of the English Village*, Harlow.

Roebuck, P. (1980) *Yorkshire Baronets*, Oxford.

Scrutton, T. E. (1887) *Commons and common fields*, New York.

Short, S. trans. (1994) *Aneirin: The Gododdin*, Felinfach.

Simmons, I. (1996) *The Environmental Impact of Later Mesolithic Cultures*, Edinburgh.

Slingsby, F. W. ed. (1905) *The Registers of the Parish Church of Grinton in Swaledale*, Leeds.

Smith, A. H. (1928) *The Place-Names of the North Riding of Yorkshire*, Cambridge.

Smith, A. H. (1956) *English Place-Name Elements*, Cambridge.

Smith, A. H. (1967) *The Place-Names of Westmorland*, Cambridge.

Smith, W. (1889) *Old Yorkshire*, London.

Speight, H. (1897) *Romantic Richmondshire*, London.

Spencer, T. (1901) *Spencer's Visitors' Handbook to Swaledale and Arkengarthdale*, Richmond.

Spratt, D. A. ed. (1993) *Prehistoric and Roman Archaeology of North-East Yorkshire*, York.

Taylor, C. T. (1989) 'Whittlesford: the study of a river-edge village', in M. Aston, D. Austin and C. Dyer eds *The Rural Settlement of Medieval England*, Oxford, 207–27.

Toulmin Smith, L. ed. (1906–10) *Leland's Itinerary in England and Wales*, London.

Turner, J. (1979) 'The environment of northeast England during Roman times as shown by pollen analysis', *Journal of Archaeological Science*, **6**, 285–90.

Tweddle, D. (1990) *Marrick Priory Research Project* (typescript ms.).

Tyson, L. O. (1989) *A History of the Manor and Lead Mines of Marrick, Swaledale*, Sheffield.

VCH (1914) *Victoria County History: Yorkshire North Riding*, vol. I. London.

Waterson, E. and Meadows, P. (1990) *Lost Houses of York and the North Riding*, Thornton-le-Clay.

Watts, V. E. (1982) 'The place name Hindrelac', *Journal of the English Place-Name Society*, **15**, 3–4.

Wheeler, M. (1954) *The Stanwick Fortifications*, Oxford.

Whitaker, T. D. (1823) *An History of Richmondshire*, London.

Whitehead, N. (nd.) *Swaledale Dialect Dictionary* (unpublished ms. in North Yorkshire County Record Office).

Williams, C. T. (1985) *Mesolithic Exploitation in the Central Pennines: A Palynological Study of Soyland Moor*, Oxford.

Williams, I. (1975) *The Poems of Taliesin*, Dublin.

Williamson, T. (1993) *The Origins of Norfolk*, Manchester.

Winchester, A. (1987) *Landscape and Society in Medieval Cumbria*, Edinburgh.

Wood, P. N. (1996) 'On the little British kingdom of Craven', *Northern History*, **32**, 1–20.

Index